LEAVING REALITY BEHIND

Adam Wishart is an award-winning BBC documentary film-maker. He has been the director of the series 'The Dome: Trouble at the Big Top', and made films for 'Blood on the Carpet', 'Back to the Floor' and 'Tomorrow's World'. He has written for the *New Statesman*, *New Scientist*, *Guardian* and *Independent*.

Regula Bochsler has worked for more than a decade as a reporter, producer and presenter for Swiss National TV and has made several documentaries about the history of media and everyday life. She has a PhD in Modern History and is currently writing a biography of Margarethe Hardegger, a political activist and pioneer for women's rights.

www.4thestate.com

'A sober yet engaging account of the forces that meshed in those crazy times.' *New Statesman*

'Thoroughly researched and reported.' *New Scientist*

LEAVING REALITY BEHIND
The Battle for the Soul of the Internet

Adam Wishart and Regula Bochsler

FOURTH ESTATE • London

For our friends and family, and for Julian whose delivery date was the same as the manuscript.

This paperback edition first published in 2003
First published in Great Britain in 2002 by
Fourth Estate
A Division of HarperCollins*Publishers*
77–85 Fulham Palace Road
London w6 8jb
www.4thestate.com

A catalogue record for this book is available from the British Library

isbn 1-84115-594-2

Typeset by Rowland Phototypesetting Ltd,
Bury St Edmunds, Suffolk
Printed in Great Britain by
Clays Ltd, St Ives plc

Contents

Authors' Note

This book is about the history of the Internet. It is also about two organisations and the extraordinary people who built them, and tells the story of the battle between them.

First there is etoy®TM, created by a group of thrill-seeking young men. It masqueraded as a corporation, with a brand, a corporate identity, a logo, a system of global offices and tradable shares. Yet really it was little more than a fiction, a series of myths created by artists. All it sold was itself.

Then there is eToys®TM, a real corporation, characterised as the Web's leading toy retailer. Its purpose was to sell millions of dollars' worth of Barbies and Pokémon. At one point, this company was worth $8 billion. Yet it too was a kind of fiction, a set of myths created by legions of institutions and small investors fired up by the Internet bubble.

This book recounts a true story based on more than a hundred interviews and thousands of pages of sources – gleaned from archives, the global media, the Securities and Exchange Commission, the LA Superior and Federal courts and the Internet.

We have striven hard to distinguish between the truth, as witnessed and reported, and the stories that were told; this distinction is made evident in the text.

However, we have deviated from fact in the following instances. etoy was created with artistic intent; for the purpose of continuing their art-world conceit, the existing etoy members insisted that our text make no mention of the group's founding members' real names. To secure some co-operation, we agreed – despite the fact that these names can be easily found on the Internet, in court records and even listed in telephone books. Thus we have used pseudonymous first names in the first two chapters, and then referred to them using the names they chose as artists. Similarly, the etoy members insisted that we conceal their family backgrounds and details of their early lives. We conceded this point because, in our opinion, such information is not germane to our story.

In a number of other cases we were asked to conceal contributors' true identities by using pseudonyms or were refused their real names to begin with. Such instances are mentioned in the text.

Beyond these points, everything written in this book is, as far as we can tell, fact . . . even the fictions.

Prologue

At 8.30 a.m. on 29 November 1999, seven lawyers arrived for a hearing on the fifth floor of the Los Angeles County Courthouse. They waited at the back of Department 53, a small, wood-panelled courtroom, for the judge to call the hearing to order. In preparation for this day, these lawyers had spent months submitting hundreds of pages of evidence and arguments to the court. Those on one team had determinedly manœuvred to prevent the hearing taking place at all; those on the other had offered increasing amounts of cash for a speedy resolution of the case. Now their arguments were to be heard in open court.

The plaintiff was a corporation, based ten miles away on the Californian coast in Santa Monica. The firm was personified by the character of its founder, Chief Executive Officer and archly self-described Uncle of the Board, Toby Lenk. This bald, slouch-shouldered thirty-eight-year-old had a fondness for mimicry and silly voices, and such a passion for work that at the time of the hearing he had gone for three years without taking the time off even to buy himself a pair of shoes. He had built his corporation – a toy shop – in less than a thousand days, with the dream to make life easier for parents and relations the world over. Like a fairytale come true, it was now worth $8 billion, and a darling of Wall Street. It was considered to be among the best companies of its kind and Lenk had filled it with only the smartest people, who between them could pack a trophy cabinet with their business diplomas from some of the world's most prestigious universities.

The Monday morning of the hearing followed a gang-busting Thanksgiving weekend during which Lenk's toy shop had sold record numbers of Barbie Dolls and *Star Wars* figurines. Toby Lenk, it seemed, could do no wrong. The powerful global brand that he could proudly call his own was eToys.

The defendants had proved tricky to pin down. Indeed, eToys' lawyers had failed to serve these renegades with all the necessary papers. They were supposedly at large somewhere in Europe; at the time of the hearing one of them, who calls himself agent.ZAI, was in the dank basement of a scruffy townhouse in a run-down neighbourhood in Zürich, Switzerland, eagerly awaiting news.

Physically as well as materially, the opponents were worlds apart. They were never to meet.

Zai was then a slim, diminutive, brown-haired twenty-eight-year-old who over time had nurtured his growing reputation in the arcane world of digital art. Meticulously he had constructed an art project that satirised the dot-com frenzy. Even before Lenk's toy shop sold its first Mr Potato Head, Zai had described himself as the Chief Executive Officer of a group called etoy and behaved as if he was the leader of a global corporation. But in reality etoy had no employees and little corporate infrastructure. It did have a logo, a brand and a Web site and it sold a series of graphic posters that its members called 'shares'. There was some serious-ness to this apparently comic endeavour; it held up an intriguing mirror, as only art could, to a corporate and financial world that was being seduced by its own cheerleading. The etoy vision had been lent credibility and support beyond that received from the art world – even Austria's Chancellor Viktor Klima had bought shares.

The legal suit filed by eToys in the Los Angeles Superior Court attacked the entire edifice of etoy's ludicrous 'corporate' venture – its brand, trademark and greatest achievements – in a desperate attempt to shut down the artists' Web site. Absurdly, the world's most valuable toy shop had launched an explosive battery against the chimera, accusing etoy of 'unfair competition'.

*   *   *

Neither Toby Lenk nor Zai made it to the courthouse. Lenk was busy finalising a deal to raise a further $150 million from his investors. Zai had not managed to get a flight to Los Angeles from Zürich over the busy Thanksgiving weekend. In any case, he had been advised that were he to step foot in America he might be arrested for securities fraud, one of the most heinous crimes against capital.

The details of how etoy and eToys built their respective companies and brands say much about the divergent histories of the Internet. On one hand was a new and fragile corporation that Wall Street pushed into the clouds. There eToys perfectly surfed a wave of euphoria about business and the capital markets, inspiring almost devotional loyalty because of the wealth the company created for its investors and employees and because of its customer-pleasing service culture. etoy, on the other hand, was a conceptual-art project that brilliantly summed up the times. It inspired a community that personified the Internet's alternative history and was uneasy with its eventual corporate colonisation.

Both parties had spent years skilfully positioning themselves to benefit from the Internet goldrush. Now their values – monetary and moral – were clashing.

The conflict not only expressed the divides and fissures that had developed since the formation of the Internet; it also turned on an altogether larger dispute, concerning the very identity of the Internet. The reason for this acrimonious and hard-fought battle was a single, 250-line document now kept in a guarded, bomb-proof room in Herndon, Virginia: the key to the map of the Internet itself, through which domain names – Internet addresses like amazon.com or 4thestate.com – are controlled. The consequences of the domain battle were to play a central and decisive role in the Los Angeles courtroom.

By 10.30 a.m., Judge John P. Shook had stated his judgment. But this was not to be the end of the war . . .

1
Discovering a New Toy

'The new artist protests, he no longer paints.'
Dadaist artist Tristan Tzara, Zürich, 1916

On the balmy evening of 1 June 1990, fleets of expensive cars pulled up outside the Zürich Opera House. Stepping out and passing through the pillared porticoes was a *Who's Who* of Swiss society – the Head of State, national sports icons, former ministers, and army generals – all of whom had come to celebrate the sixty-fifth birthday of Werner Spross, the owner of a huge horticultural business-empire. As one of Zürich's wealthiest and best-connected men, it was perhaps fitting that 650 of his 'close friends' had been invited to attend the event, a lavish banquet followed by a performance of *Romeo and Juliet*.

Defiantly welcoming the grandees were 200 demonstrators standing in the square in front of the Opera House. Mostly young with scruffy clothes and punky haircuts, they whistled and booed, angry that the Opera House had been sold out, allowed for the first time to be taken over by a rich patron. They were also chanting slogans about the inequity of Swiss society and the wealth of Spross's guests. The glittering horde did their very best to ignore the disturbance.

The protest had the added significance of being held on the tenth anniversary and in the same spot as the first spark of the city's most explosive youth revolt of recent years, The Movement.

In 1980 the Opera Riot was started by young people returning from a Bob Marley concert, and ended with barricades on the street, burning cars and police firing teargas and rubber bullets. The television pictures came as a shock to Switzerland's staid community. In the following months The Movement staged many demonstrations, some of which also resulted in riots, as they made their demands: an end to the country's 'oppressive' drugs policy; the introduction of a cultural policy that did not exclude the young (as the Opera did); and the funding of an 'autonomous' youth centre. The anti-consumerist protests were often wrapped in humour. Their chants on demonstrations included the Dadaist 'Turn the State into a Cucumber Salad' and 'Down with the Alps, for a direct view of the Mediterranean!' The demonstrations climaxed when 200 naked young people marched down Zürich's Bahnhofstrasse, one of the world's most exclusive shopping streets. The atmosphere was edgy, the crowd shouting, 'We are the dead bodies of the cultural life of this city!'

Ten years on, the demonstrators outside Spross's party lacked the impact of the previous generation but shared their spirit. They hung around in small groups, rousing themselves at the arrival of each new limousine.

One individual stood out from the crowd. Seventeen years old with carefully spiked blond hair, he wore a scruffy black leather jacket emblazoned with the words 'Nazis Raus' – Nazis Out – and bright-green Doctor Marten boots he had customised himself. The young man Herbert (though he later adopted the name agent.ZAI) was spotted by a producer from Swiss National Television who was on the talent trail for the youth programme *Seismo*, which needed reporters and presenters. When approached, Herbert railed against the authorities and talked about his involvement in the Students' Union that he helped run at his high school. He was invited to a casting, where his fast-talking wit quickly secured him a starring role.

Herbert worked for the production for the next year, gaining special permission from his school to attend recordings and meetings. A two-hour discussion programme for young people, each episode covering a single topic, *Seismo* involved numerous guests, a live audience and band performances. The shows were brash, arresting spectacles that were always staged in strange locations – on one occasion it was set among the machinery at a water-purifying plant. Herbert gave compelling performances, interviewing guests and presenting recorded segments. The contrast between this spirited, jagged young man and Switzerland's elder politicians and pundits made particularly engaging television.

Seismo taught Herbert much about the inner workings of the media, of which he was a keen and diligent student. The show also brought him a certain kudos. The press described him and his three fellow youth reporters as 'lively, competent and cheeky'; they were interviewed and had their pictures published in the media, and occasionally Herbert was recognised in the street. During the course of that year he became more self-regarding than he had been before, and dyed his hair black to show off his good looks and intense eyes all the better on-screen. For the first time in his life he had achieved a kind of recognition. In a world where the old and comfortable truths of youth rebellion – the battles between East and West, between capital and labour – were no longer so easily grasped, the delights of the media and the celebrity that it brought were all the more enticing. It was a seduction that, as the years went on, Herbert found himself unable to resist.

At high school Herbert was not having such a good time. His bristling intelligence together with his rebelliousness annoyed his teachers at the straitlaced and traditional establishment that had a reputation as the proving ground for the Swiss elite. So he left, travelling to Basel to attend the most radical of all Swiss schools, the Anna Göldin-Gymnasium, named after the last Swiss witch to have been burned at the stake. The school was anti-authoritarian, governed for the most part by the students themselves, who democratically set and enforced the rules. But even in this most liberal of environments Herbert soon became embroiled in conflicts with both students and teachers. His free spirit did not flourish: without qualifications he moved back to Zürich.

The move left Herbert at a loose end, and by the spring of 1991 he was keen to find a place where he could feel comfortable and use his estimable skills. With a group of political activists and friends he broke into an old gas-meter factory called Wohlgrot and occupied the site. It was situated right in the centre of town, just behind Zürich's main railway station, and included a cluster of buildings surrounding a courtyard, and a villa where the factory manager had once lived. The place became a popular and heavily populated squat, the most significant of countercultural happenings in the city since The Movement, and its existence was proclaimed by a huge parody of a station sign. Instead of 'Zürich', it read 'Zureich' – 'Too Rich'.

During the coming months Herbert spent much of his time in the squat. With a café, a bar, a cinema and a concert venue, the place quickly took on the character of an underground cultural centre; it was illegal, for a start, but perhaps its most subversive feature was the 'junkie room', where heroin addicts could go either to shoot up or to receive medical help. But, as with Herbert's radical school, amid the anarchy at the squat there was conflict. Late in 1991, when the new dance-beats of techno had arrived in the city, the squat's first rave was held in a basement. A squatter threw a teargas grenade into the crowd in protest because he considered techno too 'commercial' for this fiercely anti-capitalist space. Herbert and his friends and everyone else present were forced to make a speedy exit up a narrow staircase. The event turned him against the puritan spirit of the protestors.

As time wore on, the idyllic utopia that Herbert had envisioned became the venue for more and more rancorous arguments. As he remembers, 'We wanted the villa to be a special place, a nice place, but the others took over and it became dirty and fucked up.' And so he began to dream of organising something independent, something over which he could wield more control.

* * *

Herbert's yearning for his own thing resulted in his decision to stage a shocking performance. It was the summer of 1992, and Switzerland's 156 numbers – the equivalent of America's 1-900 numbers and Britain's 0898 numbers – had just appeared and had immediately become synonymous with phone sex and pornographic chatlines. Hungry for this latest sordid, circulation-boosting story, newspaper editors had given the subject acres of newsprint, simultaneously titillating their readers with the details of what the phone services offered and condemning the lucrative schemes' operators. To Herbert, too, this new phenomenon presented a glimmer of opportunity.

He remembers, 'I wanted to be a pioneer at any price, because everything else seemed to be too boring.' What he wanted to do was run his own 156 number, to use this very new technology to challenge the hypocrisy of the media and to pointedly shock the culture of the dull, lifeless and extraordinarily wealthy city of Zürich. He loved The Sex Pistols, the British band who in 1977 had reached Number One in Britain in the week of the Queen's Silver Jubilee and subsequently shocked the nation with their angry lyrics and by swearing on national television. Perhaps Herbert's scam could do the same. Zürich, after all, had a history of bizarre events. Dada, the art movement that first shocked polite society by performing nonsense poetry, making collages and championing tomfoolery in the face of the horrors of the First World War, had begun here, and went on to influence almost every aspect of conceptual art in the twentieth century.

Herbert also liked the 156 idea because it made him feel like a grown-up. 'We wanted our own company, our stickers, our logo, our publicity,' he recalls. The 156 line might even make some money, and he particularly liked the fact that this partly entrepreneurial venture would irritate the pious protestors, the po-faced squatters and the bickering politically correct alumni of his old school, all of whom were critical of any sort of commerce.

Herbert registered a phone line and set about gathering a team to execute the project. He called on his old friend Juri to handle the technology and set up the equipment. Juri was an apprentice electrician, but hated the dull monotony of a professional life that demanded so little of his skills. He had spent his younger years locked in front of computers, trying to break into computer networks as part of the tiny and highly specialised underground world of phone-phreakers and hackers. As he would later prove, he was extremely talented when armed with a computer, a modem and a few bits of elegantly written code. In person he was shy and rather wordless, and computer technology provided him with a way of communicating with the world. At high school, where Herbert met him, Juri shoplifted-to-order computer accessories for his classmates and ploughed the profits back into his enormous phonebills. He was tall and clumsy, with an unmemorable face; his fearlessness was the key to his successful career as a hacker.

Another friend whom Herbert contacted for help was Alberto. Herbert and Alberto's families had known each other for ever; by 1992, Alberto, two years older than Herbert, was already committed to a career as a student of architecture at the Zürich Technical University. By contrast to the scruffy punks and slackers squatting the Wohlgrot, he was always neat, his vivid dark eyes framed by delicate black-rimmed glasses. Herbert and his friends had nicknamed him Master Proper, the name of a cleaning product. More distant and ultimately more calculating than his friends, Alberto would in the years to come bring a cold, intellectual grounding, the brains to their sloganeering rebellion.

Thomas was the third of Herbert's friends to be recruited. Tall, with a rectangular-shaped head, he posed as a violent bruiser and loved what he considered to be the glamorous chic of motorbikes and guns. He would happily spend hours cooking barbecues, drinking beer and watching Formula One. However, this muscled exterior concealed a clever soul; Thomas was a gifted storyteller, and laced his deft observations with a dry and inscrutable humour.

The name that Herbert, Juri, Alberto and Thomas chose for their scam was HIRN-lein, meaning 'small brain' but in Swiss-German sounding just like 'brain line'.

Soon the posters they had painted were pasted all over Zürich.

They screamed 'BLOODBATH' in large print, alongside an assurance to readers that the words had been splattered with real pigs' blood. Herbert ascribed the action to a new organisation called *Verein der Freunde Monopolistischer Märkte* (VFMM) – The Association of the Friends of Monopolistic Markets – a joke at the expense of the anti-capitalist squatters.

Anyone who responded to the gruesome poster and phoned HIRN-lein's 1½-franc-a-minute line (about 50 pence Sterling, or 90 American cents) was greeted by machine-gun fire and the screams of a hysterical woman. This was followed by the moralising and portentous voice of a man: 'Dear listener, is this what you want to listen to? Is a bloodbath a reason to call us? It is sad if not tragic that you too are part of this pitiable crowd who feels attracted by a bloodbath, a massacre, even misery and death of fellow human beings.' In the background, symphonic film-music reached a crescendo. The narrator continued in an imploring tone: 'You have dialled this number; reflect on it, be honest with yourself. Is it worth throwing life away to obscene lust?' The tape ended with HIRN-lein's slogan, 'The Modesty of Truth'.

Hardly anyone but their friends called, and the story was not picked up by the press. Only Marc Ziegler, a prosecutor known as 'the hunter of the 156 numbers' for his determined attempt to shut down the more pornographic lines, seemed to notice HIRN-lein at all. When interviewed by a reporter on a local radio station about the 156 phenomenon, he said that someone should take the HIRN-lein boys by the ear and give them a good talking-to.

Still they remained desperate for a reaction to their work, and thus recorded further tasteless stories and produced yet more shocking posters. It was a poster bearing the slogan 'Somehow we find it completely perverted to fuck in front of a dead body' that provoked a complaint to another Zürich prosecutor, Lino Esseiva. He then launched a pornography investigation against Alberto, as registrant of the phone number – the boys had discovered that it was illegal for Herbert, as a minor, to have the phone line registered in his name, so had cautiously transferred it into Alberto's, the only one of the group who was over twenty years old. Alberto was summoned to Esseiva's office and closely questioned about his intentions; his response was to cleverly explain that HIRN-lein was a media-and-art experiment, rather than a porn line. This seemed to satisfy Lino Esseiva, who accepted that the group's actions weren't criminal – even if he thought they were disgusting.

The boys were happy that their oeuvre finally had been noticed. They cheered themselves on with the thought, 'The more people hate us, the better.' To up the ante, Herbert asked his friend Nico Wieland to write a letter to *Tages-Anzeiger*, Switzerland's most popular broadsheet newspaper. After outlining his puritan disdain of the antics of HIRN-lein, Nico signed off: 'I rely on the tiny remains of intelligence that are left in our society to fight this and other perversions.' The letter was published and had the desired effect: the much dreamed-of journalists started calling.

To the boys' delight, the journalists mostly wrote sanctimonious condemnations. 'We are the Saddam Husseins of the 156 lines,' Herbert gloated in response to press questions. When a journalist from Switzerland's biggest tabloid newspaper called, they told her that they were students who believed in the imminent arrival of extra-terrestrials and wanted to use the line to finance the building of a landing strip in Ethiopia. The credulous journalist agreed to meet them, and under the expert supervision of architecture student Alberto they spent the whole night drawing plans and building a model. The following Sunday the tabloid ran the headline '*Hallo Ufo, bitte landen!*' ('Hello UFO, please land!') accompanied by a picture: Thomas, in jacket and tie, with a map of Africa; Alberto, smiling under his spectacles, with his model of the landing strip; and Herbert, in a baseball cap, holding a poster bearing their 156 number, looking like a geeky high-school student.

Herbert also used his contacts to persuade Swiss National Television to carry a report on their youth show. He dictated his terms. Instead of giving interviews, Alberto pretended to be a phone-line addict; Juri and Thomas, in suits and ties, played the

HIRN-lein entrepreneurs; and Herbert acted as the group's chief ideologist.

The project was a triumph in media manipulation, but after a couple of months Herbert had to wind it down – for all the publicity, it hadn't made any money.

By the spring of 1993, Herbert again felt under pressure to make his way in the world and find something new to do. More than anything, he hated the idea of getting a job, of joining the plodding masses in their grey offices. He wanted something that combined the adrenaline hit of his TV performances with the thrill of HIRN-lein's provocation. But most avenues were closed to him because he had not graduated from high school. One hope of an interesting life came in the chance to go to art school in neighbour-ing Austria, where the entry requirements were less rigorous than those in Switzerland. To bolster his resolve and to prevent his return to Zürich, he gave up his apartment and gave away most of his belongings. After a lavish final HIRN-lein party, Herbert left for Vienna.

At the same time, his friend Hans – another failed student from the Anna Göldin-Gymnasium – decided that he would also apply. As large as Herbert was small, Hans was a skinhead whose mood-changing drinking habits and aggression made him a dominating force. His real love, however, was more sublime. 'I wanted to be a poet, a voice in the world,' he remembers. He had spent his teens writing acres of poetic rants that he described as WORDWAR. In 'Reality' he wrote, 'my brain is splattering in the flames' and that he was suffering 'the permanent reduction of the physical-body functions, the retracting of the limbs, mutilation of the extremities, medical dependence on the higher lifeforms in the body'. Much of his poetry was nonsensical, testosterone-fuelled adolescent rant-ing, but it had energy and force nonetheless.

The relationship of Herbert and Hans was intense, borne of teenage enthusiasm for each other. Together they felt much stronger and more likely to succeed than they did on their own. Though they were not lovers, they behaved like a couple –

finishing each other's sentences, sharing confidences and trust in one another. Hans had a kind of immediate and spontaneous courage that fired Herbert up, and in the past they had goaded each other into doing increasingly outrageous stunts. But their friendship masked a rivalry and was, in part, an expedient alliance. 'I know that I am greedy,' says Herbert, 'but Hans is endlessly greedy. I always said that, if you let him, he empties the buffet without caring about other people.' Hans remembers, 'We decided to be friends rather than enemies.'

Enthusiastically the two forged plans of how they would conquer Vienna together. Herbert used an illustrated portfolio of the HIRN-lein project to gain a place in the graphics department of the Vienna Academy of Applied Arts. Hans was determined to be radical, so chose not to submit any images to the same department. Instead he presented the text of the WORDWAR poems and was summarily rejected.

Despite this set-back, Hans and Herbert were not ready to give up their desire for a common future and Hans moved to Vienna anyway. They were so short of money, though, that they were forced to share a tiny bedsit, which they crammed with their video cameras and computers. They formed another association, Elastic Worldwide 4D, which was little more than the name and their enthusiasm; days and nights were spent taking drugs, making computer animations and talking about their future. And at some point they discovered the Academy's department of visual media, run by Professor Peter Weibel, a man whose strange role in the seventies art scene they found very appealing.

Weibel had been a member of an art group called the Viennese Actionists, a bizarre descendant of Dada. The Actionists performed some of the most unsavoury and sadomasochistic public performances to have ever been described as art. One member of the group was arrested following a performance during which he sang the national anthem while masturbating. Weibel himself was led around the centre of Vienna by another Actionist, Vallie Export, on a lead as if he were a dog.

Herbert and Hans applied to join Weibel's department

together, but were required to submit their portfolios as individuals. Both boys were offered places and both were delighted. But by the autumn of 1994 this was not enough. They wanted to create a larger vehicle for their ambition, and felt that their combined skills alone were insufficient for them to make it to the big-time. So they decided to gather together a group of likeminded friends.

Herbert's HIRN-lein collaborators were also interested in doing something else. Alberto continued to study architecture; Thomas, to everyone's surprise, had enrolled at law school, but felt uncomfortable with his conservative colleagues; Juri was still an apprentice electrician and was desperate to give it up.

Herbert also got in touch with a couple of other friends, who had lent a hand at the beginning of HIRN-lein: Peter, a singer and charmer, and Franco, a keyboard player and guitarist, both of whom used computers to make and record music. Aged fourteen the pair and Herbert had founded their first club, the *Gesellschaft für professionelle Amiga-Anwendung* (GPA) – the Society for the Professional Use of the Amiga – to feed a shared enthusiasm for Amiga computers.

The Amiga computer was released in June 1985. The lineage of the computers dominating the market at that time could ultimately be traced back to the telegraph; the user could communicate only in letters and numerals, typing in complicated commands that would appear on the monochrome screens. By contrast Amiga was the first truly multimedia machine, with capabilities for sound, moving images and colour. At the launch Blondie's Debbie Harry sang along to one. The computers were marketed under the tag line 'Only Amiga Makes it Possible'; even Andy Warhol was said to own one.

The Amiga was never very popular but did develop a cult following. In a forerunner of today's free-software movement, Amiga enthusiasts created an entire set of publicly available software which they distributed via bulletin-board systems and through small-advertisement sections in the back of magazines. And, in the mid-1980s in Switzerland, Herbert and his friends

Peter and Franco jumped on the bandwagon. They produced a regular fanzine for their pro-Amiga society and recruited hundreds of members from around Europe – mostly from behind the Iron Curtain, where kids were desperate for contact with the computer magazines and software of the West. The society eventually disbanded, but the three boys remained friends.

While the others were provoking Zürich with HIRN-lein, Peter and Franco had set off on a pilgrimage to the heartland of world rave-culture: Manchester. The place was engulfed by the latest, ecstasy-fuelled dance phenomenon – *Newsweek* even splashed its cover with the city and its clubs, under the title 'Madchester'. Peter and Franco had gone there thinking that it would be the perfect proving ground for their band, SuperSex, but they landed in the most violent part of the city, Moss Side. They met a lot of musicians, but nobody really understood why they had come. 'We wanted to feel like pop stars – at least for a couple of months,' remembers Franco. They finally ran out of money and their immigration status became perilous. Back in Zürich, both were only too happy to hear from Herbert.

In the early autumn of 1994, Herbert sent an invitation to his chosen friends, requesting their attendance at a meeting in the Swiss resort of Weggis on Lake Lucerne. Herbert titled the invitations 'The Company – The Family' and outlined his and Hans's ideas for possible collaboration. The front of the invitation asked, 'Fun, money and the new world?' On the back was the icon of an attaché case in front of an emerging and radiating sun, in the centre of which was a dollar symbol.

The Magnificent Seven – Herbert, Alberto the brainy architecture student, Juri the shy hacker, Thomas the muscled law student, Peter and Franco the musicians, and Hans the radical poet – piled into two cars and drove the two hours from Zürich to Weggis. A century previously, Weggis had been an opulent resort that had played host to royalty and celebrity. It was also the place where Hans Arp, one of the founders of Dada, had come to break away from the tradition of representational art.

Amid an alpine landscape of old farmhouses, stables and orchards, the location for the meeting was an eyesore of a seventies concrete apartment-building. The borrowed apartment might in another time have been the location of a family holiday – happy snaps taken on the long balcony, the snow-capped mountains as backdrop.

As the boys rolled out their sleeping bags and cracked open beers, they were still uncertain as to what was about to happen. Their motivations and aspirations were a confused desire for fame amalgamated with a determination for political change and a belief in the power of art. All seven of them shared a rebellious sensibility, wanting to poke fun at and denounce the overbearing and monotonous tone of the society in which they lived. They all hoped that this meeting would produce something new and innovative that would further their collective anarchistic take on the world. More than anything, they hoped they could find a way to control their own destinies, to save themselves from dull, office-bound careers. Like young men the world over, they were also in search of visceral excitement and both emotional and geographic adventure. As Herbert puts it, 'All of us were extremely greedy – for excitement, for drugs, for success.'

For a week they sat around the dining-room table in the holiday apartment and deliberated about their future. Everyone had been asked to prepare a paper to present to the others about their special interests and aspirations. Herbert submitted his thoughts about commercial sponsorship. Hans spoke about corporate identity; he admired Andy Warhol and the way he had used the aesthetic of commercial art to satirise and celebrate advertising. Peter, the plastic pop-boy, and Franco, his tall charming collaborator, talked about music and the use of multimedia, and about their desire to be pop stars, like David Bowie, the Sex Pistols or Madonna. Alberto lectured about Archigram, a 1960s collective of architects who became famous for their visions of 'plug-in cities'.

The arduous meetings lasted for up to eighteen hours a day. The atmosphere was combative and exhausting. 'We were searching for ideas, but it was no fun at all,' Peter recalls. 'The process of creating a group with these people who are so different was very strenuous.' For Alberto, the very impossibility of agreement was the purpose. 'It was a test, whether we could manage to spend one week together. It had a symbolic character,' he recalls. Herbert taped all the meetings with a cheap video camera, convinced that they would later have some historical value – and because they all wanted a record of them in case arguments broke out in the future about what had been agreed.

The group acknowledged that, in this 'multimedia' world, becoming 'pop stars' or just being 'artists' would not necessarily guarantee their success. They spent hours discussing their collective view that the world was undergoing a 'multimedialisation' – by which they meant that the separate disciplines of text, images and sound were collapsing together, since all now relied to a greater or lesser degree on computers. The co-operation between artists of different media was required. They saw the success of manufactured boy-bands and avant-garde art groups as a demonstration of the need for some kind of collaboration. Also they had all witnessed the power of their combined forces in the clubs that Herbert had so avidly formed in previous years: the HIRN-lein, the Society for the Professional Use of the Amiga and – to a lesser degree – Elastic Worldwide 4D.

Instead of a club they decided to form a corporation. Says Juri, 'We were kids who pretended we were doing business.' Previous generations might have blanched at such a commercial take on youth rebellion. But this group felt no guilt. Capitalism dominated the world and had just 'won' the Cold War; the Berlin Wall had crumbled only a few years before. Indeed, brands – of sneakers, in fashion and music – were often the heroic icons of the moment. 'We were fascinated by multinational corporations – millions of people, one name, one brand. Like Sony,' says Alberto, who especially admired anything Japanese.

For these young men it was as if there was no alternative to 'a company' as an engine of ideas, cultural change and defiant rebellion. The bickering, political correctness of the Old Left in the squat and in the radical Anna Göldin-Gymnasium was hardly a compelling alternative. Indeed it was clear that the furthering of their opinions would be better done by creating a corporation and a brand than by employing the outdated and singular methods of music, art or literature. This was how to triumph in the nineties.

It was as if they were going to turn on its head the behaviour of big-brand corporations that 'steal' the cool of rebel music and the *élan* of street fashion for marketing their burgers, sneakers and clothes. As a lyric of Peter's favourite band, Chumbawamba, said, 'They think it is funny turning rebellion into money'. Now Herbert and his friends were going to steal from the power of the dominant corporate ideal and turn it to their own defiant ends. And if it could make some kind of profit too, then all the better.

The boys set out to codify this 'just do it' philosophy into the constitution of their corporation. But they could not finally do away with the collectivist ideology employed by the protesters and squatters. They agreed that on the inside they were to be a collective, that no one would have any hierarchical power over any other, that everything was to be agreed by democratic vote. Once a rule was agreed it would be followed like a corporate diktat, and policed with determined and aggressive diligence. The first rule to be instituted was that no one was allowed to eat during meetings – it was considered 'unprofessional'.

Despite this theoretical agreement, in practice Herbert exerted his influence. 'He was very much in the centre of the group because he established the rules,' remembers Franco. 'He was the only one that still had energy at the end of the day, when everybody else was totally exhausted. These were the moments where his opinion got accepted by the rest of the group.'

Since part of the group would be living in Vienna and the others in Zürich, they also discussed their *modus operandi*. They felt that they were in need of what they called a 'virtual office-system'. Juri, the hacker, suggested that they might use the Internet rather like a special kind of phone or fax machine, for swapping information – just a boring utility. Like most of the rest of the world, the others had little idea what the Internet was. By 1994, the Internet still had a comparatively small number of people connected to it, and the majority of those in the backwaters of the scientific-research community, in the corporate offices of Silicon Valley, or in localised enclaves, like the rave scene in San Francisco.

Juri knew his way around the Internet, but it was far from simple. The software that was used, such as it was, had been written inside the academic computer-science community and was not really intended for the average home-user. Getting online was hard in itself, and asked for dogged determination. Modems were expensive and their installation involved the typing in of many seemingly random and complicated series of numbers and letters, user names, and passwords. Mistyping meant failure to connect, with no friendly error-message – often just a blank screen. The difficulty of the logging-on process cloaked a uniquely powerful network that was about to leap into the public consciousness.

The network's success owes much to one man, Jon Postel. By 1994, he had twenty years' experience – first as a graduate student and eventually as a professor – writing and editing a number of key documents that formed the foundations of the Internet. These described how computers would be able to communicate with each other. The Internet is not so much a radical new technology but rather a set of brilliantly written rules that computer scientists call Standards. These rules are consistently applied by all computers across the network; without a set of Standards computers live on the Tower of Babel, unable to speak to each other because they do not share a common language. Like the internationally agreed size for cargo containers, or the regulations of the Universal Postal Union, Internet Standards are not especially complicated – but when the network grew large and ubiquitous it became an extraordinarily powerful way of trading information.

The first Standards were written in the late 1960s in response to the request by an obscure research agency, the Applied Research

Jon Postel, at the Information Sciences Institute, University of Southern California, Marina del Rey.

Projects Agency (ARPA), associated with the American Defense Department, that wanted, apart from anything else, to communicate at a time of war. Since then the Standards have been improved and clarified through a loose network of computer academics and consultants, nurtured and corralled by Postel and a few others. To begin with, the few constitutionally appointed organisations and the culture were very much in line with the T-shirt slogan of one of the central bodies, 'We reject kings, presidents, and voting. We believe in rough consensus and running code.'

The *Economist* once proclaimed that, 'If the Net does have a god, he is probably Jon Postel' – and, with his long hair, bushy white beard and open-toed sandals, he does have the look of an Old Testament prophet. This Professor of Computing at the University of Southern California was a product of the hippy movement, and the key Internet Standard, the Transmission

Control Protocol/Internet Protocol (TCP/IP), of which he was the co-author, chimed with his personality. Enshrined within the code was a dislike of central authorities and the promotion of individual freedom. Previously computer networks and telephone systems had depended on a central commanding authority – even making a local telephone call requires dialling a central exchange, which then routes the call back to the receiver. The US military thought this was a vulnerable way of setting up a communication system. The network that TCP/IP governed was to have none of this.

The Standards of the Internet were to eschew this kind of centrality. It was to be a network in which every computer that was attached to it was to have equal power and equal value to the network. The TCP/IP Standard was remarkable because it gave no favour to those computers on the network owned by corporations, governments or the powerful. As a consequence any computer could, in theory, attach itself to any other that would transfer information ubiquitously.

Most surprising at the time, the Standards rejected the dominant technology of networking: switches. A telephone call, for example, requires a continuous electrical circuit to be switched on – via switches at the local exchange and all the exchanges along the route. In contrast the idea of the Internet is that information – be it a voice stream, like a telephone call, or a graphic image or a text document – flows through the network in a series of discrete pieces. To send a large piece of information it is first divided up into 'packets' and then sent separately to the destination computer, where it is reassembled. The system has the power and flexibility of a central Post Office and, as with the postal system, every computer on the Internet has an address. These addresses, twelve-digit numbers, are unique. Also like a mail system, the Internet would collapse into chaos if the same information could be directed to two or more post boxes with the same address.

These two elements of the TCP/IP Standard – the distributed and equal network, and the sending of packets – make it rather like a 'Mutual Post Office', a co-operative movement of which anyone can become a member provided that they pay a small fee and follow the rules of TCP/IP. At its inception, the system offered several obvious advantages. For a start, it could not be destroyed by knocking out the central sorting office or telephone exchange; the packets of information could route around any temporary obstruction. The network could also grow like wildfire without the need for studious bureaucrats to diligently design and then control it. To become a member of the Mutual Post Office, one simply needed to attach a computer to another already on the network and agree to play by the rules.

The mutuality had a radical cultural impact. The system's lack of control and regulation defined the early incipient Internet community. As wrote Kevin Kelly, former editor of *WIRED* magazine, 'The US government, which indirectly subsidizes the Net, woke up one day to find that the Net had spun itself, without much administration or oversight, among the terminals of the techno-elite. The Internet is, as its users are proud to boast, the largest functioning *anarchy* in the world.' This anarchy would not be easily controlled by governments, corporations or even by lawyers. Indeed, over the coming years it seemed as though the Internet's many conflicts and lawsuits had their foundation hard-wired into the mutual details of this technology.

In the concrete building in Weggis, Juri and Franco were charged with getting the company on the Internet as a cheap and practical form of communication between Zürich and Vienna. Nobody considered the Internet as an important new medium, let alone as their new company's focus or platform.

Eventually, after days of debate, the friends also managed to agree on a name, Combination-Combination, which was supposed to express their intention to combine the efforts of different people with different specialities in different places. It was in the universal language of hip youth – English – and contained an allusion to their technical know-how.

They decided to raise the money to fund the setting up of the necessary infrastructure and offices by servicing the rave scene, using their many multimedia skills to contribute to the experience. Five of them could contribute to this venture: Herbert, Hans and Juri were to create images to project on club walls using computers, and musicians Franco and Peter would compose sounds. The others were to think about their possible contribution to the larger group project – it was hoped that this would be the first step towards something bigger.

On the last evening in Weggis the group staged the official founding ceremony of Combination-Combination. They were thrilled that the bonds of old friendships were now united in a common destiny. In the meadow in front of the apartment they lit a firework and toasted their future with champagne. Franco, who had been given the position of the group's 'specialist in human resources', was designated to make the official speech. He told the others that he hoped 'we would succeed in shaping not only pioneering new technologies but also promising human relationships. And that we were a very special team and would be able to do so.' Even today, Herbert goes into raptures when he remembers the founding of the group that he would so relentlessly drive. 'It was a magic moment when all these brains came together to form a common will.'

Back home in Zürich, Thomas – the law student – wrote his first business letter, to the company founders. It contained a budget and asked everybody to send 5,000 Swiss francs (£2,000) as their individual share of the founding capital. 'Dear Business Partners,' it read. 'How each one gets hold of this money is his private matter (fantasy and creativity!).' With the money, the boys rented a tiny room in an empty office building and set about making parties happen.

Soon they were asked to provide the visuals for a rave in Basel. Dozens of TV screens were dragged into an old factory, where Juri hooked them up to his computers and fed them whirling graphics. The friends all wore the same clothes for the event, a uniform of a black suit with a Pepsi logo on the sleeve, pointedly turning the brand on itself.

After Basel, Hans and Herbert returned to Vienna and convinced a nightclub promoter to hire them. The plan was that Juri, who remained in Zürich, would produce the visuals on his computer and then send them down the line directly from one computer to another.

The day before the party, Juri set his computer in Zürich to dial the computer lab of the Academy of Applied Arts in Vienna, where Hans and Herbert were waiting. Nowadays computer files containing graphic images and animations amounting to the equivalent libraries of data are regularly swapped across large distances. Juri's graphic file was tiny by comparison, but that did not make his task any easier. In Vienna Hans and Herbert watched as the line was connected and part of the file was slowly transferred. Then the connection broke, and Juri had to start again. It was a frustrating process. The boys were worried that failure to get the images on time would put their careers as party organisers in jeopardy.

Four hours later, the pictures arrived. The group knew that neither their nerves nor their wallets could cope with this sort of lengthy international transmission, so they found a more old-fashioned way to go about their business. From then on, when in similar straits, Juri would take out his computer's hard drive and tape it to the underside of a seat on the express train from Zürich to Vienna. Herbert or Hans would wait at the station to retrieve it.

Combination-Combination might have continued to be party organisers, or they might have tried seriously to achieve success as a band or become defiant political artists, had it not been for the intervention in autumn 1994 of Franz Penz, one of Herbert and Hans's teachers at the Academy. In his thirties, with an ill-cut beard to match his ill-fitting pullovers, Penz had wanted to show the two students something novel and exciting that wasn't available in the art school. Penz was not, however, a great talker and refused to describe the new phenomenon. The boys had begged him to tell them more, but Penz simply said, 'This is way too cool; I really can't explain.' So they went with him across town, to the Technical University's computer laboratory.

What Penz showed them was the World Wide Web – an easy-to-use information system with a graphical user-interface. Using a mouse to control a pointer on a computer screen, one could click on various parts of the display and bring up new information. It was simple and freewheeling – and, of course, soon to become known as 'Web surfing'. Within half an hour, Hans had negotiated his way around the Web, from New York to Tokyo to Madrid. 'I had stars in my brain, and I knew this was exactly what I wanted for the next couple of years. This was the future.'

The World Wide Web began in Switzerland in 1990. A taciturn, idealistic Englishman, Tim Berners-Lee, was working as a researcher at CERN, the European Particle Physics Laboratory, in Geneva, where he had decided that he wanted to create a common Standard for sharing information. At the time, outside a small community of academics and publishers, this was not thought to be the most exciting task. Berners-Lee's idea was to create something new for the common good, agreed upon between many parties, of which he would be a catalyst and consensus-builder. Dale Dougherty, a publisher of computer books, met Tim Berners-Lee during this time and was struck by his fervour. 'His idealism was his driving force; that appealed to me,' he recalls. 'There was the idea that information online could be linked together and used.'

Previously, using the Internet to find a useful document on a remote machine was tricky. Postel's Standards focused on the network and the transferring of information, not on the organisation of information – which usually ended up in tree-like hierarchical file systems, rather like those of a computer's hard drive. The casual user would have to send a command requesting a list of the contents of a particular directory. To find anything useful required a trawl through directory after subdirectory until one chanced upon something interesting.

Berners-Lee wanted to replace these old and difficult methods by enhancing the existing network with a new information system.

His models were academic papers: generally full of links, with citations, references and footnotes scarring the texts. His hope was that the ability to jump directly to the source of a citation, rather than having to plod to the library and search for it, would be immensely useful to the research community.

There were some precedents for this idea. Vannevar Bush, Franklin Roosevelt's scientific advisor and for many the father of the military-industrial complex, had written an article about such a system way back in 1945. Ted Nelson, a self-described 'paradigm creator', had dreamed up an information system named Xanadu in the early 1960s, in which he called the connections between documents 'hyperlinks'. But nobody had ever managed to get such a system to work across a network of computers. Nor had any single system been widely adopted by sufficient numbers of people to be of real use. At the time of Berners-Lee's investigation, a competing system called Gopher – much beloved of librarians because it allowed remote access to large databases such as catalogues – seemed like it might become ubiquitous enough for users to invest the time in getting and installing its software. But Berners-Lee was undaunted, and soon adopted the name Hypertext for his document system.

Just as the Internet relies on the Standards of TCP/IP, Tim Berners-Lee needed a set of Standards which would enable computers using Hypertext to communicate and which would dovetail with the Internet itself. Late in 1990 he finalised those Standards. The idea was that the sharable information would be held on a remote computer, which Berners-Lee called the server, and these would be available and accessible to a global audience across the Internet. Other computers within the network would run a different sort of computer application; these would be known as browsers, and could request information from the server. Once the information had made its way to the browser it would appear in a window; the user could then pull up other information by clicking on any of the hyperlinks that were displayed in the browser window.

This transfer of information was regulated by the Standards.

The 'http' that is now a prefix to Web addresses stands for Hypertext Transfer Protocol, which is just a way of ensuring that computers are speaking the same language. One of the most important parts of the Standards that Berners-Lee created, and which has underlain every dispute about Web domains, is the Uniform Resource Locator, or URL. Just as every computer on the Internet has a unique address, which is akin to the location of a house on a street, so the Web needed a definition for the precise location of individual pieces of information – like that of a book or document within the house. That definition is the URL. With it, every music file, program or document can have a specific and precise place on the Internet.

In defining these Standards, Berners-Lee wrote the rudimentary software, as a sort of test, but not on a widely accepted operating system. While touring conferences and writing papers trying to promote what he now called the World Wide Web, he received a muted response. The truth was that Berners-Lee's Web was just one of a number of different protocols and applications then competing for critical mass in the information community.

In late 1992, Marc Andreessen, the son of a seed salesman from provincial Wisconsin, was a twenty-one-year-old computer programmer finishing his final year at the University of Illinois at Urbana-Champaign and working for $7 an hour at the University's National Center for Super-Computing Applications (NCSA). Ambitious and arrogant, he was searching for something new to do when another researcher suggested that he write a browser for the barely known but potentially interesting World Wide Web.

In the middle of November 1992, Andreessen contacted Tim Berners-Lee and the Web community for the first time, in a note to the www-talk mailing list, the notice board for the tiny population of Web developers, in which he said that he was 'starting the game late'. Over the following weeks, he did everything he could do to catch up – working feverishly, posting messages at all times of the day and night – behaviour that he would later describe as 'obsessive-compulsive'. Almost from the beginning he referred to the Web and his browser as a 'product'.

On 29 January 1993, Andreessen made a historic announcement to the www-talk mailing list. 'By the power vested in me by nobody in particular, alpha/beta version 0.5 of NCSA's . . . World Wide Web browser, X Mosaic, is hereby released.' Two months after they'd started their task, he and Eric Bina, his colleague and collaborator, had created their first Web browser. It was for the computer-operating system favoured by the computer-science community, Unix. Remarkably easy to install, more importantly, it *worked*; Andreessen pushed it out with aggressive fervour to email groups and bulletin-board services around the Internet. It was adopted with a genuine excitement, in the belief that it really was going to make the difficult world of the Internet popular and easy to use.

There were already other browser developers at work but none shared Andreessen and Bina's single minded determination. Nor could they match the speed of their codewriting or focus on creating new features to meet the demands of the users. Mosaic would come to dominate the Internet. In the free-for-all of the Internet, the ability to put out software that worked trumped everything else.

Andreessen wasn't content just to work within the Standards that Berners-Lee had created – he wanted to extend them. Just a month after releasing his first browser, he proposed that it should be possible to view images in the midst of documents. Berners-Lee suggested that it would be better if the images were a hyperlink that when clicked would open up in a separate window. Two weeks later Andreessen announced his unilateral decision to display images in his forthcoming browser Mosaic. He wrote, 'I don't see an alternative [to this other] than to . . . wait for the perfect solution to come along.'

In March of 1993, Tim Berners-Lee happened to be in Chicago. He thought it would be interesting to meet the new enthusiasts for his Web a couple of hours away in Urbana-Champaign. There, in the Center's basement meeting room, Andreessen and Berners-Lee and their various allies sat face to face.

The purpose of the meeting was ostensibly to agree further

extensions to Berners-Lee's Standards, but beneath the surface of their discussion bubbled genuine hostility between the protagonists. Tim Berners-Lee later remembered it with discomfort: 'All my previous meetings with browser developers had been meetings of minds, with a pooling of enthusiasm. But this meeting had a strange tension to it.' For Berners-Lee the universal system that he had created seemed as if it was about to be taken over by a group determined to claim it as their own. Also at the meeting was Tom Bruce, a researcher from Cornell University, who had travelled to Urbana-Champaign with Berners-Lee. When he surprised the Andreessen team by announcing that he was writing the first browser for the Windows operating system, he sensed that he was now characterised as competition (rather than a fellow collaborator) and as such he was the foe to be beaten.

Joseph Hardin, then Andreessen's boss, recalled that Berners-Lee was upset. 'This was one of the first times that he really saw the group that was moving so fast. And the technology was taking on a life of its own. It's like a parent who sees a child grow up all of a sudden. We were playing with his baby.' Hardin and his team had no qualms about being competitive; they thought that they could be really successful only if their software was adopted by huge numbers of computer users.

The young hacker and the older researcher had very different personalities. Tim Berners-Lee was idealistic, he wanted to create a common standard for sharing information. As Dale Dougherty describes him, 'Tim wants to talk about ideas, and get you excited about them, rattling through them so fast, he doesn't care for nuts if you get them all and he doesn't necessarily care to sell you on something.'

Andreessen was quite different, he was a champion, a salesman, challenging people, and arguing with them. Forceful, determined, persuasive and desperate to push ideas in exactly the directions that he chose. Even his boss at the time, Joseph Hardin, describes his arrogance, 'He very much felt that he was the leader of the thing.'

On leaving this first meeting in Illinois, Berners-Lee felt that his Web was in danger of fatally fracturing, because Andreessen's team was running 'single-handedly' towards the goal line. As he recalled: 'Evidence was mounting that "the Web" could splinter into various factions – some commercial, some academic; some free, some not. This would defeat the very purpose of the Web: to be a single, universal accessible Hypertext medium for sharing information.'

To prevent this, soon afterwards Berners-Lee released the Standards under a 'public license' which meant that the World Wide Web could never be controlled by a single institution or corporation. He also established the World Wide Web Consortium, a not-for-profit organisation whose sole purpose is to guard the Standards that make the Web work. This was in order to guarantee that the Standards would not be perverted by corporations seeking to extend them to the exclusion of other users, and as a way of preventing any individual, including Berners-Lee himself, from profiting from his innovation.

In various subsequent meetings, tension continued to be felt between the consensual Tim Berners-Lee and the determined and singular Marc Andreessen. Observers describe the young hacker's behaviour as childish, with his wisecracking to the sniggers of his team, making sarcastic, deprecating comments about his elders, and 'we are going to conquer the world' attitude. Nonetheless, this gung-ho spirit did inspire incredible productivity from the Mosaic team. During 1993 the Mosaic Web browser was released first for Windows and then Macintosh – and it was the Mosaic browser that Hans and Herbert discovered via Franz Penz. The Web phenomenon had begun, and growth in traffic suddenly became exponential as new users flocked to the easy-to-use Internet. In the one year until the end of 1993, the number of Web sites grew from a few hundred to more than 10,000.

The opposing characters of the Web's main protagonists did much for its ultimate success. While Tim Berners-Lee built the Web, safeguarded the Standards and kept order, the younger Marc Andreessen made a compelling browser and fought aggressively to make the World Wide Web a simple, accessible technology.

Marc Andreessen went on to set up a corporation that made browsers – and in doing so became the first of the boyish Internet millionaires, a role model for a new generation of entrepreneurs using the Internet as a platform for profit. For their cover, *Time* magazine placed him barefoot on a gold throne – the rebel king.

By contrast, Tim Berners-Lee adopted the role of consummate politician, defending his creation from avaricious colonisation by any commercial interest. *Fortune* magazine in turn depicted him as Saint Tim. Always the European, he would later write, 'Many people ask why I didn't commercialize the Web. It's a strange question. By asking the question, people are suggesting that they respect people as a function of their net worth. That's worrying. It's not an assumption I was brought up with; and it is disturbing, the extent to which it pervades [the USA].'

Without these two notes the Web phenomenon could not have had such explosive resonance. What Berners-Lee and Andreessen achieved was remarkable: despite the anarchistic sensibility of the Internet community, they had built order, a set of common rules that was widely adopted because nobody owned or controlled it. Yet the Web would not have been so massive had a singular individual and the company that he became part of not dominated the process in the first years. This struggle between self-interest and public good, between wilful individualism and determined collectivism, was the defining conflict of the birthing of Web technology. This conflict would set the framework for and determine the path of many others of the coming years.

From Vienna, Hans and Herbert quickly communicated their discovery of the World Wide Web to the other members of the gang. 'A world opened up to me that I did not know existed. It was like a parallel universe, and it seemed to be incredibly huge,' says Franco. 'I had this impression despite the fact that there was almost exclusively university stuff up there.' Almost immediately, the group came to see the Internet as more than a vehicle for simple communication – they began to realise that it was a medium through which they could define their identity.

Herbert and Hans were so excited about their discovery that they demanded Internet access at their art school, and even set about organising access for the rest of their class (though their efforts were met with derision from the archly hip art students, who thought that the latest cool media was video, not the Internet). In Zürich, the rest of the crew wangled passwords for the computer lab at the university.

One of the first things the friends used the Web for was to search for a new name, because Thomas hated Combination-Combination. He thought it was both too long and too dull ever to be seen as anything cool. Instead, the story goes that Juri created a little computer program called the Term Shooter, a script that was able to generate names. It created four-letter words with a vowel in the middle, like that of their role model Sony, and descenders or ascenders for graphic effect. Supposedly, one night towards the end of 1994, they were huddled around their respective computers in Vienna and Zürich with the Term Shooter spewing out thousands of scrolling names. It was like a transnational shoot-'em-up word game; if a name didn't stick immediately, it wasn't worth considering. At first they found nothing. Then one name resonated across the collective. Herbert, Juri and the others danced on their keyboards. It was better than Sony. It looked good and it had comic connotations. They liked it for its whimsy, for its drug reference and its playfulness. The name was etoy.

Later in 1994, Peter was using Mosaic to navigate his way around the Web one day when he chanced upon a Web site, based at a polar-research centre in Ohio, that also hosted Web sites for free. There he created the beginnings of etoy's first site; it was dreary, with black text on a grey background. It had a Web address and a URL with so many parts that it was impossible to remember: http://www-bprc.mps.ohio-state.edu/cgi-bin/hppetoy.html. Next to the icon of a little bomb, Peter had written, 'etoy, here we are now! . . . etoy is THE new lifestyle for the coming generation. Please visit us when this site will be finished, in mid-January.'

Leaving Reality Behind

The boys celebrated in the way they knew best: by getting drunk at a party. Elated by their new discovery, they ran round scribbling the '@' symbol on to party-goers' hands. As Peter remembers, 'We were so excited that we told everybody how brilliant the future would be.'

2
Leaving Reality Behind

'Branding, in its truest and most advanced incarnations, is about corporate transcendence.'

Naomi Klein, *No Logo*, 2000

'It is impossible that old prejudices and hostilities should longer exist, while such an instrument has been created for the exchange of thought between all the nations of the earth.'

The Times, about the telegraph, 1858

In early 1995, the etoy gang worked relentlessly for their common aims. Hans and Herbert considered the strategy, created graphics and wrote manifestos and poetry. Peter and Franco wrote and recorded music. Juri explored the working of Web technology. Alberto worked on three-dimensional graphic representations that he hoped would become a 'virtual disco'. Thomas wrote witty essays about their lifestyle. There was no central direction, but the seven of them had a shared sensibility and all seemed to push in roughly the same direction. 'It was as if we were ants,' remembers Juri, 'and we all knew independently where the sugar was.'

They also began planning a more extensive Web site. They wanted to show its visitors their work – Herbert's images and Hans's WORDWAR poems. In the 'disco', Peter and Franco were going to make their soundtracks available. To launch themselves and their first steps on the World Wide Web, they decided to hold a party, which they initially hoped could be online, with party-goers logging on around the world, listening to their music and chatting and smooching with each other across the Internet. But while they were confounded by the impossibility of virtual drinks and drugs, their biggest problem was that the technology didn't quite live up to their expectations: the network was slow and the computers lacked power. In the end, the online-party idea was abandoned in favour of an offline event at a converted Zürich sports-centre. They called their launch party etoy. FASTLANE as a homage to the information superhighway.

Prior to the event, Thomas had filled hundreds of plastic bags with capsules of icing sugar; on the day, many guests thought these contained drugs, thinking the 'e' in etoy stood for ecstasy. Laughing gas was served alongside the beer and snacks at the bar. Dominating the room was a huge black box on which Peter danced in a silver dress and sunglasses – trying to be a digital David Bowie – lip-synching his way through two of etoy's Internet-inspired techno tracks, 'Mail Me' and 'We Can't Stop'.

Coco, a beautiful blonde transsexual and Swiss tabloid celebrity on the way to greater fame on the Paris catwalks, produced the evening's climax. Suspended on a rope, she flew across the room dressed in a silver angel costume and singing a Japanese song, while a Russian TV crew filmed the event as the perfect expression of decadent Zürich youth. Coco had recently discovered her own fascination with cyberspace, along with a crush on Herbert. She had offered to be his muse and to use her media connections and photogenic posturing to help the group. In return, Herbert would declare her 'etoy's lifestyle angel'. It was as if the Seven Dwarves had discovered their Snow White.

All the members of etoy were pleased with what they considered to be an edgy and glamorous party. For those guests who made it into the VIP area, there was the added thrill of an Internet connection – which many of them were seeing for the first time. It was as etoy had promised in their pre-party press release: 'Navigate with a mouse-click through worlds that recently were not even imaginable. Cyberspace for everybody! THE FUTURE IS NOW!'

However, the future they thought they had launched didn't come quickly. A slot they had been promised on a local TV station in Zürich under the tag line 'etoy – the first street gang on the international super data highway' fell through, and attempts by Herbert and Peter to secure a record deal in London also came to nothing. Herbert was convinced that the dullards of the entertainment industry didn't understand quite how the world had moved on. etoy decided that from then on they would only release their music and other creations on the Internet – 'a non-material platform, the virtual stage for the new travelling generation', as they called it. For this new world of Internet stardom they coined a new slogan: 'etoy: the pop star is the pilot is the coder is the designer is the architect is the manager is the system is etoy.'

The Internet and pop stars were not the only influences to be fuelling etoy's dreams. 'At the core of etoy are the computer and LSD,' Herbert explains. LSD had been their favourite vice as adolescents; they all remember their first acid trip. Together they had gone to Zürich's Bahnhofstrasse, the home territory of the city's financial gnomes, and watched hallucinations of blood running down the façades of the banks, which then metamorphosed into the red-and-white Swiss flag. 'We took these common drug experiences back into reality. It glued us together as a group,' says Peter. The experience of tripping together welded the bonds of their friendships closer and created a common understanding about their lives and work.

Nowadays the conjunction between computers and LSD seems surreal. Most computers have become simply the dull cogs of the global economy. But in the early 1990s this symbiosis of technology and narcotics did not seem at all strange; even the sixties drug guru Timothy Leary was promoting his latest passion: computers. Although etoy never met him, they came to know his friends, some of whom were to have a profound influence on the gang. In the pantheon of etoy influences Tim Leary is another angel.

In his days as a Harvard professor of psychology, Leary had

advocated the benefit of hallucinatory drugs such as LSD to the Flower Power generation. Described by President Richard Nixon in the 1970s as the most dangerous man in America, he had escaped from a twenty-year jail sentence, fleeing first to Algeria and then to Switzerland, only returning to Beverly Hills in the 1980s.

From its outset, Leary was fascinated by the life-altering possibilities of the personal-computer revolution. One of his first endeavours was to create a computer program to analyse the human mind. By the early 1990s he was committed to pushing the computer as a social force, saying that, 'The PC is the LSD of the nineties' and reworking his famous drug slogan 'Turn On, Tune In, Drop Out' into 'Turn On, Tune In, *Log on*.' He encouraged his audiences to connect to the Internet as a method of political empowerment, and advocated 'digital power to the people'.

A regular performer at raves and technology conferences alike, Leary became a guru to a small and peculiar scene in the Bay Area of Northern California that centred around a magazine called *Mondo 2000*, the self-declared 'User's Guide to the New Edge' which hit American news-stands in 1989 and was soon to become the bible of a new counterculture called cyberculture. The so-called cyberpunks drew their identity from an amalgam of science-fiction literature, the drug rebellion of the sixties and the computer culture of nearby Silicon Valley. By 1993 they had made it to the cover of *Time* magazine in an article that called cyberculture the 'defining counterculture of the computer age' and described it as 'bubbling up from the underground, popping out of computer screens like a piece of futuristic HYPERTEXT'.

Mondo 2000's contributors ranged across the spectrum, from writer William Burroughs to the anarchistic promoter of magic mushrooms Terence McKenna. Also involved were the Grateful Dead's ex-lyricist and Wyoming farmer John Perry Barlow; monologist Spalding Gray; New Age dolphin researcher John Lilly; and Eric Gullichsen, who had helped develop virtual reality. At *Mondo 2000*, partying was integral to the cyclic editorial process:

ideas for articles appeared at parties; parties happened as a result of articles. In this 'far out' environment, *Mondo 2000* and Timothy Leary provided each other with a mutual fan club – *Mondo* declared Leary a 'cyberdelic guru' and 'MVP (Most Valuable Philosopher) of the twentieth century', while Leary saw the magazine as 'a really remarkable institution' for its 'beautiful merger of the psychedelic, the cybernetic, the cultural, the literary, and the artistic'.

One idea that captured the collective imagination of the *Mondo 2000* group more than any other – because it promised a kind of technology-assisted acid trip – was virtual reality: the simulation of a three-dimensional environment experienced through a computer. By the late 1980s the world's press had become fascinated by the prospect of existence in another world – the broadsheets by the manipulation of molecules in another three-dimensional space; the tabloids by the prospect of virtual sex, absurdly called teledildonics.

'Cyberspace', the term used to describe this 'other world' created between computers, was coined by the novelist William Gibson in his novel *Neuromancer*. In this cult classic he described the new place as a 'consensual hallucination experienced daily by billions of legitimate operators, in every nation'. Gibson's dystopian future saw an alternative space, in which people would interact. This was 'a graphic representation of data abstracted from the banks of every computer in the human system. Unthinkable complexity.' Tim Leary loved the idea of cyberspace, believing that it was possible to create 'electronic realities' on the other side of the computer screen in which one could talk, dance, swim and float.

By this time Leary, in his seventies and increasingly fragile, became enraptured by thoughts of a non-corporeal future. He reckoned that 'within ten years many of us will not have to "go" to work. We will get up in the morning, shower, dress in our cyberwear suits, and "beam" our brains to work . . . Tomorrow our brains will soar on the wings of electrons into the offices of friends in Tokyo, then beam at light speed to a restaurant in Paris for a flirtatious lunch, pay a quick, ten-minute visit to our folks in Seattle – all without physically leaving our living rooms.'

In the coming years, the influences of the acid-head guru and the strange magazine persisted. Their countercultural ideas were currency to the newly established Internet community; and, later, as this community was forced into conflict under the pressure of corporate incomers' colonisation of cyberspace, it was Leary and *Mondo*'s philosophies that lent galvanising force to the battles of opposition.

By 1995, etoy had really taken to heart the idea of virtual reality. For the boys, cyberspace was a new and open territory that they were intent on squatting. As with their real-world activities of a few years before, they wanted to create a place in cyberspace that was an alternative cultural centre, as a means of bringing their radical, alternative lifestyle and ideas online.

However, their rudimentary Web site did not fulfil this ambition and their resources were not sufficient to turn it into a fully functioning virtual space. So, despite their rebellious sensibilities, they turned to government and private agencies for financial help. They were pioneers, and the grant givers did not understand them. One member of the Swiss Arts Council was wrong-footed by the unfamiliar '@' sign on etoy's business cards and asked what email addresses were; etoy soon realised that the funding bodies had no real idea what the Internet was – never mind the Web. One cultural bureaucrat even suggested to them that a CD-rom would be a more suitable project. This only made etoy all the more determined to prove themselves right.

To find a stage for their Web-based countercultural ideas, in April 1995 Herbert travelled to Linz in Austria in a bid to persuade the organisers of the prestigious arts festival Ars Electronica to hold an etoy event. Situated on the River Danube, with its tourist boats and cargo freighters, Linz had gained unwelcome notoriety as the place where Hitler attended school and was an unusual setting for such a forward-looking event. The festival was first held in the late 1970s, developed initially by the city council as a fringe programme to their annual festival celebrating the Victorian composer Anton Bruckner. The event soon flourished into a fully fledged festival of its own, exploring the relationship of art, technology and society and so becoming a draw for a stellar list of Big Thinkers such as Richard Dawkins, author of *The Selfish Gene*; William Gibson and Bruce Sterling, the fathers of cyberpunk; Jean Baudrillard, France's favourite post-modern philosopher; Kevin Kelly, author of *Out of Control* and executive editor of the seminal magazine *WIRED*; Vilém Flusser, philosopher of communication, and his colleague, the philosopher and psychoanalyst Slavoj Žižek.

Each year, Ars Electronica has a different theme; and in 1995 it was 'Welcome to the Wired World'. This was the first time that the festival celebrated the World Wide Web, and included in the schedule was a special prize category for innovative use of this new medium. Herbert hoped that etoy could organise a party there as a means of promoting themselves, but to his disappointment their project was outshone and undercut by some art students from Linz who had offered to organise a cheaper 'Netnite' party.

Even without an official role, etoy planned to use the festival as their stage. In preparation they brainstormed how best they could present themselves to the digital-arts world. They remained adamant that their countercultural ideas were best furthered not by a manifesto, a poem or a painting, but by a corporation. Herbert gave out the order that the whole crew must show up in Linz because, as he put it, 'this is one of etoy's markets'. The festival would be etoy's first opportunity to launch their 'corporation' to the world of art and culture.

They had big dreams. As Franco remembers, 'We were dreaming of a headquarters that was a skyscraper, all in glass with a big logo on top of it.' The key to their venture was etoy's 'brand'. Hans borrowed a corporate-identity booklet from his father's company; what they learned from this led to their decision to establish a rigorously defined set of rules concerning company presentation. Their first step was to design the etoy logo. It was agreed that the name would always appear only in lower case; they chose a typeface – Microstyle Bold Extended Oblique – with a precise stretch of 135 per cent; and then their corporate colour – orange – because it reminded them of warning signals.

One of the boys' more remarkable moves was to jettison individual fashions in favour of a uniform corporate look. Throughout the Western world, people were 'dressing down' and wearing casuals – even Silicon Valley's millionaires were increasingly jeans- and sneaker-clad – but Herbert and his gang were determined to follow a more time-honoured corporate aesthetic. Just as IBM had once been seen as an army of executives in identical blue jackets and pressed shirts, etoy would from now on adopt a consistent company style. They chose what would become their most notable icon: an orange bomber jacket with the etoy logo on the back. These were set off by black trousers, mirrored pilot sunglasses and little black attaché cases. The final touch was that they all shaved their heads. Spectators described them variously as resembling a group of astronauts, a security squad and a fascist street-gang.

etoy's corporate identity was a striking break from normal modes of behaviour. It was as if they were forcing themselves into the most radical position with their look and their rigorous graphic style. They seemed to revel in – and criticise – the power of 'brands', precisely mirroring one of the era's dominant themes.

Branding, in 1995, was in the middle of its magisterial rise to prominence. By the end of the nineties, Tom Peters – the pre-eminent management guru of the decade – would write, 'It's a new brand world.' It was estimated that corporations were spending an annual $465 billion supporting the logos, tag lines and philosophies that gave 'value' to their products. Many of the world's leading corporations divested themselves of responsibility for producing anything at all, instead positioning themselves at the centre of networks of independent contractors and establishing their role simply as 'managers' of the all-encompassing world-view of their various brands. As Naomi Klein would write in *No Logo*, 'Overnight, "brands, not products!" became the rallying cry for a marketing renaissance led by a new breed of companies that saw themselves as "meaning brokers" instead of product producers.'

The etoy brand's 'meaning' was the group's antagonistic sensibility itself, standing against the banality of the ordinary, the dullness of life. They would steal the clothes of corporations – the branding, the rhetoric and the aesthetic – to create an absurdist critique of corporate culture. Theirs was a satire of the overbearing power of corporations, and yet they simultaneously paid a kind of twisted homage to the heroic brands that had dominated their youth. They were not afraid of playing both ends against the middle, paradoxically celebrating and lampooning corporate life in demonstration of their cynicism. Even their intentions became couched in the language of enterprise, as Herbert remembers, 'We wanted to enter a market, the market of entertainment, art and culture. It's a limited market, so we had to fight for recognition and promote etoy internationally . . . We played it hard.'

Beyond the thin epidermis of branding, the corporate ideal was to have a profound effect on how the gang behaved. Again like IBM, which in the 1950s had a corporate ideology that extended to a song book containing such lyrics as 'All Hail to the IBM', the etoy members resolved to push their absolutist dogma to its limits and submit to the will of the corporation. The source of this will was not to be a CEO or a Board of Directors, but rather a computer. As if the boys had canonised their computer system, they vested in it a power beyond their control. 'The system itself was at the centre,' says Herbert. 'The server [computer] was like our god, being superhuman and incomprehensible.'

The commandments that this computer-Moses brought down from the mountain were absurd. The most important rule was that etoy members should always put the company first, which meant being reachable at all hours of the day and night and dedicating most of their energy to the company's success. The corporation also determined when members were allowed to go on holiday – and even when they were allowed to see their girlfriends.

The commandments in a sense codified the dominant work-ethic of the contemporary technology industry. After all, computer scientists and early hackers had for years worked eccentrically long hours – a tendency only exacerbated by the arrival of the Web, when everything was always online and always available. In the frenzied ethos of the day, each moment spent away from a terminal came to seem like a missed opportunity. By the time one came in to work, who knew, the world might have changed again, another future forged by someone who had not gone out for dinner.

etoy's company rules also insisted that members keep the group's inner workings secret from outsiders; any transgression of this was fiercely punished. It was an intensely claustrophobic adventure that Herbert remembers being like a journey into space. 'We often used the metaphor of the spacemen. They can only concentrate on their work when they are isolated from the rest of the world. The spaceship is also a symbol for risk and loneliness, for setting off and leaving many things behind.'

Their ultimate sacrifice on the altar of company 'professionalism' was their decision to give up their names. It was at this point that they began to call themselves 'agents' and adopted new titles. Peter, the charming musician, had already taken a different name because he hated his own; he had chosen Goldstein when he became a radio DJ after the character in the novel *1984* whom Orwell described as 'the primal traitor, the earliest defiler of the Party's purity'. Therefore when the others chose their new names the obvious choice for him was to stick to what he had and simply become agent.GOLDSTEIN. The new monikers would be capitalised as part of the group's obsessive rules of corporate identity.

Hans searched for a name that would match his aspirations and chose to become agent.BRAINHARD. Herbert called himself agent.ZAI and for years afterwards would symbolically spell it for journalists, Zoo, America, Idiot. Alberto used Gramazio; Franco chose Esposto; Juri opted for Udatny and Thomas became Kubli. Henceforth they would only be known by these titles, except on occasions when the group swapped names to confuse

etoy in 1995. Clockwise
from top left: Zai,
Brainhard, Esposto, Udatny,
Goldstein, Kubli and
Gramazio.

journalists. Despite the boys' real names being easily available on the Web, Zai still sweats with anger when journalists reveal his.

As time wore on, the boys' intonation and vocabulary sounded increasingly similar; this, along with their orange jackets and skinheads and interchangeable names, ensured that it became nearly impossible for anyone to tell them apart. In some ways they were merging into a single character, played out by seven individuals, their own identities more and more difficult to distinguish. In uniformity, the etoy group found a salve for their explosive egos, because, as Zai explains, 'It prevented members from putting their individual characters into the foreground. No one could stick out, and this guaranteed the group's equilibrium; it solved several problems at once. That the members were interchangeable was good for the art aspect also.'

Submitting to the company was a painful process that most of the group did not enjoy, but they were prisoners of ambition and friendship. 'It was a collective decision,' Brainhard (formerly the blustering poet Hans) remembers. 'It was, in a very cool way, radical, experimental and completely crazy.' They all thought they were playing an 'edge game' pushing ideas about identity and technology to their limits in the hope of provoking a response both from the world's staid institutions and from their peers, who they dreamed of as their fans. The result was a complicated intellectual construct, an absurd fantasy-world of branding that was a sort of amalgamation of a company, an artists' club, and an absolutist sect.

They hoped also that this weird world might be able to make them a living. Like the designer of Diesel Jeans, Renzo Rosso, who piously claims, 'We don't sell a product, we sell a style of life', etoy declares, 'The notion of lifestyle is central to what we were searching for. We wanted to create our own lifestyle and sell it.' More specifically, they wanted to sell what they called 'Digital Lifestyle', which would include their products, projected images and music for parties.

* * *

It was with this rigorous formation in place that etoy set forth to conquer Ars Electronica, determined to make their mark although still without an official role. The festival was opened in June 1995 by the Mayor of Linz and comprised, among other things, a collection of performances, including one by the New York artist and musician Laurie Anderson. There was also what the programme esoterically described as 'an attempt to do a critical analysis of Wagner's works on the basis of Bernard Shaw's simultaneous reading of Wagner's operas and Karl Marx's *Kapital*.'

Heads turned as the seven orange-clad shaven-headed youths wandered the streets of Linz. 'We staged ourselves like a boy-band, and we always drank too much,' Zai recalls. But when they gatecrashed the gala party and tried to shock the celebrating crowd, they were received with only wry amusement from the openhearted liberals.

One of the festival events was a symposium to which a dozen speakers had been invited to share their visions of a wired future. As the programme stated, 'no longer do we live in streets and houses alone, but also in cable channels, telegraph wires, email boxes, and global digital Net-worlds'. Zai and the gang were diligent attendees, while one of the major stars to appear was Tim Berners-Lee, inventor of the World Wide Web.

Another was John Perry Barlow, former Grateful Dead lyricist, now a pre-eminent defender of liberty on the Internet. In the five years prior to this Ars Electronica, he had established himself as a sort of roving ambassador, travelling the world promoting the Internet community. Some of this time had been spent as an advisor to US Vice President Al Gore and also to Newt Gingrich, yet in conflicts and court cases against the government he was often taking the side of hackers and community insiders.

In the auditorium at Ars Electronica, John Perry Barlow told the assembled mass – including the attentive etoy crew – how he had initially found his way on to the Internet, in the late 1980s. At the time he was a farmer, running a cattle ranch in Wyoming, and he had wanted to eavesdrop on a community of Grateful Dead fans – the Deadheads. Someone pointed him towards the

Whole Earth 'Lectronic Link (WELL), an early online service that had started in 1985 and was for the most part a collection of bulletin boards. Users could send a message to whichever board they found of particular interest, and in turn provoke responses from others in lively strings of discussion that would continue intermittently. These debates about politics, music, culture and technology were often thoughtful, erudite and long-running. As a result, the WELL was regarded for years to come as the prototypical model for all 'online communities'.

Barlow told the audience at the festival of how he won his struggle with modems and cables to gain access to the WELL: 'I found myself looking at the glowing yellow word "Login", beyond which lay my future . . . I was delighted. I felt I had found the new locale of human community.' Remarkably, for a community where people had no physical contact, he thought it much like his home in Pinedale, Wyoming, because its members 'had a place [where] their hearts could remain as the companies they worked for shuffled their bodies around America. They could put down roots which could not be ripped out by forces of economic history. They had a collective stake.'

What had most intrigued Barlow was that this was a self-governing community, pioneering its own set of laws about member behaviour and applying its own sanctions against those who transgressed them. Consequently Barlow was one of the first to identify the Internet as being a place with real politics, where interest groups and individuals could struggle for power between themselves. To distinguish the Internet as an arena for social forces, power and politics, he decided to name it borrowing William Gibson's word, *cyberspace*, and in so doing gave it political intent.

Almost as soon as he found cyberspace, Barlow became concerned that governments and corporations were trying to impose their will on 'the desperadoes and mountain men and vigilantes' of the digital Wild West. Thus in 1990 he co-founded the Electronic Frontier Foundation (EFF) to defend freedom of speech online. His partner was Mitch Kapor, the man who founded Lotus Computers and who was by 1990 a *bona fide* member of Silicon Valley royalty. Together, Barlow and Kapor corralled a collection of their friends – some of them the founders of Sun Microsystems and Apple Computers – to sit on the board and make hundreds of thousands of dollars' worth of donations. The EFF began by defending kids who were victims of an FBI crackdown on computer crime, and went on to fight attempts by the US government to impose censorship on the Internet.

With the rhetoric he used and the images he painted, Barlow positioned himself as a kind of cowboy survivalist, armed and ready to defend his cyberspace wilderness from the approaching posse of Federal forces. Barlow's most grandiose and historic political stand came when he proclaimed himself as the Thomas Jefferson of the new world. At the World Economic Forum in Davos, Switzerland, he wrote 'A Declaration of the Independence of Cyberspace', in which he demanded that governments back off.

A Declaration of the Independence of Cyberspace

Governments of the Industrial World, you weary giants of flesh and steel, I come from Cyberspace, the new home of Mind. On behalf of the future, I ask you of the past to leave us alone. You are not welcome among us. You have no sovereignty where we gather.

We have no elected government, nor are we likely to have one, so I address you with no greater authority than that with which liberty itself always speaks. I declare the global social space we are building to be naturally independent of the tyrannies you seek to impose on us. You have no moral right to rule us nor do you possess any methods of enforcement we have true reason to fear . . . We are forming our own Social Contract. This governance will arise according to the conditions of our world, not yours. Our world is different.

The declaration, which runs to more than a thousand words, was posted on hundreds of Web sites and was a clarion call to regulators, lawyers and courts to leave the Internet community alone. As the Internet became more commercial and the space more contested, various new conflicts erupted between governments and the community and between individuals and corporations. In these it was often the spirit of this declaration – its wilful libertarianism and plea for independence from the laws and courts of the corporeal world – that was invoked.

When etoy heard John Perry Barlow talking at Ars Electronica, they were struck most of all by his question about cyberspace, 'Does it supplant the real or is there, in it, reality itself?' Barlow drenched his answer in the utopianism of the euphoric believers in the Californian technological dream. The new world that he was describing was not just going to be a replacement for the real one; it could, he hoped, be an improvement on it, more humanistic and wonderful. 'When we are all together in cyberspace then we will see what the human spirit, and the basic desire to connect, can create there . . . Despite its current (and, perhaps, in some areas permanent) insufficiencies, we should go to cyberspace with hope. Groundless hope, like unconditional love, may be the only kind that counts.'

Zai, Brainhard, Gramazio, Kubli, Esposto, Udatny and Goldstein had now found real motivation to explore the new world. They were willing to go into cyberspace with dreams that it could perhaps be a more interesting place than the real world. They were also ready and willing to protect this new space from the drones of the old world who were intent on imposing a dull morality on it. They were to be the 'the First Street Gang of the Information Super Data Highway'.

After the festival, Zai and Brainhard returned to Vienna, the others to Zürich. Their determination to live online crystallised. The only impediment was their need for a catchy and distinctive domain name of their own – like in cnn.com or bbc.co.uk – the address where they would park their Web site. To continue the metaphor of cyberspace as the digital West, the domain name was like a homestead, the claim of the frontiersman. During the Internet's goldrush years, millions of hopeful punters bought such claims, in the belief that a name was all it took to strike Internet gold. Indeed, some did win out, selling simple names – such as events.com or business.com – for hundreds of thousands of dollars, and later millions. etoy were conscious that their decision to acquire a domain name was vital to their future.

When the Domain Name System was invented, the possibility for avaricious demand was never even contemplated; it was simply designed to make the locating of information easier and to organise the network more efficiently. But, as the Internet grew more commercial, the Domain Name System became the focus of a heated and rancorous conflict, at the heart of which lay the question of who should control the Internet itself.

At the epicentre of this battle was Jon Postel, of TCP/IP Standards fame. Since co-authoring the Standards, he had gone on to edit the documents that further improved the working of the network. It was his work on the Domain Name System, however, that ultimately gained him heroic status.

The Domain Name System began life in 1983. Postel had asked his colleague Paul Mockapetris to write a specification about how a naming system for the Internet could work. Already in place was the system of giving every computer on the network a number, the so-called IP number, but these were difficult to remember. Also, rather like the old telephone system, there was no easy way to carry the numbers between computers – in effect meaning that every time a user switched computers they had to take a new email address. The Domain Name System was to overlay the IP numbers with a portable and easy-to-remember name system.

The central idea of Mockapetris's Domain Name System is that there is only one 'address book', which accurately locates every computer on the Internet. Without a unique address for each computer, information intended for one machine could end up at another; were this to happen, the Internet would no longer be a unified and universal information system, but rather a set of fragmented, networked fiefdoms. In deciding on this single naming system, Mockapetris gave enormous power to the authorities in control of the registration and stewardship of the domain names, in that they could decide to delete any entry from the Internet without offering an alternative.

Essential to Mockapetris's system is arguably the most powerful document on the Internet, the A-Root, containing the key to the complete road map – all the addresses for every named computer connected to the Internet. Following the creation of the Domain Name System, this document became the Royal Standard, the Holy Grail over which competing armies in the domain wars would fight. What is most remarkable about the all-important A-Root is that it contains only 250 lines of information. Yet this tiny record, while not a list of every computer sitting on the Internet, can determine the addresses of the hundreds of millions of computers on the Internet; it is a collection of pointers to where this information can be found.

The distribution of the singular address book among many hands was not only an elegant technical solution to the problem of managing what would become such a big network, but also an ideological one. As Mockapetris – in whose Silicon Valley office now hangs a rebellious skull-and-crossbones flag – remembers, 'At that time I was a true believer in the idea of distributing the authority, rather than having it centrally.'

Mockapetris wrote the specification for the Domain Name System and gave it to Jon Postel, who became the pre-eminent domain-name politician. At first, this simply meant that he was the one who stewarded the technical details through the consensus-gathering process of Internet engineering. But it was also Postel who later determined the precise contents of the A-Root; as if he controlled the address book which in turn contained the addresses of the other 250 address books of the top-level domains. Postel chaired the committee that decided there should be 243 top-level domains named as country codes – .uk for Britain, .ch for Switzerland, etc. – and seven generic domains – .com for companies, .edu for academic institutions, .org for not-for-profit organisations, .net for networks, and so on.

The first dot-com domain name was registered on 15 March

1985 by a software company called symbolics.com. The registration process involved Postel creating the first entry in the database of dot-com domains, the dot-com address book. This in turn pointed to the database for the symbolics.com address book in which their own systems administrators could allocate numbered computers to specific sub-domains. For example, they would later take 'www' for their Web site – www.symbolics.com – but they would also have an email computer, at something like mail.symbolics.com. As the Internet grew, the fact that system administrators could name additional computers without resorting to a central command made it all the easier for the network to expand at incredible rates.

Jon Postel reigned benign and supreme across the Domain Name System from its inception until the 1990s. He was at the head of a shell organisation, the Internet Assigned Numbers of Authority (IANA), that had control over the A-Root and its future. But as the Net became more commercialised, so his authority was challenged. The biggest such threat came from an organisation that was initially brought in to help him out. In 1993, the US Government's National Science Foundation (NSF), which subsidised the Internet and funded Postel, gave a contract to a small company based in Herndon, Virginia, called Network Solutions. They were charged with physically looking after the A-Root while Postel kept control of the policies relating to the ways in which it could be changed. Network Solutions was also required to maintain the database of new generic-domain registrations like dot-com.

By 1995, this somewhat lowly administrative contract was on the verge of radical change. As the Internet blossomed and increasing numbers of for-profit firms and foreign organisations registered names, those at the National Science Foundation began to feel queasy about the prospect of continuing to subsidise these operations. In addition, Network Solutions was faced with developing legal liability as the first 'domain dispute' – between the owner of a trademarked brand and the owner of a domain name – was filed in a Chicago court and named Network Solutions as a co-defendant. As the problem grew, the company had no real idea of the kind of liability such a dispute might entail – there was the possibility of bankruptcy, which could have forced the collapse of the naming system and even the Internet itself.

It was at this time that Don Telage, who worked for a secretive defence contractor, Science Applications Industries Corporation (SAIC), stepped into the fray, when his company bought the struggling Network Solutions. Really he had hoped to exploit the other side of Network Solutions' business, telecom consultancy, but almost by accident he found he was sitting on a registration venture that might soon prove to be a goldmine. Encouraged by Telage, and to prevent the collapse of the Domain Name System, the National Science Foundation agreed that Network Solutions should be allowed to charge $100 for each new two-year regis-tration and $50 annually thereafter. Thirty per cent of the fees would revert to an 'Internet intellectual infrastructure fund', while the remainder would go towards Network Solutions' costs and to their profit. Charging for registration was to be introduced on 1 October 1995. When the news leaked out, speculators rushed in their thousands to register for free before the deadline. Thus it was brought forward to 12 September.

This event rocked the Internet engineering community – which until then had been organised around grindingly slow opinion-gathering processes. Around the Web campaigners, engineers and entrepreneurs began to complain about the new system, hope-lessly fracturing the rough consensus that Postel had nurtured for twenty years. Many felt that domain space was a public resource that should not be pursued for private profit. The shift also created a monopoly for the registration of dot-com and other top-level domains; and this monopoly was in the hands of Net-work Solutions, which now had every reason to guard jealously its singular right to register and charge.

When etoy first discussed where to build its home on the World Wide Web, etoy.ch with the Swiss country code was dismissed as being parochial. etoy.net was favoured because it had the essence of the underground hacker-scene and a sense of community. Soon, however, etoy.com became the group's preferred option because 'dot-com is an Internet status symbol (at least for primitive people like me)', as agent Kubli wrote in an email. 'And status symbols stand for power and power, in the end, stands for money.' The mischievous and musical Goldstein was the only group member to disagree; he thought that etoy should be pushing 'love', not power. His objections were eventually overcome. In Vienna Brainhard spoke for the rest of the group when he argued that 'dot-com is the commercial image, beautiful, brilliant like steel and hard'. The decision was made.

On 15 October 1995, the etoy members registered their domain name – etoy.com – with Network Solutions for a fee of $100 under the new rules. Had they completed the process one month earlier it would have cost them nothing. In registering they gave Network Solutions enormous power over their destiny. At the time, however, they foresaw no apparent danger – and anyway, they had no choice.

With the domain name registered, the boys relentlessly finished work on their Web site. Everywhere trailblazers were reaching for metaphors to describe the perfect Web site. Some thought the Web would deliver the written word like a magazine; others thought that Web sites were actually more like TV shows, streaming images and sound. To enable users to navigate around the sites, some contained headline-blaring front pages, structured like a newspaper, while others gave maps of information. For the etoy site, Zai and Gramazio proposed a metaphor which was a network of tanks and pipes – like a sewage farm. Initially the front page was to be a picture of the system, a sort of schematic plan, linking the various components. Gramazio remembers, 'We wanted to create an environment with surreal content, to build a parallel world and put the content of this world into tanks.'

During these intense months of creativity, etoy was also developing its own language. The word 'professional', for instance, came to be used as the primary aspiration and injunction of the company, and the word 'unprofessional' the central pejorative.

These became, as Esposto recalls, Zai's favourite terms. 'He always said that we had to be "professional". The word "professional" was used to paper over the weak spots of the organisation. I didn't understand all the company details any more, but I was very impressed by this guy who thought of everything.'

Slightly more surprising was their use of the word 'hardcore' in almost every sentence. For them, it denoted determination, wild and adrenaline-fuelled, as well as alluding to the beat-heavy industrial house music of that name. Interestingly, and unbeknown to the boys, the only corporation to regularly use the word 'hardcore' as much as they did was Microsoft. *New Yorker* writer Ken Auletta called a whole chapter of his book *World War 3.0* about Microsoft 'Hardcore'. As Rob Glaser, CEO of Real Networks, who used to work with Bill Gates, said: 'I do think the Microsoft culture was one where being hardcore and not being seen as less than hardcore was very important and very highly valued. The Microsoft culture is one where people are not chastised for being paranoid or over-competitive.'

Eventually the etoy Web site was completed, named the etoy. TANKSYSTEM and described as a 'parallel world somewhere in between LEGO-land, Internet training camp, virtual fairground, hypermedia test ground, sound & vision dump and Internet motel for travellers of the new kind'. Visitors could navigate through the tanks by clicking on arrows at the top of the screen. In the Supermarket tank they could order online etoy sunglasses and laughing-gas cylinders – though these were never delivered. In the Gallery the IP numbers of Web-surfers were checked and printed on the screen, while a Big Brother-ish eye, created by the brilliant hacker Udatny, looked on. etoy also built the first suite of its cybermotel. Coco, the transsexual who had flown through their launch party, furnished it with pictures of and interviews with herself.

The most visited tank was called Underground. There, etoy featured the forbidden – pornography, violence and drug abuse. This was the place where the boys were determined to repudiate the stuffy and constricted sensibilities of the communities they came from, pushing to the absolute limit their critique of the middle-class righteousness and virtue that they so despised. As Zai remembers, 'etoy, at that time, thought that any moral was bad.' Their method was to shock in the most extreme and distasteful ways. The Underground tank contained a photograph of the Federal Building in Oklahoma City after it had been bombed; underneath it was the caption 'Such work needs a lot of training'. There was also a picture of a woman's naked breasts pierced with dozens of needles, and a naked man bound and hung upside-down. It was not that the boys supported terrorism or were enamoured by sadomasochism; rather, it was that they thought these shocking images would serve to both get them noticed and provoke and move on the world in which they lived.

When the Web site was completed, Zai was euphoric, exhibiting a hubris that would in time become overwhelming. He wrote to the Zürich crew, 'We are now the biggest, strongest and most beautiful of the world! This is the first time in my life that we have done something really great. My partners Brainhard and Udatny, and me today worked for the tank for 12 hours without stopping, online, non-linear, not local! HARDCORE! nobody can catch up with us. fuck mtv. fuck netscape. fuck all.'

Soon etoy would announce to the world that they were the first people ever to have emigrated to the Internet to live a digital existence. This 'emigration' led to them relying more and more on the robustness of the Domain Name System to protect their homestead at etoy.com. Within a year, they had left their hair, their clothes, their names and, of course, their personal freedom on the altar of the etoy brand; they were henceforth committed to following the etoy corporate identity. And from now on, all communiqués were signed 'etoy, leaving reality behind'.

In the hills above Hollywood, Timothy Leary, now an old and sick man, was also preparing to leave reality behind, with the support of his 'godson', Joichi Ito. They had first met each other at Ito's twenty-fourth birthday party, in Tokyo in the summer of

1990, when Ito – then a DJ entrepreneur – who had been reading books about Leary, asked him if he ever really had received messages from aliens. Leary laughed. 'That's just a lie; we made it up.' They broke away from the party and strolled across the Ropongi district, where Ito showed the older man the hip, technology-loving children of Japan's economic bubble at play. 'He got really excited,' Ito recalls; Leary was also intrigued by this representative of tech-savvy Japanese youth and soon began describing him as his godson.

Less than a month later, Leary took Ito – along with Ito's Los Angeles-based mother and sister – to a party in northern California at the *Mondo 2000* house in the Berkeley hills. There, Joichi Ito met the scene. Soon he was appearing with Leary on stage in a show called 'Psychedelics to Cybernetics', and was staying with the liberty-defending John Perry Barlow in Pinedale, Wyoming. In the summer of 1990, he wrote in his diary, 'I got a call from Timothy just now, what a godfather, I'm having trouble keeping up with all this energy, I feel an almost ecstatic vertigo from the acceleration of progress.'

But if Timothy Leary introduced Joichi Ito to his world it was Ito who introduced the older man to the World Wide Web, and opened up for him another dimension beyond the disappointment of virtual reality. Ito – like the etoy boys – had a previous history with computers, that he had all but forgotten. In 1981, as a teenager in Tokyo, he'd managed to hack his way into university computer systems and then jump from one location to another. He eventually found the first interactive game, the Multi-User Dungeon (MUD) at the University of Essex, in England. For weeks he played this text-based adventure game, as a character whom he called Sid – after the Sex Pistols' Sid Vicious. When Sid met a gruesome virtual death, Ito wept for a whole night.

By the time the Web browser Mosaic was released, Ito was in Tokyo running clubs and various other businesses. The Web was a medium to which he took with great ease. As Howard Rheingold, a writer from the West Coast technology elite, wrote,

'Mosaic in Joi's hands had that instantly recognisable look of the future to it.' Tim Leary had a similar revelation on seeing Mosaic. On his Web site he wrote: 'A few years ago, a young Cyber-Wizard named Joichi Ito said, "Our computer screens are windows into Cyber Worlds which we can explore. The first step is to design, construct, and furnish our personal-private Home, where friends can hang out." And that's when I realized the empowerment that inter-personal computers offer individuals.'

Joining Leary's vision to Ito's ideas, in the middle of 1995 the pair began to create a 'Home on the Internet' for Timothy Leary. So enamoured of the future was Timothy Leary that he sold his car, leaving behind what he thought of as the old fossil-fuel economy, and transformed his garage into the workspace for a number of young Web designers and hackers; this he called his 'digital garage'. Ito, meanwhile, had been using his bicultural and technical knowledge to translate the Internet to the Japanese. He founded a company called Eccosys and set up Japan's first Web server in the bathroom of his apartment, then sent his godfather and mentor the computers he would need to implement his final dream.

Tim Leary wanted his Web presence to replicate his real-life house, for viewers to be able to see inside the living room and dining room and to 'pick' books off his shelves. The concept was simple, as Chris Graves, Leary's Webmaster, remembers, 'He wanted people to have as much access to his life and his work as he gave them in real life.' Graves and his friends mapped out the house, photographing it from top to bottom and uploading the pictures on to the Web. 'Tim was the mastermind of the whole thing; he was directing the whole process,' recalls Graves.

Leary was dying of prostate cancer, and he planned for the Web site to be his swansong. He registered his drug intake on it, and in one rash moment even claimed that he would broadcast his death live over the Internet. The global media reported hysteri-cally this strange final twist from the great provocateur of the sixties; it seemed so new, so radical and so innovative. In the event, Leary did not go ahead with the broadcast.

In the spring of 1996 Joichi Ito had his last cigar with the dying Timothy Leary. When Ito left the house, he took a plane from LAX to Austria in order to attend that year's jury deliberations for the Prix Ars Electronica. The following night, Timothy Leary quietly died in his bedroom, surrounded by his friends and the various people who had been looking after his Web site. John Perry Barlow was at home that night. 'The phone just rang in the middle of this rainy Wyoming night, and now I'm here naked in the dark trying to think of something to follow him out with,' he wrote hours after the call. His eulogy spread across the Internet, posted as a memorial on hundreds of Web sites and email lists; the symbol of the sixties had died and it seemed like the end of an epoch.

Meanwhile Ito had arrived at Ars Electronica, where etoy, almost a year after their first attendance as a group, were about to step from the shadows into the spotlight. For them, a new era was about to begin.

3
Kool-Aid Kings and Castles in the Air

'This emerging new economy . . . has its own distinct opportunities and its own new rules. Those who play by the new rules will prosper; those who ignore them will not.'

Kevin Kelly, 'New Rules for the New Economy',
WIRED, 1997

'Computer hackers . . . their programs are like surrealist paintings.'

Nicholas Negroponte, *Being Digital*, 1995

When John Perry Barlow founded his Electronic Frontier Foundation in 1990, he was determined not only to fight for freedom of speech in cyberspace, but also to open the network to the free market. At that time, the Internet was an academic resource and commerce was restricted from it. For years the US Government's National Science Foundation which subsidised the Internet had controlled access to it by making new users agree to an Acceptable Use Policy that precluded any profit-seeking activities.

But Barlow – along with various other campaigners – worked hard to repeal these restrictions. In his capacity as an advisor to Speaker of the House Newt Gingrich and Vice President Al Gore, Barlow took his belief in the economic potential of the utterly unregulated Internet to the very highest levels. (He even joked that his favourite mode of transport was *Airforce Two* – the Vice Presidential plane.) Key pieces of legislation were gradually put in place, allowing the National Science Foundation to foster economic growth and enabling commercial service-providers to hook up to the public network.

Hucksters soon got online, and those who failed to learn the strange language and customs of the early cyberspace pioneers were cruelly punished by a community that was sceptical of their free space being colonised by commerce. One key spat, a precursor to many that followed, began when husband-and-wife lawyers, Laurence Canter and Martha Siegel, sent an email advertising their services to every bulletin board on the Internet. This amounted to some five and a half thousand postings, ensuring that hundreds of thousands of users would see it, over and over again. This was considered to be 'spamming', and extremely bad-mannered. Many of the victims of this unwanted attention were already loosely organised as communities within email lists and online discussion-boards. They declared war on the lawyers, filling the firm's inbox with thousands of useless emails – many containing threats and obscenities – and bunging up their fax machine. The story made it to the cover of *Time* magazine and was viewed as a warning to those who sought precipitous commercialisation of the not-for-profit cyberspace.

Despite such hostility from some sections of the old Internet community, the forces of commercialisation were too strong to resist and Barlow's libertarian ideas came to dominate. As he took on a new role, as a corporate consultant and contributing writer to *WIRED* magazine – which promoted a business ethic wrapped in party-going clothes of *Mondo 2000*'s dayglo graphics – Barlow perfectly embodied the Internet's transformation from hippy playground to new capitalist marketplace. One significant point of inflection on this journey happened in April 1995, when, after years of bureaucratic wrangling, the US National Science Foundation formally privatised the Internet. The key parts of the infrastructure – the hubs that routed traffic, and the transcontinental telecom links – were handed over to commercial organisations;

as a consequence, the Acceptable Use Policy was repealed and the age of the commercial Internet truly began.

At about this time, thirty-six-year-old nebbish computer entrepreneur Bill Gross was away from his home in Pasadena, California, to attend a family wedding in New York. As ever, his mind was racing through new possibilities for his existing businesses, radical technical innovations and the possibilities of the Web as a new toy. Just before the wedding, he decided that he needed a haircut, so took a look through the New York *Yellow Pages* to find a barber. Hundreds were listed, but Gross had no idea where any of them were located or of how good they were. He was not about to wait for a recommendation. Instead, he hailed a cab and chose a barber at random. Arriving outside his selected shop, he immediately realised, just from the look of it, that it wasn't the kind of place for a man who was already a multi-millionaire. But it was too late.

The experience led to a typical 'eureka' moment for the entrepreneur, who loved finding solutions to the world's problems in the form of snazzy new business ideas. It made him wonder: if pictures of all the city's barber shops were accessible on the Internet, surely he could have been saved the fruitless journey. In contrast to many of the virtual-reality concepts that were the currency of the moment, Gross's plan was to use the Internet as a means to help real people in the real world. The trouble was that he didn't have the time to focus on a new project himself, so he persuaded his old friend Charles Conn, a partner at the management consultancy McKinsey, to look at the idea. Conn didn't care much for Gross's initial and limited concept of a photographic directory, but he did think it could be the starting point of a much larger idea. And so, in the summer of 1995, Bill Gross managed to persuade his friend to start an online city-directory company, CitySearch. As Gross said: 'What lured him there was the opportunity to direct his own drama, to own his own destiny.'

Gross may have been busy with other businesses, but he did

help Conn by finding high-profile investors like Steven Spielberg and Michael Douglas for the venture. He also assisted in making the Web site easy to use. Conn remembers, Gross was 'a sort of strange combination of geek, technologist and a huckster marketer all rolled into one.' Gross's other role was to entertain and cajole potential employees, persuading them to jump ship from their steady careers and join the risky world of a new company and a new frontier. At the time, nobody really imagined that the Internet was going to make them huge amounts of money, but it did seem to be exciting and to have the potential to change the way the world worked.

CitySearch's emerging success placed Bill Gross at the vanguard of the Internet revolution, and demonstrated that he had a Midas touch in this new arena too. He was now beautifully poised to benefit from the coming boom with the absolute belief that he had seen the future. He enthused, 'I'm unbelievably bullish on the Internet. I think the Internet is going to be in everybody's home, on everybody's watch, in everybody's pocket, pretty much by the end of this century.' Soon he had set up more than twenty different Internet businesses – among them a toy company. And in due course he would be catching private planes, being driven in limousines and chased by groupies, as well as being hailed as the most important entrepreneur since J. D. Rockefeller. Not bad for a man well into his thirties who gave the impression – perhaps because he was short, wore simple clothes and scurried around with his gaze fixed on the floor – that he could still be a teenager. Whatever, in the midst of a world of inexperienced entrepreneurs, Bill Gross's unique asset was that he had a history.

Gross enjoyed telling journalists his perfect entrepreneurial-creation myth. The son of an orthodontist in Encino, California, he had become a candy salesman (a start like that of both Rockefeller and Thomas Edison) at the age of twelve, buying confectionery in bulk and undercutting the local drug store. By the time he reached high school, Gross had employed a few salesmen to work for him.

His next venture, at high school, saw him enter the world of engineering – selling, via adverts he placed in the back of *Popular Electronics* magazine, hundreds of kits of tin foil and cardboard along with instructions on how to make parabolic dishes for solar energy. This venture paid for his tuition at the California Institute of Technology, where he sold stereo loudspeakers to his classmates. Upon his graduation, in 1981, he started his own audio shop in Pasadena, vaingloriously called Gross National Products.

However, when it came to convincing potential investors and a hungry media that he was a substantial force in the Internet boom, Bill Gross's real asset was the fact that he'd previously built two multi-million-dollar software businesses. And both had been exactly in sync with two fundamental shifts within the computer business over the precious decade.

The first of these shifts began in August 1981 with the launch of IBM's personal computer, marketed as their 'smallest, lowest-priced computer system, designed for business, school and home'. Until then, PCs had been thought of as hobby machines and were only properly used by esoteric academics; IBM's endorsement jump-started the micro-computer market for business. The computer even became *Time*'s 'Man of the Year'.

Bill Gross soon bought a PC for his audio shop. At first the small and not very powerful desktop computer sat unused in the basement – under a blanket, to protect it from the sawdust of the shop floor. 'You couldn't do anything with it,' Bill Gross recalled. The PC was anaemically powered and also lacked a suite of software programs that would make it useful for everyday business. Back then, applications for it were often slow to run and cumbersome to use, having been designed for different kinds of machines and hastily translated to work on the IBM PC.

The lack of software programs was seen as an opportunity by Mitch Kapor (later he co-founded the Electronic Frontier Foundation with John Perry Barlow). A self-confessed dilettante, he was known for wearing Hawaiian shirts and had been both a DJ and a mental-health worker. Having made some money from a graphical software program he was as much a veteran as there was in the tiny software industry. More than anything else, though, he was a 'hacker' – not in the criminal sense but as defined by journalist Steven Levy: 'adventurers, visionaries, risk-takers, artists . . . And the ones who most clearly saw why the computer was a truly revolutionary tool.'

Kapor's idea was to make an existing computer program – Visicalc, the first spreadsheet software – work on the new IBM PC. Before Visicalc, budding entrepreneurs had planned their business on squared paper or huge blackboards, divided into matrices of rows and columns; each space was filled with scribbles, some cells related via complex calculations. Visicalc mimicked and automated this cumbersome process. Now, just by inputting a list of figures – the set of assumptions – one could easily speculate how to run one's business by allowing the spreadsheet to calculate future profit or loss. The strange and bizarre 'business models' of the Internet revolution could only have come about with this capacity to imagine and balance the impossible.

Mitch Kapor set up a new company, which he called Lotus (because he was a follower of transcendental meditation), and created a spreadsheet program for the PC that was faster than any other and included an onscreen-help application. On 23 January 1983, Lotus 1-2-3 was launched on the back of an unprecedented marketing campaign that cost more than a million dollars. As a result, business adoption of the IBM PC went into overdrive and sales quadrupled in the first few months following the launch. Just one year later, Lotus had $157 million worth of annual sales, were employing 700 people and had become the largest software company in the world.

Bill Gross was on holiday when his brother and business partner Larry installed Lotus 1-2-3 on to their basement PC. When he returned, Bill began to use it to computerise the shop's accounts. The brothers soon found that their customers were coming to them for advice about how to use 1-2-3; despite the benefits of the program, it was still difficult to use. A complex line of code was required to instruct the computer to perform even simple tasks. Printing out a section of grid, for example, necessitated the input of '/ppral..f17-om14-escagq'. One mistyped character and the command would fail to execute. So the brothers guided their customers in installing applications and computerising their businesses. As Bill recalled, 'Everyone trusted us and wanted our advice on computers and software.'

Bill Gross loved tinkering with the software. He worked long hours, had fun, hacked code. As he told one journalist, 'We do our best work after midnight, sitting around with pizzas and computers, being creative.' Gross, like Mitch Kapor, was part of a new generation of businessmen who came from a culture of hacking. According to the Finnish academic Pekka Himanen, the 'hacker ethic is a new work ethic that challenges the attitude toward work that has held us in its thrall for so long, the Protestant work ethic'. In this new mode of work, it was not money that was the motivating force; it was the desire to create something better and smarter than one's peers. The ethic meant that work was characterised not as a drudgery, carried out within rigid hours set by employers, but as a joyful pursuit, eroding the distinction between work and play. The ever cool Mitch Kapor became one of the very first poster boys to this new generation of hackers, as well as being one of the first software millionaires. Eventually, Bill Gross would follow suit.

The Gross brothers soon began writing and selling their own programs. Their first attempt was something called CPA+, an easy-to-use accounting template using Lotus 1-2-3 as its foundation – as if an account book was laid over the program's simple grid. Designed for use by small businesses, it included a rudimentary layout and some basic linking between various cells to allow customers to make profit-and-loss balance sheets like the ones the brothers had already created for their shop. Their next, more sophisticated idea was to simplify the tricky coded commands of Lotus 1-2-3 with easy-to-understand English. They worked hard to write a program that would allow the user to type in 'print this' instead of cumbersome commands.

Mitch Kapor discovered the Gross brothers' language-based product and, as Bill Gross remembered, his reaction was 'wow,

wow, wow, incredible'. For the young Bill, still only twenty-six years old, this was truly a moment to remember. 'It was like we achieved everything we could dream of with a compliment like that from Mitch.' For Bill Gross, praise from one of the industry's leading lights carried real import. In what was becoming a typical strategy of the fast-moving software industry, Lotus bought up their competition, paying $10 million for the Gross brothers' software company. Henceforth Bill and Larry commuted between their offices in Pasadena and Lotus's in Boston.

By this time, Lotus had more than a thousand employees and had become a huge bureaucracy. Shortly after buying out the Gross brothers, Mitch Kapor resigned from his post as Lotus's Chief Executive, bored of the dull, operational command. Within Lotus, Bill Gross was intrigued by what he saw as the growing indolence of his new colleagues, and came to believe that they lacked inspiration and commitment purely because they had no stake in the business beyond their monthly salary. As a company man, he felt that his body was changing – the 'new chemistry' taking the edge off his ambition. No longer was he selling 'his' product; he was just a cog in a huge machine. As the 'fun' aspects of business began to fade, Gross resolved to remember the lessons he'd learned during this period as a salary man. He left Lotus in 1990, after five years, to become once again the master of his own destiny.

Not long afterwards, Bill Gross started the second of the businesses that later gave him credibility in the Internet boom. When discussing this period in the years to come, he would tell the press that his original intention had been to take a year off to pursue his creative yen. Now that work and play were no longer distinguishable, he had planned to pursue his leisure interests with the same determined diligence – not to mention hubristic grand ambition – as that with which he had coded software. To some, he mentioned that he had wanted to write a symphony; to others, that he had wanted to paint. He took up the hobby of copying Old Masters, brushstroke by brushstroke; his copy of Van Gogh's

Sunflowers hung above his desk for years. He explained, 'There's all kinds of violence in the brushstrokes. I love to see what it feels like being creative in different areas.' But the power of the computer – a computer with the capacity to make art – was enough to divert him from his own artistic ambitions.

Late in 1989, the press began trumpeting a new type of computer and related method of communication: multimedia. The idea that a computer ought to be able to play music, display pictures and movies as well as running text programs had already been around for a while. However, until the middle of the 1980s, most micro-computers – besides game consoles or niche products like the Amiga – were text-based, because they were not powerful enough to accommodate the complex demands of graphics. Computer memory, though, had rapidly decreased in cost, while the speed of central processors had accelerated. And so, by the autumn of 1989, Apple and IBM were busy promoting 'multimedia machines', promising interactive *son et lumières*. *Business Week* hurrahed in a headline 'It's a PC, it's a TV – It's Multimedia', and claimed it would 'change the way people work, learn and play'. The rest of the press followed, and multimedia was soon a fully fledged business fashion.

Bill Gross's first experience of this new technology came courtesy of Beethoven's *Symphony No. 9*, one of the first multimedia CDs, on which users could not only listen to the entire work but also hear a full-length running commentary and read essays about the composer's life and work. Gross bought a $5,500 Apple computer just so he could play it. He described his reaction as having 'goosebumps all over my body about how great Beethoven was. It let me in on a non-academic way to discover beautiful things on my own . . . It opened me up to the beauty of music.' The discovery coincided with the first day of school of his four-year-old son, David. Waving goodbye to him from the family car, Gross thought, 'Oh my God, I'm handing him off to the educational system. Their software stinks, and teachers aren't paid enough. I really should do something about that.'

For Gross, the solution to these problems was to begin hacking code again. He had leaped on the bandwagon of a rising trend once before, with Lotus 1-2-3. Now he was about to do it again, by taking the new power of multimedia computing to the world of education. If children could play with software programs as if they were games, he reasoned, they could discover knowledge along the way. To make this happen, he set up a company, Knowledge Adventure.

Their first product was self-titled and hit the retailers' shelves at the end of 1991, promising 'The Most Exciting Journey of All'. Once the home user had installed the software on to their PC, an image would appear on screen: Neil Armstrong planting the American flag on the moon; hidden behind this were many further layers of information. The computer mouse – at the time a relatively new addition to the PC – allowed the user to manipulate an onscreen pointer and to click on various parts of a chosen image to reveal these further levels. For example, click on the flag on the first image and the program would deliver a section containing text and images about Betsy Ross sewing the first American flag in 1770. Click on Armstrong's lunar-landing module and a photo of the space-shuttle *Columbia*'s maiden voyage in 1981 would appear. And so on. Each of these new images in turn could be explored further. What *Knowledge Adventure* lacked in coherent narrative it more than made up for with its barrage of pretty pictures and fascinating factoids.

Knowledge Adventure went on to release *Bug Adventure*, *Body Adventure*, *Dinosaur Adventure* and *Space Adventure*, all featuring similar journeys through their respective subjects. And as home-computer technology improved, Gross added more sophisticated features to his software – first sound and then video.

Knowledge Adventure was a very successful venture. Within a few years, the company was selling almost $20 million worth of products a year and became a media darling. In 1993, it was chosen as one of *Fortune* magazine's '25 Cool Companies'. Gross had proved that not only could he write programs for the business sector, but also that he had the common touch with that most difficult of consumer targets: the children's market. As a consequence he developed his glorious reputation as a serial entrepreneur, someone who could repeatedly hit the jackpot of turning ideas into profitable reality.

Nonetheless Gross stuck to his hacker lifestyle. He often worked from home, and held parties to help his employees dream up new ideas for products. One reporter wrote that Gross spent his time sitting in the dark in the study of his Pasadena home, listening to Mozart, reading history and directing the efforts of other programmers. Gross himself said, 'I couldn't have imagined a better life.'

As he became more successful, he dealt less with the dull, everyday details of running a business and was increasingly sought out by the media, investors and potential partners as a kind of visionary. Michael Wolff, who ran a publishing company at the time, recalls: 'I was about to meet with Gross when someone I knew said, in a cautionary tone, "Remember he's drunk the Kool-Aid."' This was a Silicon Valley phrase that became a widely adopted idiom to describe the irrational excitement and exuberance of the Internet goldrush years. The term was an allusion to cult leader Jim Jones who in 1978 forced his followers to live in the Guyanese jungle where, in his final show of strength, he gave them the softdrink Kool-Aid laced with cyanide; 638 adults and 276 children were killed. Bill Gross had 'drunk the Kool-Aid' insofar as he fervently cast technology, new media and the seismic transformation of life by the Internet in truly messianic terms. So Michael Wolff hit on a simple strategy to impress the evangelist, 'He was a believer, therefore I should be a believer too.'

Having this kind of visionary talent made it difficult for Gross to concentrate on the more menial tasks involved in running a business. He described himself as 'the most unfocused man on the planet', and constantly flitted from one idea for a new company to another, squirrelling money away for special projects. At times, Knowledge Adventure was more of a buzzing chaos than an orderly bureaucracy.

This often led to conflict with his brother Larry, still his business partner, who wanted to focus on a smaller number of things in order to ensure that everything was executed with excellence. The two would shout at each other, but whatever the outcome Bill would still 'lose interest in something when it started becoming mature', remembers Rick Gibson, who worked with them at the time.

An unlikely encounter finally pushed Bill to radically rethink his working methods and question whether he should listen to his brother at all. The story goes that a money manager on behalf of a potential investor once visited Knowledge Adventure but Bill Gross had no time to speak to him. Instead, his son David, by this time aged eight, introduced the visitor to the products; the man was duly impressed. It was only afterwards that anyone discovered that the visitor had been representing Steven Spielberg.

Spielberg was then at the height of his success, and about to win a raft of Oscars for *Schindler's List*. He used computers to create the sophisticated graphics that distinguished his films, but was sceptical of them for independent, cinema-like entertainment; he certainly saw no reason to abdicate the director's storytelling responsibility to a brigade of mouse-clicking viewers. Nevertheless, he was intrigued by the educational potential computers offered and had heard that Knowledge Adventure were at the cutting edge.

So, one day in late 1993, Steven Spielberg himself travelled to Knowledge Adventure's nondescript offices in the Los Angeles suburb La Crescenta. There, some seventy staff awaited him, nervous and on their best behaviour – Gross had carefully choreographed Spielberg's visit, and had even excluded some of the most senior management from this audience with the king of entertainment. Gross's bravura performance introduced Spielberg to the complete range of Knowledge Adventure's products, and allowed his guest time to play on them for himself. Larry Gross remembered looking on at Spielberg's enthusiasm. 'He played every single module. It was pretty fun to see my brother . . . knocking the socks off Steven Spielberg.'

What was immediately remarkable was the way that Spielberg

and Gross identified with each other – almost as if they were bright kids who had just happened to meet on a suburban street-corner and found shared interests. A reporter from *WIRED* described Gross as 'genuinely unpretentious, projecting a sincere, childlike charm'; in fact, Gross seems to act like the heroes of Spielberg's movies – who are often drawn to discovery, having their key shots at moments of wonderful revelation. Said Spielberg, 'In many ways, we're very similar.'

Spielberg liked Gross and his company. He invested millions in Knowledge Adventure and also offered to add his creative wisdom to the project. As Bill Gross remembered, 'He took one look at *Body Adventure* and said, "That human body should walk on, look down, and notice he has no clothes on." We would never have thought of that.'

In the months after their first meeting, the two spent time together. On one occasion, Gross hitched a ride in a golf cart with Spielberg as he was driven from meeting to meeting around Universal Studios. He watched as the great film-director made suggestions about TV scripts or the shooting of movies, constantly adding his creative thoughts and energy. Previously, Gross had been burdened by the thought that rather than dreaming up new ideas he should be singlemindedly dealing with business, prosaically managing employees and the minutiae of profit-and-loss statements. Being creative, Gross had thought, was only a tiny part of an entrepreneur's overall value. Seeing Spielberg in action, he realised it might be possible to do things the way that came naturally to him.

Gross hatched a plan: to create an environment in which he could run around, and think, without the distractions of mundane paperwork and management politics. He recalled: 'I knew that's what I wanted to do next – create a playroom where I could work with ideas.'

It was a good moment to be thinking along these lines. Pre-eminent management guru Tom Peters wrote at the time: 'Welcome to the world where imagination is the source of value in the economy.' The current management and economic theory was prophesying the death of the old economy, in which manufacturers produced goods from raw materials and manual labour. In its place was rising the New Economy, in which corporations traded information, brands and patents, and their employees were called 'knowledge workers'. More than ever before, ideas were now *the* most valuable commodity – and nowhere more so than on the Internet, where there was no history and no set way to make money.

In the summer of 1995, Gross began to prepare himself for the emerging opportunities of online business as the Internet had been privatised and around the world millions of new consumers were eagerly logging on. But these changes were nothing compared to the explosion of Internet commerce that began on 9 August that year. This was the day that Netscape, the world's leading Web-browser company, sold shares on the stock exchange for the first time. The amazing success of the venture led to a huge change in perception of what constituted 'appropriate' business and how money could be made on the capital markets.

Netscape was the bastard child of the Mosaic Web browser developed by Marc Andreessen's team at the National Center for Super-Computing Applications (NCSA) in Illinois.

When Andreessen graduated at the end of 1993, he left Illinois and went to Silicon Valley, the strip of land between San Francisco and San Jose that had become the heartland of American technological innovation. Soon after arriving in California, Andreessen met Jim Clark, the visionary founder of Silicon Graphics, a company that made powerful computers for the animation and defence industries. Clark was more than anything an impresario; feverishly he dreamed up new projects, searching for the 'new, new thing', as writer Michael Lewis noted. Like Gross, he was a serial entrepreneur, interested in the realisation of his ideas rather than the operating of corporations.

In 1994, Clark and Andreessen hired the team that had built Mosaic at the NCSA, and set about building a company to make a better, faster and easier-to-use browser. That company was

Netscape. Like many other business people at the time, Clark was asking himself how anyone could actually make money on the Internet: 'I didn't have a specific answer to that yet, but I figured that with the Web- and Mosaic-enabled Internet already growing exponentially how could you not make money? It was just the law of large numbers at work – even a small amount of money per user would yield a big business.'

By the spring of 1995, more than six million copies of the browser Netscape Navigator had been given away for free. But Netscape was still a tiny company, barely a year old; its only real money was made through selling server software that enabled Web sites to take payments via secure credit-card transactions. Netscape's revenue in its first quarter was less than $5 million, while its outgoings amounted to more than $7 million – the difference being paid by Clark and with some venture capital.

Despite the modest size of the company, in the summer of 1995 Netscape's Chairman Jim Clark, its Chief Technology Officer Andreessen and the Board had much faith and vision. Although the Internet was not in general use and was, in some parts of the media, still being criticised as a faddish, soon to be out-of-date craze, they made an extraordinary decision. They agreed to sell a stake in the privately owned company, taking it on to the public-capital market: the stock exchange. This was a very brave move – even the Morgan Stanley bankers in charge of the deal had no email addresses on their business cards.

Before the heady days of the Internet goldrush, most Initial Public Offerings (IPOs) were the culmination of the long and arduous journey of company formation, and occurred only once a company was properly established and its management's ability had been demonstrated. Most importantly, they usually took place when a company had already made a profit. Wal-Mart's shares weren't sold until the company was eight years old; Microsoft's were presented eleven years after Bill Gates and Paul Allen first decided to create a computer application, by which time it had annual revenues of almost $200 million and more than a thousand employees.

Netscape was going to be different. In early June 1995, the Morgan Stanley bankers decided that Netscape could sell 3.5 million shares at $13 each, which would have set the company's value at almost half a billion dollars – more than twenty times its annual revenue. However, on the evening before the IPO following a rush of interest in the stock, they decided to sell the shares at $28 each. Jim Clark would later call the day of the IPO 'D-Day, with me trying to have a normal day while knowing that my life would never be the same again'.

The event made stock-market history. As is traditional with IPOs, the shares were sold only to the banks' big customers – the pension funds and money-management firms – who eventually placed them on the public market. When trading of the shares first began, such was the demand that the first price they went for was $71 – two and a half times the starting price. The market capitalisation of Netscape at that moment was an extraordinary $2.7 billion, more than a hundred times its annual revenue. Netscape's was one of the most stunning debuts ever seen on Wall Street; a tiny, loss-making company had been lifted to the heavens by the frenzy of an excitable market desperate to pour money into cyberspace.

The valuation of Netscape divided investors. As Professor Burton Malkiel of Princeton University in his *A Random Walk Down Wall Street* stated, there have always been roughly two schools in the valuing of companies. Those in the first use a method that Malkiel calls the 'firm foundation', which tries to anchor a share price in the intrinsic value of the corporation. In a manufacturing industry, this is roughly calculated by considering the assets of the company, the possible market, the cost of the machinery, the land, and the investment in patented processes combined with the size of the revenue and the profits that can be returned to investors.

To those belonging to this school, the Netscape corporate valuation was almost incomprehensible. Throughout the years of the Internet boom, Warren Buffett – arguably the greatest American investor of his generation – diligently followed the 'firm foundation' approach, only buying into companies such as furniture retailers and utility businesses, ventures that he could understand and that could reasonably be expected to make a profit. As the market ballooned, Buffett was derided for not being clever enough to second-guess the exploding share prices of the fashionable Internet businesses.

The second method of calculating value is what Malkiel calls the 'castles in the air' theory, which does away with any analysis of a company's intrinsic worth. Instead, investors consider how the hordes in the marketplace are likely to react in the future. The successful investor calculates what situations are likely to lead to rising share prices, then buys before the crowd and sells before the fickle market has got bored. No less an investor than the twentieth century's pre-eminent economist John Maynard Keynes advocated this approach, and became a millionaire as a result. He wrote that most people are 'largely concerned not with making superior long-term forecasts of the probable yield of an investment over its whole life, but with foreseeing changes in the conventional basis of valuation a short time ahead of the general public.' He stressed that investors should concentrate on the behaviour of the market above the insular world of the company.

Some investors and commentators tried to argue that the value of Netscape and of the other Internet companies that soon followed suit were in fact based on a firm foundation. In the New Economy there were to be New Rules which would benefit a different sort of corporation. By giving away their product, Netscape had come to dominate the browser market – surely this would prove to be incredibly valuable in the future. In addition, Netscape had a thriving corporate culture, the loyalty and satisfaction of its customers and the power of a brand; enduring market-dominance and profit would surely follow. But Netscape's firm foundation was built in virtual reality, and its Initial Public Offering was mostly a triumph for the castles-in-the-air method of valuation.

Jim Clark said that his Initial Public Offering proved that the market saw the future through his eyes. 'People started drinking my Kool-Aid. Netscape obviously didn't create the Internet. But if Netscape had not forced the issue on the Internet, it would have just burbled in the background. It would have remained a counter-intuitive kind of thing. The criticism of it was that it was anarchy. What the IPO did was give anarchy credibility.' From 9 August 1995, the capital markets were pitched into chaos, uncertainly gyrating as belief in the Internet wavered. The Netscape IPO was the Internet's breakthrough as a commercial medium. What had been a playground for researchers and idealistic online communities became a dreamscape for entrepreneurs.

The IPO had profound consequences for the coming years. The capital markets were now ready for a new kind of business, one that hadn't yet made a profit but had loudly staked its claim and would presumably make a mint in the years to come. From then on the investment community was happy to rely on the unfamiliar rules of Net economy and leave reality behind. 'There was an unbelievable frenzy,' one important investor remembers. 'You [might get] these four kids who didn't even finish college, [and] they would say, "We know how to sell insurance on the Internet" or "We can sell pet food, or toys", and me and Kleiner Perkins and Soros, we were rushing to sign huge cheques to these kids. And everybody said, "They won't make money for twenty years, but you have to get the space". It was incredible.'

The Netscape Initial Public Offering took place on Bill Gross's thirty-seventh birthday, and only added to his general excitement about the possibilities offered by the New Economy. His own online venture CitySearch was about to be launched, and elsewhere the first of the online merchants were embryonic. In the middle of July 1995, amazon.com had been launched in Seattle by thirty-year-old entrepreneur Jeff Bezos, who touted it as 'Earth's Biggest Bookstore'. Legend has it that Bezos wrote the business plan on a laptop while being driven west from New York by his wife; he chose the book industry because it was large, fragmented and had an already well-established distribution system. The company's debut came with no great hullabaloo and no anxious editorialising about this being the future of business. Yet in its first week amazon.com took more than $12,000 worth of orders; within only a couple of years it was worth hundreds of millions of dollars, and later billions. More importantly, it spawned a series of copycat businesses, in various areas of retail, from groceries to toys.

Gross was well aware of the new companies springing up across the Internet, and was keen to jump on the bandwagon. Soon he sold Knowledge Adventure, which by then was valued at $100 million and his stake in that at a little less than $20 million. Free and with money in the bank, Gross was now able to concentrate full time on his new baby, the Spielberg-inspired 'idea factory', which he christened Bill Gross's idealab!.

His radical innovation was to create something like a movie studio but which turned out new businesses rather than films. Some of them might fail; but if a few were 'blockbusters' and could be sold to the ravenous capital markets, then he would be made. His challenge was to bring a touch of brilliance to new corporations – just as Spielberg did to films. 'I don't compare myself to Steven Spielberg,' he said. 'But in the same way he has this expertise about what things should ultimately look like onscreen, I have a very good vision for pure business concepts.'

The new project Gross described as an 'incubator', like those that had been around for years, particularly on university campuses, as the 'nursery slopes' of company formation – providing office space and a little advice to aspiring entrepreneurs. One particular role model for Gross was George Hatsopoulos, founder of the Thermo Electric conglomerate, who had created and then taken public nineteen companies, keeping an interest in each. Gross's insight was that a slow-moving and conservative institution could be re-focused as a speedy engine for the creation of Internet companies. He said, 'I felt if someone else could make this work with the physical processes, it would work way better on the Internet.'

Bill Gross's core skill, and the one he most prized, was creativity. A great brainstorming session, he once said, was 'a little bit like having sex'. Characterising himself as the everyman fixer, he wandered around the world spotting problems and trying to fix them. He has described how, in order to properly contemplate problems, he meditates to the sounds of Yosemite's Merced River or listening to classical music. As Steven Spielberg said, 'He's kind of like a mad genius. His brain works like a roundhouse in a train station, spinning off ideas in seven directions at once, yet not losing its focus on any one of them.'

Having formulated the idealab! business plan, Gross approached and seduced a number of investors and asked each to put up at least $500,000. As one of them remembers, '[Gross] talked to us about the Internet; I didn't know what the Internet was, zero, but he got money from me.' Oscar-winning actor and producer Michael Douglas was among those to put money in, as was Jean Pigozzi, the heir of the Simca car-manufacturing fortune. Steven Spielberg also came along for the party, having said about Gross, 'If he's involved with it I want to invest in it.' And Ben Rosen, the founding investor in Lotus and Compaq computers, invested too. Rosen's reasoning was that 'Bill has a chance of having a dozen hits. I think in five years' time Bill Gross will be as much of a household name as any household name in technology, even though today he's barely known outside of a very small circle.'

With these people's investment and what Gross described as his '50,000 nuggets of business experience', idealab! was officially incorporated in March 1996. For the first eighteen months, it squatted the offices of Knowledge Adventure and CitySearch while Gross, with the help of a theme-park designer, planned a new office space. In this, his desk would be enclosed in glass at the middle of one wall, like a command centre. He would face out towards the empire of hatching companies, which would be arranged in segments, divided by low walls, radiating out from his desk. Between them and Gross's desk would be a sort of no man's land where eager managers would loiter, hoping to catch his fickle attention.

idealab! was to forge a radical, speedy, cheap and multiplex way of manufacturing corporations, very different from the slow

Bill Gross at his workstation at idealab!. His glassed-in cubicle looks out across his broods of hatchling companies.

and prudent methods of the old economy. As one early headline about the venture happily proclaimed, 'To be an online company, first throw out old rules.'

Gross's intention was to create an environment that was perfect for frenzied entrepreneurs like himself. Most importantly, idealab! would take responsibility for the dull procedural elements of Internet-company set-up – such as providing office space, recruiting senior managers and legally incorporating the companies. Gross considered that the economy of scale would allow his managers to singlemindedly focus on the problems unique to their individual businesses and so come up with creative solutions. The key to successful business, he was convinced, was the 'maximization of time and efficiency: having everybody spend every minute of every day doing precisely what maximizes the organization's prospects.' The Netscape IPO had demonstrated that the speed at which ideas were executed was the essential ingredient of Internet success. Indeed this was so fast that Silicon

Valley types began talking 'Netscape Time'. As *Fast Company* magazine headlined in November 1995: 'Are you fast enough? Are you hungry enough? Are you tough enough? To work, live, compete in Netscape time?' Bill Gross thought that the idealab! companies would benefit from shared knowledge across the various start-ups, proudly declaring that idealab! would 'do in four and a half months what would take another Internet start-up nine months to do.'

Gross also wanted to capitalise on the uniquely low cost of creating an online business. 'It used to be that the main thing you needed was money to start a company, but you don't need that anymore,' he said. At only marginal expense, it was possible to have a window on the world. This meant that idealab! could create a shoal of tiny companies, some of which would barely see the light of day while others would stumble towards independence. Those that made it to the starting gate were given $250,000 and told to find their way in the world.

Despite his enthusiasm for his own ideas and his ability to create companies, Gross was faced with an enormous obstacle: he lacked people to run the various businesses. There was no cohort of bright, experienced managers wanting to take a chance on a risky new venture – why would there be, when they could happily earn fat salaries in stable blue-chip corporations or management consultancies?

To solve this tricky problem he recalled an insight gleaned during his time at Lotus: that a stake in the company is the greatest of motivations. So he came up with a remarkable new form of corporate ideology, which he called the New Math of Ownership. Whereas traditionally companies would own the majority of their subsidiaries, Gross would re-calculate the balance and give his top managers substantial chunks of their businesses – normally about ten per cent. Gross would keep about fifty per cent, the remainder being divided between other founding staff. He said he had 'decided to put this arithmetic – this notion of relinquishing ownership and of letting go – at the very heart of a new venture.' This striking break from the norm allowed him to recruit a group of managers from blue-chip corporations such as Disney and Lotus.

During the first year of idealab!, Bill Gross became a weather vane for the fashions of Internet-business models, creating companies that seemed to mimic almost every possible fad. The first of these to appear was PeopleLink, which created software for servicing online chat rooms, instant messaging and message boards. It was a brave move that PeopleLink should set out to commercialise these not-for-profit online forums where people discussed their common interests. These had existed for years but had not been used for commerce.

It was hoped that following the influx of new users, PeopleLink would create new and profitable Web communities. Similar ideas concerning radical shifts in the meaning and purpose of Internet communities had been expounded by John Hagel and Arthur Armstrong in their book *net.gain*, which Bill Gross once recommended to the readers of *WIRED*. Online message boards and email lists were no longer to be about nurturing kinship but about reaping a profit. *net.gain* contained the promise that those who nurtured, listened and empowered these communities would leap ahead of their online rivals; now, Internet users were not individuals who had logged on but customers to be sold to. Gross was enthusiastic, saying, 'It is a business model we've adopted.'

The book also warned that corporations that failed to acknowledge the power of online communities or that tried to control them would themselves fail. The authors went so far as to say that 'virtual communities have the power to re-order greatly the relationship between companies and their customers.' In the years to come this early fear was not taken to heart by all of Gross's chief executives, and the lessons were not always learned or implemented.

Another of Gross's ventures sprung from his frustration about not being able to share his knowledge and experience with the world. 'Every time I sit on the beach in Hawaii and have an idea, I get incredibly frustrated that I can't put it in the hands of the people who can use it.' So began Ideamarket, a market for 'intellectual property', which promised to become a stock exchange linking buyers with sellers of everything from recipes to business plans.

Gross quickly managed to snap up two of the top names in computer journalism to run this business, Jim Seymour, editor of *PC Week*, and Peter Lewis of *The New York Times*. One of the first intellectual properties for sales was Gross's own opus, 'Raising Money Successfully: Secrets of an Entrepreneur'. This 3,200-word article cost $19.95 and pledged to 'increase your chances of success by using tips and lessons that [Gross] learned over the past 15 years.' Gross was confident about Ideamarket, declaring one of his favourite ideas and boasting that it would quickly become a billion-dollar corporation. Six months after its launch, it was in *Fortune*'s list of '25 Cool Companies'; one week later, it collapsed and all but one of its staff abandoned the project. Despite Gross's enthusiasm, Internet users had not bothered to use the service.

Throughout the first year of idealab!, Gross had an incredible promiscuity of ideas – some of which had barely one outing in the press. When he wanted to watch old episodes of *Seinfeld* on the Web, he set up Bandwidth+ to speed up the Internet. He also came up with I-Map, a means of visualising large amounts of information; Datamining, which could find gems in swamps of information; Visual Search, designed to search the world of virtual reality on the Web; and Recomentor, a service that made collaborative recommendations about anything, from movies to music.

The atmosphere at idealab! was driven and feverish, with meetings often carrying on late into the night. Gross would sometimes organise meetings of all the employees of all the companies, in the hope of coming up with yet more ideas. As he recalled, he would 'run around like a hummingbird, plugging my ideas into multiple, highly focused companies.'

One early investor remembers this period. 'I used to go and see him in Pasadena, and he would have seven hundred messages on his computer, and he was talking to you doing emails at the same time. He had this glass office, and he was talking to people from five different companies. I thought, "Oh my God, this man is a genius."' The CEO of another company remembers a time when Gross would only book in meetings that were five minutes long, while Hollywood movie stars waited in the idealab! reception area to spend a moment with him.

By autumn 1996, idealab! had already created eighteen enterprises. Though none of them had as yet been successful, Gross was insistent that only one 'hit' was needed in order for idealab! to be funded for ever. He seemed utterly confident that this would happen, and told one radio host, 'We've extracted the Internet genetic code for success, and then we try to inject that code into each start-up that we create to guarantee its success and give it the advantage of the shared knowledge of all the companies in this incubation lab.'

Gross was later raised into the pantheon of great entrepreneurs. Just as Henry Ford's car lines in Detroit had profoundly affected the creation of products through mass manufacture, so Bill Gross was praised as a huge influence on how corporations were created. He became a star of the Internet, indulging in the cars and private planes of the trappings of wealth. Remembers an investor, 'I went to a conference with him and there were women, you know, there were groupies. He had ugly tech groupies running after him, it was incredible.' He received the ultimate seal of approval when the pre-eminent American entrepreneur Jack Welch, CEO of General Electric since 1981, joined the Board of idealab!.

Back in late 1996, though, Gross was still looking for his first blockbuster idea. One of the people he brought into assess business plans had just left Disney's Strategic Planning department. This was a ferociously clever man called Toby Lenk.

4
'This is a Digital Hijack'

'I saw myself as an electronic joy rider; I was like James
Bond behind the computer; I was just having a blast.'
Kevin Mitnick, convicted computer criminal

In October 1995, etoy convened a meeting in a room they'd
booked at Zürich's official youth centre, Dynamo, a seventies
concrete block located beneath a flyover. The email sent out prior
to the event stated, 'Project etoy: How to proceed? What concept
will enable us to reach our instinctive goals?' Morning and afternoon meetings were rigorously timetabled to discuss their Web
site, music projects, decision making and how to find 'freelancers'.
Everyone was asked to bring 'your laptops and your inspiration'
and to 'be as punctual as etoy is able'.

The gang gathered for almost three days – a Friday morning
until midnight on Sunday. Saturday afternoon's session turned
out to be the most important, as it dealt with a central problem
with the etoy.TANKSYSTEM: that it was not the blockbuster
they had hoped it would be as very few Internet users were
calling up www.etoy.com with their Web browsers. Over the
previous weeks, the plastic pop-boy Goldstein had tried to
increase etoy's prominence by registering the site with search
engines, the popular and easy-to-use directories that index the
Web. But this had barely increased the TANKSYSTEM's paltry
number of visitors. Zai's words after the site's completion – 'We

are now the biggest, strongest and most beautiful of the world!'
– now rang hollow; for etoy, this failure was a savage disappointment. Now, on this Saturday afternoon, they were to discuss what
was billed as 'How do we gain omnipresence and worldwide
fan-advertisement?'

At the meeting, Goldstein proposed the radical suggestion that
they bamboozle the Web's search engines for etoy's benefit.
Udatny, whom Zai had once described as the 'high priest of
code', was asked if he could help; having spent years hacking
networks, he had an intense knowledge of the way they worked.
Although he found his methods hard to explain, he thought there
was a chance of implementing Goldstein's idea of exploiting the
technical vulnerabilities of search engines to capture unsuspecting
users for etoy. Were it to succeed, the plan would be a brilliant
way to gain etoy the unfair advantage needed in their fight for a
global audience.

After the meeting dissolved, Udatny decided to devote himself
to the new project and moved from Zürich to Vienna, where Zai
and Brainhard helped him secure a place at the Academy of
Applied Arts. Udatny used the academy's computer lab to
research the inner workings of search engines, aggressively fighting for one of the few work-stations in the morning and being
evicted by security guards at night. What little sleep he got was
on a platform built over the desks in the etoy office, housed in
an old elevator factory. So wrapped up was he in his machines
that most of his fellow students never heard him speak more than
a few sentences.

Easy-to-use, index-everything search engines first came to the Web
from the Scottish town of Stirling, situated in the no-man's land
between Glasgow and Edinburgh. In 1993, Jonathon Fletcher,
the gifted son of a Yorkshire doctor, was having a difficult year:
with Europe still in the grips of recession, the graduate grant
he had been praying for had failed to materialise. So he found
himself hanging around Stirling University with little sense of his
future. Eventually the university's systems administrator found

Fletcher a small salary and put him in charge of the seventy Unix machines in the computer-teaching labs. With nowhere to live, Fletcher camped on friends' floors and was occasionally forced to stay in his sleeping bag in the computer lab among the buzzing machines, his life, work and computers merging into one.

Always ingenious, as a child Fletcher had built gadgets and programmed games on his Sinclair Spectrum, the first mass market British colour computer. When he was a computer-science undergraduate he had used the Internet well before the Web became popular. Now what little spare time he had was spent playing games or hacking programs to test his newly found knowledge of networks. By the end of 1993, he had created a small project for himself. 'What I wanted to do,' he remembers, 'was see how big the Web was.'

When Fletcher set out to answer this question, he wrote a program that relied on Tim Berners-Lee's idea that Web pages are linked by Uniform Resource Locators (URLs), each of which precisely describes a document's unique location on the Internet. Fletcher's simple program would take a Web page and then identify all the URLs it contained (which would normally direct a user to other pages) and copy these into a database. Having done this with one page, the program would then take an already collected but as yet unsearched Web page address from the database and re-run the whole process with that. Again and again and again the robot performed this task, slowly sucking thousands of URLs into the database. As each of these pointed to another page, Fletcher soon realised that the Web numbered at least 10,000 pages.

This exercise was not difficult and Fletcher was not the first person to try it; but he did wonder what else might be done with the information. Inspired by the search engines of huge government and institutional databases, he decided to create a searchable database of Web site locations. There was one rudimentary precursor, called Northstar, but this had been clumsily converted from another information system and only indexed

5,000 pages, and was rapidly out of date as the number of Web pages was blooming.

So Fletcher now wrote a new computer program, which he called a robot and which collected not only the URLs but also the titles of each page and stored both sets of information in a database. He then created his own Web page that would allow remote users to interrogate this. It was simple enough to use: enter a word; click on the search button; then wait for the site to offer up a new page containing a list of Web sites, all with the search term in their title. Each had a hyperlink to the page itself. Fletcher thought of the site as a means for users to jump from one site to another, and the name JumpStation stuck. It was the first wide-ranging search engine on the World Wide Web. And, though Fletcher's initial trawl had produced 25,000 pages, pretty soon he had some 200,000 pages indexed.

In 1993, the easiest way to find new and interesting destinations on the World Wide Web was to click through the Whats New pages, updated by Marc Andreessen's team at the University of Illinois. At the end of December 1993, Fletcher submitted his creation to these pages, announcing, 'The JumpStation is a WWW form for finding other WWW pages. At present it is in its Alpha state and cannot be relied upon too heavily. Problem. The current problem is the search speed (it is SLOW!).' Very quickly he found that thousands of people were using JumpStation to navigate their way around the information on the Web.

Jonathon Fletcher is too modest to acknowledge that he was doing anything special. But he was ahead of the rest of the game, if only by a few months. By early spring 1994, there were a number of competitors. Two Stanford graduate students – Jerry Yang and David Filo – began swapping lists of their favourite Web sites and while doing so discovered that they had almost involuntarily created an invaluable resource for other Internet users. They called their list Yahoo!.

Fletcher's most direct rival was Brian Pinkerton, a graduate student at the University of Washington. By the spring of 1994, he had decided to create his own search engine. Having seen

JumpStation and others, like RBSE (which only indexed com-
puter-science-related pages) and the World Wide Web Worm
(later bought by Bill Gross once he had set up idealab!), Pinkerton
was convinced that he could improve on them. His novel idea was
to index every word on a page – not just document titles, as the
other early search engines had done – the point being to direct users
to the Web pages that bore the most relevance to their queries.

Pinkerton's search engine comprised three parts just like
JumpStation. The first was a program that scoured the Web.
This robot cleverly collected not only the URLs and titles of
Web pages but also the text that was written on the pages. The
second part of the engine was the database where the robot
program stored the information. The third part was the mechanism that allowed users to interrogate the database – a Web page
featuring a box in which search terms could be typed. Pinkerton
called his device WebCrawler.

Pinkerton's crucial innovation was to apply 'relevance' to the
search method. His way of determining relevance was very simple:
whenever a search word was entered, WebCrawler counted the
number of times that word appeared in every page that was
indexed in its database. The more times the search word appeared
in a page, the more 'relevant' the page was deemed to be. And
the more relevant the page, the higher it was placed in the list
of search results delivered to the user. It was this crucial element
of Pinkerton's system that etoy soon exploited for their own
peculiar reasons. It was also what made WebCrawler the most
popular search engine for a number of years.

At much the same time that WebCrawler, with its cuddly
spider-logo and the motto 'Lightning-Fast Web Search', was going
live, Jonathon Fletcher was facing a challenge with JumpStation.
His employers at Stirling University had told him that, because
his work had been carried out on their computers, with their
Internet connection, *they* were the ones who owned it. 'The
impression that I was given was that I had no claim to it,' he
remembers. 'Back then, out of ignorance, lack of self-confidence
and immaturity, I didn't think I could fight it.'

And worse was to come. He was officially classed as technical-support staff by the university, not as an academic. So, when he wrote a research paper which was accepted by Tim Berners-Lee's First World Wide Web Conference, in Geneva, he was unable to persuade the university to fund him to travel to it. This was particularly disappointing for Fletcher, but he was not the type for fighting: 'If there hadn't been ownership issues and if I had presented my paper, then there would certainly have been other opportunities. What I would have made of them I don't know.'

So Jonathon Fletcher abandoned JumpStation in October 1994, although, in a roundabout way, it did secure him a job at a merchant bank in Tokyo. He wrote an email to one of his friends, entitled 'The death of the robot', which included the observation, 'Indexing the Web doesn't bring in much money.' After Fletcher left Scotland, JumpStation slowly withered; without subsequent modification it didn't keep up with the ever-changing Web.

By contrast Brian Pinkerton was far more savvy, having seen the commercial world in action during three years he had worked in Silicon Valley. He reported the findings of WebCrawler at the Second World Wide Web Conference in Chicago. Shortly afterwards he secured a letter from the University of Washington's Office of Technology Transfer confirming that he, and not the University, owned the technology. This was the prerequisite for raising further research money from the private sector. Six months later, Pinkerton sold WebCrawler to America Online for $2 million in cash and stock – over the course of the boom period, this stock came to be worth much more.

Between them, Brian Pinkerton and Jonathon Fletcher demonstrated that on the Internet the brilliant, innovative idea was never enough. Despite grandiose claims about bringing together the global village, what dictated the reception of a new service was whether it had come out of California or the hinterland of Europe. And though Internet evangelists promised it would stimulate a liberating exchange of ideas, what really mattered was who owned them. The University of Stirling still controls the intellectual-property rights to JumpStation.

Throughout the autumn of 1995, Udatny continued his research into search engines with the hope of finding surreptitious ways of diverting Web users off course and towards the etoy Web site. He found a whole collection of competing services, including WebCrawler and Lycos, which focused on maintaining the largest index of Web sites, and Infoseek, which also indexed newswires and Internet news groups. One of the largest computer companies in the world, Digital Equipment, launched Altavista and soon six Stanford students were boasting 'concept searching' with the launch of Excite!. As the months wore on, it seemed to Udatny as though everybody was trying to get in on the search-engine game.

In an effort to understand how search-engine robots worked, Udatny hacked a simple program that operated much like the first part of Jonathon Fletcher's code. It worked by sucking in the URLs of hundreds of Web pages, but had one crucial addition: a feature that collected any email address that was on those pages.

He named his creation Ivana the Grabber. 'She was a radical 'bot. That's why I gave her a radical name from the East. Somehow I thought about the angry, radical Russian that was incorporated into the name.' On 12 December 1995, Udatny sent a proud email to all@etoy.com with the announcement that his beloved Ivana would begin work at 10.02 p.m. She came back the next morning carrying the first entries in what soon became a list of several thousand email addresses. This etoy would later use when sending out unsolicited mass mailings.

Udatny's intuitive ingenuity came into play with the next step in his creation. The plan was that when a Web user keyed a certain word into a search engine and after clicking on a link, they would not be directed to the selected subject but would be 'captured' by etoy. Determined to show off his technical sophistication he wanted to have control over exactly which links in a search engine's list of results would divert the user to etoy. So he set about further analysing search-engine results. In fact, he programmed Ivana to precisely target Brian Pinkerton's technical innovation, which ascribed 'relevance' to Web pages based on the frequency of search-word appearances within them.

The secret was to make Ivana behave like an ordinary Web user. First the robot would submit a particular word to a search engine; then it would scour each page that it pointed to and count the number of times the chosen word occurred. For each word, Ivana produced a table relating the position of each page in the results lists to how many instances of the search word it contained. For example, the Porsche Web site in the fifth slot of WebCrawler's top-results page might include thirteen mentions of the word 'Porsche', while the page in the sixth slot might contain only ten.

The next stage was to create Web pages purporting to be about particular words, and then to place them on etoy's Web site so that they would eventually appear in various search engines' results lists. All these dummy pages were headed 'The best information about . . .' or 'The best pictures about . . .' followed by one of the key words that it was hoped users would submit searches for. Wanting to elegantly place these pages into precise locations in the results lists, Udatny programmed Ivana to create texts containing specific numbers of instances of the chosen search words like 'Porsche'. Brian Pinkerton's bright idea for giving users relevant results was being turned on its head by Udatny's inventive coding for etoy's purposes. To begin with, for fear of being discovered, he tested the theory by keeping search-word frequencies low and thus placing his pages way down on the results lists.

Although the Internet porn industry already used a similar technique (called spamdexing) to generate trade, filling Web pages with sexually explicit words, etoy were unique in creating pages that exactly targeted positions on the results pages. Also unlike the porn merchants, they were creating a performance to which the redirection of hapless users was the sinister end – not a brash method of advertising.

The boys sent emails to each other discussing what words should be used as their traps, in order to capture exactly the right cross-section of Web users, and Goldstein in Zürich was made responsible for compiling the final list. They wanted to ensnare a broad range of people, from those searching for famous movie-directors to those looking for porn; at the same time, they aspired to a collection of words that in some way described the purpose and sensibilities of etoy and included their favourite bands, from punk to nineties anarchists. Eventually, after much argument, a list of about 350 different words was agreed. This was:

Abba, abuse, AC/DC, accessories, ace, architecture, advertising, Amsterdam, Arnold, art, Ash, Atari, athletics, Austria, baby, bands, base, baseball, Beatles, Belgium, Berlin, bitch, Björk, black, Blur, bobo, bomb, bondage, Brasil, breakbeat, Brussels, Bullock, business, cars, Castro, censorship, Che, Chirac, Chumbawamba, cinema, city, classics, Claude, Clint, Clinton, clockwork, cocaine, cock, communications, communism, companies, computers, Costner, crack, crime, culture, cunt, cyberculture, cyberia, cybersex, cyberspace, dance, David Bowie, Dead Kennedy, Dean, design, designernews, designers, Detroit, dick, disco, DJ, Doom, Doom2, drinking, drugs, Eastwood, EBM, economy, ecstasy, electronic, Elvis, England, entertainment, Europe, events, experimental, fashion, Ferrari, fiction, Fidel, firearms, football, formula, Formula1, France, ftp, fuck, future, gabber, game, games, generation, generationx, genx, Germany, Goldie, Goldwyn, graphic design, Green Day, Greenpeace, Guevara, gun, health, heavy, hell, heroin, hi-fish, highheels, hill, hiphop, Hiroshima, Hitler, holidays, house, hustler, i-D, individuals, intelligence, international, Internet, Internet guide, interview, Italy, Jack, Jackson, James, Jean, Johnny, jungle, Jurassic, Kant, Kelly Family, Kerouac, Kevin, kiss, Kraftwerk, Le Pen, lifestyle, literature, London, Lou Reed, love, LSD, Madonna, magazines, marketing, Marusha, masochism, Massive Attack, Mayer, media, Melody Maker, men, metal, Metro, Michael, Milano, military, miss djax, Mondrian, movies, MTV, Mururoa, music, naked, NATO, nature, Nazi, Net, Netbomb, Netheads, Netherlands, networks, news, nigger, Nintendo, Nirvana, NME, nuclear, Oasis, OJ, online, orange, Orb, organisations, paradise, Paramount, parc, Paris, parties, party, Penthouse, people, performing arts, Petshop Boys, pharmacology, philosophy, pictures, pistols, plastic, Playboy, PlayStation, police, politics, pop, popstars, porno, pornography, Porsche, Portishead, products, promotion, Prost, Proust, Pulp, pussy, racing, rebel, recreation, religion, REM, republique, residents, revolution, riot, roboter, rock'n'roll, rollerblades, rolling, Rolling Stone, Rolls Royce, rubber, sado, Sandra, Schumacher, Schwarzenegger, secret, Saga, Senna, services, Seveso, sex, Sex Pistols, Simpson, skating, skin, slave, sm, society, sound, SoundGarden, space, speed, spex, Spielberg, sports, Stalin, star, Steven, Stones, Switzerland, T-shirt, Tarantino, TCP, techno, technology, teenage, Terminator, terror, tits, tng, toys, trade, trek, triphop, UK, uncensored, underground, underwear, underworld, universal, uno, VanDamme, velvet, virtual reality, viva, Vogue, VRML, war, Waterworld, Westbam, white, WIRED, women, wordwar, XTC, Yello, youth, Zürich

These words were grist to Ivana's mill, the bait she would scatter across dummy Web pages to misdirect users.

Towards the end of 1995, etoy's project had crystallised with the name of the Digital Hijack. Unintentionally they were to answer the question that the Ars Electronica catalogue had posed the previous summer, 'Who will be the hitchhikers and hijackers of the information super-highways?'

At this point, Zai's contribution to the project was the promise of some graphics. In Vienna, he and Brainhard the one-time poet were also planning how best to communicate the Hijack to the public, though to Zai their ideas seemed inadequate. Increasingly dissatisfied, and determined to do something hip, with global resonance, he felt that there had to be a way of turning the Hijack into something more than an elegant technical event. So he began, as he described it, 'analysing the world'.

In the pages of *WIRED*, he stumbled across an article about Kevin Mitnick, a computer criminal who had been captured in February 1995 after a thrilling chase by the FBI. Mitnick had gained illegal entry into networks of big companies like Motorola and Sun Microsystems, and had eventually published some of their secret computer code online. He was reviled by the Federal authorities but worshipped by many Internet kids. The story gave Zai the inspiration he needed. He decided that the Digital Hijack would benefit from having a political issue as its apparent purpose, and a campaign for the release of this infamous criminal seemed appropriate. He felt certain that it would provide 'the hype we had been looking for', because it would help etoy 'take part in the myth of the underground', and hoped to create a scandal. He remembers, 'We abused Mitnick as a perfect character for our story.'

The other boys were enthusiastic because focusing the Hijack on the demand for Mitnick's release promised real digital adventures, a route to fame and, eventually, money too. Goldstein wrote an explanatory mail to the other etoy agents, 'We will have to be cautious not to be overrun by groupies. I'll need a bodyguard. This project could become the genius stroke of modern times . . . Chaos on the Internet will be perfect, orientation will belong to the past, only thoughts directed by etoy will be left. In the end the big sponsors will participate, we will drive Ferraris and have beautiful women. And everybody will call us traitors. But we will be free, like the birds. Long live the Sex Pistols!!!' Zai continued where Goldstein's excitable rhetoric left off. 'MTV is doomed to die. They will conduct interviews with their slaughterers, etoy. And glorify us without understanding what's really going on. It's like at the time when VIDEO killed the RADIOSTAR.'

With the stakes rising, the pressure to succeed increased. Zai was convinced that the Hijack was their opportunity to graduate to superstardom; the desire was strengthened when he saw his idol David Bowie perform in Vienna. Rather than boost his confidence, the concert demoralised him. 'Hardcore. We will never be like this,' he wrote. Increasingly he made the target of his frustration his fellow agent Goldstein, etoy's sound-department front man.

In Zürich, Goldstein and Esposto were working on a musical accompaniment to the Digital Hijack, a track called 'Electronic Highway Riot'. Zai did not like the composition from the outset and continuously asked for changes. But Goldstein had his own ideas and insisted upon a certain independence for his artistic creations. 'When I participate I do interfere,' Zai wrote. 'With you too. If you don't like this, you have to tell me and our ways will split . . . etoy is demanding, you have to respect this.' Zai travelled several times to Zürich to oversee the work in the studio; he even demanded that Goldstein call in sick to his day job.

At the beginning of 1996, the conflict escalated. Zai claimed that Goldstein was not up to the job of creating the etoy music and promoting the Digital Hijack. He began calling Goldstein a 'loser', and eventually Udatny and Brainhard joined the campaign. The situation made Goldstein feel depressed and lonely, but he was desperate to remain a part of the group.

By February, the Hijack song had been recorded, with Zai's help, and Udatny had finished coding Ivana. They wanted to launch in about a month's time, Zai insisted that they should run through the project as a whole beforehand. So he called a meeting in Bratislava, the capital of Slovakia – which, using American corporate terminology, he described as an 'off-site'.

Despite the advent of the free market, this run-down Eastern Bloc city still had the feel of the old days. Its public squares remained packed with massive Communist monuments and an expressway bisected the old town, almost chipping off a corner of its medieval cathedral. Importantly for etoy, Bratislava was an easy journey from Vienna and also dirt-cheap; they booked into the Trnávka, a seedy hotel in the suburbs, so nondescript as to be remarkable only for having once hosted the Slovak football team.

Each morning for a week, the boys would appear at breakfast in their uniform black trousers and orange jackets. As was the case more than a year before in Weggis, every morning, afternoon and evening was spent in arduous and chaotic meetings that were broken up only briefly for meals. Udatny remembers that at the end of each day his legs ached from the exhaustion of sitting through these interminable arguments.

There was much to talk about. While the Digital Hijack would function technically, it required careful staging. The creation of the performance, the timing of the search-robot Ivana's release, the media strategy and the Web site design were all meticulously dissected. Throughout the discussions, the boys continued to vie with each other for power and control. Goldstein's previous responsibility for public relations was taken from him and given to Brainhard instead – to be carried out from Vienna, where Zai's influence was more pronounced. And Gramazio's place in the group was now also in jeopardy because he had failed to turn up in Bratislava at all. These were difficult meetings, and the only distraction permitted came at night, when the boys would have a couple of whiskies and watch the strip show in the hotel disco.

Beyond etoy's claustrophobic world, search engines had suddenly become the most talked about service on the Internet. The financial pages were enthusing about them; *Business Week* classed them 'among the biggest attractions on the Web', while *Fortune* included them in their cover story about the 'Ten fundamental technology trends that will spawn opportunities for thousands of companies – and for shrewd investors'.

When the etoy members returned to their respective homes in Vienna and Zürich, they did so in the knowledge that they had one month in which to prepare the Digital Hijack. On 26 February 1996, the day of their return, Brainhard registered the domain hijack.org Udatny had tested the technology on the day he left for Bratislava and now checked the log-files, finding that all but one of the chosen search engines had visited the etoy Web site. On typing etoy's key words into these search engines, he found with some satisfaction that Ivana's dummy page appeared at the positions he had predicted. By clicking on the given links he was transported to etoy's Web page and from there to the Digital Hijack page, thus becoming a 'trial hostage'. The next day, Infoseek, the last of the selected search engines, finally paid the site a visit. Udatny proudly announced to all@etoy.com, 'It seems as if we had Infoseek tightly under control! This makes a total of 5 search services under our control.'

Now that etoy knew how long each search engine needed to index a new page and refresh its database, they could fix the Digital Hijack launch date. They chose a Saturday night, 30 March 1996, as the moment when they would set the counter to zero and start counting hostages. In advance, Udatny would send out Ivana so that by that date their dummy pages would appear in all the chosen search engines. 'I felt like a pioneer,' he explains. 'A pioneer is a guy that believes in something, who the others think is crazy. And they only believe him once they can see that it is working.' A press release was also sent out to, among others, MTV, the *Face*, *i-D*, *New Musical Express*, *Rolling Stone* and *Mondo 2000*.

SPECIAL-PREVIEW + + + SPECIAL PREVIEW + + +
THIS IS NOT A BUSINESS-BASTARD-MESSAGE.
THIS IS LIFESTYLE, ART AND ROCK'n'ROLL . . .
We are ready to hijack the world-wide travelling society on the Internet! We do not hijack your bodies, we hijack your attention to show you another direction – smashing the boring style of established electronic traffic channels . . .

Udatny spent the time leading up to the launch writing an elegant hack to make the Hijack appear all the more sinister to Web surfers. Web browsers have a 'back button' that allows users to return to the page they've just visited. Udatny's efforts made it appear as though the Hijack page had a back button that did not work, so those users directed here would be forced into the dark world of etoy and find it difficult to return to the calmer pages elsewhere on the Web. At the same time Zai and Brainhard borrowed a strange textual design from the best-known digital artists of the time – jodi.org – to frame their message.

Late in the evening of the launch date, Udatny, Zai and Brainhard gathered around a computer in the Vienna Academy of Applied Arts. Esposto and his girlfriend did the same in Zürich. Zai welcomed them, writing that, while 'we are about to leave reality behind', he felt for the first time in his life 'the real virtual live groove'. A little later, shaking with happiness, he composed another mail to the Zürich branch – this one officially announcing the launch. 'Madness. Pure madness,' he wrote. 'Something is in the air. All the feelings, the hundred thousand downs of the last months and days condense in my head into euphoria. The next level is reached. Be happy with us. It was hard and sometimes unbearable. We will be redeemed any moment. The thing belongs to all of us. It is etoy. And tonight we show the world for the first time our FACE.' Around their respective computers, they saw the first 'hostages' appear in the log-file and shouted out with excitement. This was better than any drug they'd ever experienced together.

In Houston, two young men – self-styled sonic sculptors, DJs and bohos – were supposed to be working, designing a Web site for a company that provided seismic data systems for the oil industry. Instead, they were looking for porn on the Internet. They had typed various words into search engines, hoping they would find some sexy pictures. They pressed a link. The page they were sent to contained weird runic symbolism, in green type on a black background – by www.etoy.com. The hapless surfers scrolled down and read:

DON'T FUCKING MOVE
THIS IS A DIGITAL HIJACK

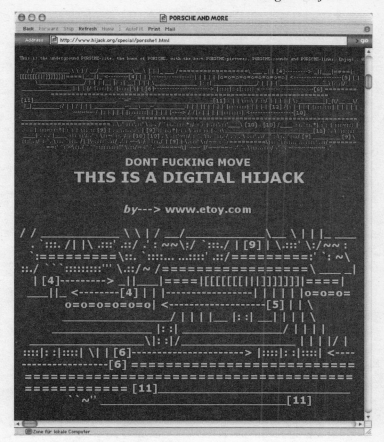

The screen that confronted hijacked 'hostages'.

The back button on their browser wouldn't work. They pressed the links on the page and were delivered into the heart of the etoy.TANKSYSTEM. Surfing their way around the site, they then wrote etoy a message: 'The amount of creativity and life involved with this site is beautiful. Fucking Beautiful!!!!!' They signed it, Ashokan and Dharmaja, and asked etoy to be a little circumspect in replying because they were squatting on their boss's machine.

In Geneva, art curator Nicolas Bonstein was sitting in his office playing on his Mac Centris 650 when he came across the site. 'I didn't understand it as art, but just the idea of some hackers who wanted to remind me that information rhymed with manipulation.'

Meanwhile Zai, Brainhard and Udatny were studying their server's logs, and realised that while many of their unwilling victims came from America there were also victims from Japan and across Europe. They counted a thousand hits before leaving for a bar to celebrate.

The Digital Hijack was timed brilliantly to coincide with the climaxing media interest in search engines. In the two weeks following the launch, three Internet-search companies held their Initial Public Offerings. Among them was the brand leader Yahoo!, whose shares tripled in value on the first day of trading, making the company worth almost $1 billion despite its revenue of just a couple of million. *The Wall Street Journal* sagely noted that 'investors are still gaga over virtually anything related to the Internet'.

An unpleasant surprise awaited Udatny when he returned to his server the day after the launch: the number of hijacked Net surfers had caused it to crash. After rebooting the computer, he was pleased to find Ashokan and Dharmaja's mail, as well as congratulations from etoy's Zürich branch. The email list Ivana had collected was now used, with more than a thousand emails sent out asking recipients to 'spread this new Internet-lifestyle to your friends and to Internet-freaks + surfers! this is an under-ground art-project not a bastard-business mail. our grab robot "etoy.IVANA" got your email-address by cruising the net.'

The email tactic provoked a passionate response from infuriated members of the Internet community. Spam should not be sent, and etoy had badly transgressed this kindly and solicitous rule of the Internet's early years. Some, like TOBY696004, threat-ened: 'this sucks if you mess with my ass you will be eating a virus buddy'. Others launched more aggressive attacks. Some filled the etoy mailbox with rubbish. George Reese, who ran one of the oldest multi-user role-playing games on the Internet, sent etoy 250 copies of his complaint: 'It seems you are too fucking STUPID to get the point. Hopefully by wasting your time in a fractional ratio to the amount of times of others you have wasted, you will get the point. DON'T FUCKING MAIL ME, MY MAILING LIST, OR ANYONE ELSE IN AN UNSOLICI- TED MANNER.' Reese was not alone. It was during this week that Udatny learned the meaning of the English word 'unsolicited'.

Soon representatives from the search engines came calling. When etoy received an email from Andy Bensky, one of the lead engineers at Infoseek, they panicked that they had been dis- covered. But Bensky had only written to enquire about one of their dummy pages, because its content did not match its title. Apologising for 'the mistake', Brainhard solicitously asked Bensky to remove the entry from the index. For the time being, etoy had escaped the search-engine scrutiny.

It actually took Infoseek almost two months to grasp what was going on. But once their technicians discovered the Hijack, they did everything in their power to fight it, erasing all the hijack.org entries from their database. 'We felt they were attacking us,' Bensky recalls. 'They were using our goodwill to further their own ends that were diametrically opposed to everything that we were trying to do, which was to make the Internet a fun place to be and an easy place to navigate. We just cut them out of the index. And we took steps to make sure they couldn't get back into the index under different domain names.'

As a consequence of the Digital Hijack, Infoseek created what they called the Spam Committee. During the following years, weekly meetings discussed how best to prevent misuse of their search engine. Despite themselves, etoy had helped to make the search engines less prone to commercial abuse. It also meant that etoy had to change tactics and refine their technique. Udatny asked all his fellow students to lend him their server spaces, but Infoseek were close on his heels and he never managed to get the same amount of pages indexed again. WebCrawler was soon to fol- low. Andrew Leonard, the first American journalist to report on etoy, informed Brian Pinkerton at WebCrawler of the etoy scam. 'Pretty funny,' Pinkerton wrote back. 'But we'll still nuke them.'

Leonard later delighted the boys by writing a critique in hot-wired.com: 'Welcome to the next step in the evolution of the Web: The invasion of the search engine snatchers ... As the Web spreads its tentacles, it is indeed becoming the ultimate stage, a low-cost platform for stunts with a potential audience of millions. Let the games begin!'

For three months, Zai and etoy left the Digital Hijack running, although they found it increasingly difficult to cope with the counter-measures of the search engines. Nevertheless, by the end of the summer, etoy would claim 1,500,000 visitors had been hijacked.

Kubli, meanwhile, responsible for legal issues, submitted the Hijack to the 1996 Ars Electronica prize.

The jury gathered a few months prior to the festival. Joichi Ito, invited as a juror for the Web category, flew in directly from Los Angeles, where he had just said his last farewells to Timothy Leary. Coincidentally, he had spent much of the spring of 1996 dealing with search engines. In his new guise as a serious Internet entrepreneur, he was in the process of establishing a Japanese version of Infoseek – at the time, lagging only a little behind Yahoo!.

Also on the Web category jury were Karen Spaink, a writer and digital artist from Holland, and David Blair, another artist, who in March 1993 had been one of the first to put his work on the Net. His film *WAX or the discovery of television among the bees* was an Internet art legend that allowed viewers to construct their own stories from the clips he had created – though for many, this advanced and novel approach did little more than crash their simple computers. The other jury members were David Traub, an American CD-rom producer; and Thomas Frommel, who worked for the Ars Electronica Center.

The jury held their deliberations in Linz in the studios of ORF, the Austrian public television station. Joichi Ito and his fellow jurors had trouble viewing the 212 submitted Web sites because of the sluggish speed of their Internet connection, and were forced to hold their meetings in the evenings, when access was faster. Through the night, they ploughed through the entries. They had to decide who to give the top prize of a *Goldene Nica* to, as well as who to nominate for 'highly commended' in the Web category. Much of the work submitted comprised of hastily established hobby home pages or dull demonstrations of technical skill – all of little interest to the jury. They were keen to find a project with what they called 'Webism', by which they meant that it could only have existed on the Web.

Amid the drudgery there were a few sites that stood out. Tim Leary's Nethome, inspired and helped by Ito, was on the list – although he naturally found this a little embarrassing to discuss. They also considered Hygrid, which allowed users to upload little images that were then merged into one enormous picture by the server. Journey into Exile played angelic music as accompaniment to a reading of a J. G. Ballard novel, while also serving up related search-engine results.

For Joichi Ito, etoy's entry was the only contender. David Blair, however, was irritated by etoy's caper; he felt that they were abusing the art community and using the Hijack as a means to promote themselves as pop stars. 'Amidst the utopian rhetoric of the time, it didn't seem very advanced irony, and there wasn't much irony in doing sales promotion as art work,' he protested. He thought it was either 'insincere or young'. The debate raged on for fourteen hours, with Blair digging in his heels while Joichi Ito and Karen Spaink became ever more vocal supporters of etoy. Finally Blair was overruled. Ito still thinks that it was justifiably so: 'The Digital Hijack was really the only example of its kind, a piece of art that used and exploited the network.' And, as Karen Spaink would later write in the jury statement, 'If something might turn out to be a spoof in the real world, that was, to reformulate a worn-out adage, "a pity for reality".'

When Christine Schöpf, Ars Electronica's Deputy Director, rang Kubli to tell him that etoy had won the *Goldene Nica* in the Web category he was asleep at home in Zürich. He thought he must be dreaming, but she continued, asking if etoy would create an installation demonstrating the Hijack for the Ars Electronica festival, in a few months' time. When the call was finished, he came to his senses and wrote an email entitled 'Fasten seatbelts!' to spread the good news.

GLORY & HONOR GET CLOSE
- -
get the champagne and the cigars ready,
- -
>>>
>>>
>>>>>>>>>>>>>>>>>>>>>>>>>
this is the netbomb!!!!!!!!!!!!!!!!!!!
$$
$$
$$
$$

The boys had trouble believing Kubli's mail. Gramazio wrote back, 'Really cool news, I have tears in my eyes, I have to admit. Except if this is only a bad joke.' In Vienna, Zai and Brainhard phoned Christine Schöpf, to check that they weren't the brunt of Kubli's acid wit.

Then, euphoria took over. 'Fuck, fuck, fuck ... We are the art bosses of World Wide Web – unanimously. What a feeling, what emotions,' Brainhard wrote. Zai was incredibly happy; it was 'like being struck by lightning – within minutes our lives changed; we felt that the world would never be the same for us. Before, we had tried to hype ourselves as the famous guys. Now suddenly we *were* the famous guys. It was like winning an Oscar.' In an email sent to the others, Zai thanked all the etoy members effusively – even the 'problem child Goldstein' for having had the original idea of the Hijack. He also thanked himself for having endured the emotional stress – despite having been its major cause.

Beneath the euphoria, Brainhard felt a little uneasy. After years spent desperately seeking fame, he was now worried that it would damage them, that etoy might be corrupted by success. He talked to Zai, who felt no such concerns. Zai, still thrilled, sent another mail – this time announcing the death of Timothy Leary. He felt that an epoch had ended: 'It was a beautiful time with the LSD. THANKS TIM! But every pain has its sunny side. Way to a new millennium. A new generation with new drugs.' He signed himself 'zai@etoy.com (always online – never stoned – but sometimes lost)'.

When Joichi Ito left Linz he kept travelling, finally arriving in Los Angeles for Leary's funeral by way of a UNESCO conference in Singapore and some business meetings in Tokyo. In California, he told his new partners at Infoseek about the award that had just been given for the Digital Hijack. To his wry amusement, his colleagues told him that they had been trying to 'stomp it out' for some time.

Before etoy could appear at Ars Electronica, they had another obstacle to scale. At six o'clock one morning in late June 1996, Brainhard was asleep in his Vienna apartment when two plain-clothed policemen arrived armed with a search warrant. At first Brainhard assumed that they were looking for drugs, but they were interested only in computers and disks – neither of which he kept at home. From the Austrian Staatsschutz, the national political police force – like MI5 or the FBI – they had tracked Brainhard down because he had been the one to register the etoy domain name. Finding nothing of interest in his apartment, they presented him with a summons to report to the Central Police Station on Schottenring, one of Vienna's main thoroughfares.

Udatny and Zai accompanied Brainhard to the station. His mouth was dry as he went through the long corridors to the back of the building, past uniformed officers and into the domain of the plainclothed spooks. In a small room containing only a plain desk and an old filing cabinet, he was met by Officer Korinek, who told him that the US Secret Service had requested an investigation into etoy's activities – and that the Staatsschutz was going to oblige them in any way they could. What intrigued Brainhard was that Korinek – the Staatsschutz's computer-crime investigator – used an old-fashioned manual typewriter.

The reason for the investigation was that several people had sent emails to president@whitehouse.gov with the subject line, 'Free Kevin Mitnick!' Many included obscenities and threats to President Clinton's family; several were signed in the name of Ulrike Meinhof, a deceased member of the 1970s German terrorist group Rote Armee Fraktion (RAF) – Red Army Faction – and had emanated from etoy's domain. Although no one in etoy had sent the offending emails, a device installed inside the TANK-SYSTEM encouraged visitors to mail the President demanding the hacker's freedom. It was anonymous – a difficult thing to achieve, at the time – and evidently some had taken advantage by posing as terrorists.

Officer Korinek cross-examined Brainhard for an hour and a half, during which time he requested that Brainhard supply him with copies of etoy's server logs – the list of all the domains of those who had visited the site. In the event, Udatny scrambled the information on the files before they were printed out, applying what Zai called 'the electronic mincer method', making the records useless for Korinek's purposes. Still, hundreds of pages were put into boxes, and Brainhard delivered them all to Korinek. It seemed he was quite satisfied with them – etoy never heard from him again.

Having dealt with the police, etoy's summer that year was filled with innocent excitement. Although the Ars Electronica jury had already announced the year's winners, prizes would not be given until a formal ceremony at the festival. By then, etoy had to create their Digital Hijack exhibition. They worked relentlessly in preparation for the event – probably the only time that all the etoy members pulled in the same direction. Kubli took a term off from his law studies and moved to Vienna to help. 'We were in seventh heaven, we were so happy,' remembers Esposto. 'We knew that nobody could ever say again that we made just weird stuff. We worked like mad, and we loved what we were doing.'

They completed the installation in early September and shipped it to Linz, where it was set up in exhibition space allocated to them. etoy had created what they described as a 'physical event in the counter-world', a kind of real-world extension of their TANKSYSTEM. Large 'tanks' – boxes constructed out of plywood – were connected by etoy wastepipes, all hand-painted orange and diligently branded, and in each tank was a computer. In the first tank, visitors could watch a simulation of the Digital Hijack; in the Disco tank, etoy soundtracks played; the so-called Striptease tank's computer printed out mails from the etoy archive and spewed them across the floor; and the Identity tank displayed a video of the etoy agents' faces morphing into each other. The final tank, Duty Check, contained a mass of statistics about each of the agents and their daily activities. They had dutifully recorded their activities every day for the previous few months. This included their exact whereabouts, what sex they'd had, how much money they'd spent and what drugs they had consumed. The information was now presented in a series of beautiful graphs, an articulation of that peculiar and increasingly complicated etoy characteristic: discipline and submission of the individual to the etoy project.

Just before the exhibition's opening, the boys were briefed by their spokesman, Brainhard, and given a set of rules, drawn up by Zai especially for their appearance at Ars Electronica. They were supposed to meet every hour during the event, to discuss each agent's duty and to decide who should talk to which journalist. Their girlfriends were banned from appearing whenever cameras were around. Alcohol was forbidden during work hours, drugs were forbidden completely and they all had to shave their heads every day. Each of them had to 'radically follow the rules', as Zai remembers. Every morning during the festival they were to have a press briefing, at which Brainhard would give out topics for the agents to push to journalists. If faced with a difficult question, they were simply to lower their sunglasses and reply with an etoy slogan. The stance that they had to adopt during interviews was also prescribed: 'soldier's fight-attitude'.

The opening of the festival included a speech by the Mayor of Linz and various champagne receptions. Around their gallery space, etoy posed for the cameras, dressed in their uniforms and sunglasses and carrying their black attaché cases and newly acquired palm computers.

The climax of the celebrations was the award ceremony, broadcast live on Austrian national television. The event was held in a television studio in front of an audience selected from the great and the good of Linz and the festival, and was presented by two Austrian television personalities. The etoy members waited in the green room for their appearance while the other *Goldene Nicas* were being handed out. John Lasseter, who had been in creative control of the first computer-animated movie, *Toy Story*, was there to pick up his.

Zai had decided that Udatny should speak in front of the cameras when etoy received their award: 'I felt that he needed this attention, that it was good for the team because normally he was in the background.' When the award was announced the seven bald young men in orange jackets climbed on to the stage. Udatny grabbed the microphone and thanked etoy's sponsors – the donors of the wastepipe and a clothes shop that had provided their uniform. This was forbidden on the public-funded TV network, and etoy were pleased to have once again been provocative. Along with the statuette of the *Goldene Nica*, they were presented with a cheque for 100,000 Austrian Schillings (about $7,500, or £5,000).

For all seven of them, it was a spectacular coup. Just a year before, they had sneaked into the Ars Electronica after-awards party as outsiders, wondering how to make names for themselves, admiring the celebrities of the technology elite. Now they were right at the heart of it. From the audience, some of their parents looked on; even their girlfriends had been allowed to share this moment of glory.

Following the ceremony was a gala reception at which the etoy agents were to collect email addresses of any important guests for their database. After an hour, the boys started celebrating – all of them got very, very drunk. They moved on to another after-party, held at a public swimming-pool; wearing only their underwear and sunglasses, etoy took their beloved *Nica* for a dive. At the end of the night, Gramazio placed the statuette as a bet on roulette and lost.

During the rest of the week-long festival, they continued to pose as celebrities. Esposto recalls, 'Success definitely went to our heads; we started being megalomaniac.' They properly met Joichi Ito, who loved their attitude. He would accompany them to parties and he and Zai would talk about how to take etoy into the future. In finding Ito, they had found one of their key advisors, sponsors and motivators for the coming years. They admired him because he was a real businessman and not an artist dependent on public subsidy. 'For me, it was magic how he fitted into our group,' Zai remembers. 'We all were into technology, pop culture, and the staging of our lives.'

For Ito, etoy was a melding of everything he found interesting – counterculture, the Internet, search engines – and he adored them, believing that they were fulfilling the promise of art by 'pushing technology to its limits to fuel its development'. To him, etoy demonstrated that while the US was defining the technical and business aspects of the Internet, the Europeans seemed to be leading the art community into the digital age.

Not everybody was so impressed by etoy. According to one radio presenter, their skinheads and uniforms made them look like the 'voluntary fire brigade' of Jörg Haider, the leader of Austria's ultra-right nationalist Freedom Party. Unsurprisingly their posturing and appearance caused great controversy in Linz, a place loaded with Nazi allusions. For etoy, however, all attention – in favour of or against them – was welcome.

When the festival was over and they checked out of their hotel, they realised that they were responsible for paying their mini-bar bill, which amounted to more than $1,000. It seemed worth it, for such a week of exhausting exuberance. And after all, Ars

Electronica faced a bill of their own – the holes etoy had drilled into the gallery walls to affix their installation would cost a lot to repair.

etoy found it hard to return to normal life. 'It was as if someone had put out the spotlights; it was a difficult moment,' Gramazio recalls. To recover, they visited the Black Sea resort of Varna in Bulgaria, where their hotel, the Ambassador, had a radiation counter installed over its front door because of a nearby nuclear reactor. Three coloured bulbs indicated radiational activity – green for 'normal', yellow for 'high' and red for 'danger'. This only depressed them further. They felt burned out, and had no ideas about how to better their achievement; when they returned to Vienna and Zürich respectively, they were disconsolate.

In Zürich, Kubli was the first to stumble under the pressure. In an argument with Goldstein, Gramazio and Esposto, he declared that they had no right to dictate how he should live his life, that he hated wearing the orange etoy jacket and that he was leaving. He wanted to take time out to decide whether he would continue to contribute to etoy.

In Vienna, Udatny voiced his own doubts about remaining in the group. He had come to hate etoy's atmosphere, particularly because he had always felt undermined by Zai. When Zai had drawn up the credit list for the Hijack it originally included only Zai and Brainhard as 'directors', while Udatny was down as 'the coder' and their 'support'. Ultimately, Udatny had compromised with the credits: 'directed by etoy.Zai & etoy.Brainhard, advised by etoy.Udatny'. He felt that even this was unfair, since he had provided the technical foundation on which the whole scheme was built.

Zai was shocked by the prospect that etoy might fall apart. In his despair, he composed a paternal email to shake the others out of their lethargy. 'Do you realize that etoy is dying! . . . I was the one that pushed you, that encouraged you, whenever I was able to, I have cursed many times, I have pushed the envelope sometimes, but I have also prayed, preached courage and chivvied you along.' If etoy was about to die, he went on, it was the mistake of 'zombies who will never manage to do what they want because they lack the WILL'.

A week later, things went from bad to worse. Udatny refused to comply with the requirements of the etoy group discipline. He had been working for etoy relentlessly, had lost almost all social contact outside the group and was running out of money. His nerves and tolerance had collapsed, and in one argument he called Zai a 'dictator'. This was more than Zai could stomach. 'DEFCON 1!' he immediately mailed to the other etoy members. 'Now it's getting dangerous. APPEAL TO ALL, HELP!' He felt that he had been ridiculed and derided by the star of the Digital Hijack, and now wanted the group to back him in his fight. He defined the rules for Udatny: 'I want you to be disciplined. that's what I ask, for gods sake. because otherwise we will go to the dogs.'

Udatny couldn't cope with the rules any more: 'It was the missing respect for the individual that stressed me out. I want to have fun; I'm not a slave; I hate being ordered around. I was continuously blamed for not following the rules. It was complete terror.'

The Zürich branch was horrified to learn about the row between Zai and Udatny. Goldstein wrote a mail, admonishing them: 'Pull yourselves together.' At the time, it was not at all clear what the outcome of the storm would be – whether Udatny, the genius coder, or Zai, the headstrong motivator, would win this particular mind game and force the other out. Zai increased the pressure on Udatny: 'I will give you the choice between UNDERSTANDING and GETTING LOST or a SUPER-FIGHT.'

In a bid to deal with the crisis, etoy booked a meeting room in a hotel in Salzburg, halfway between Zürich and Vienna. When Udatny refused to wear a tie to the meeting, the group's anger spilled out. 'I was appalled, I have to admit,' says Esposto. 'I believed that wearing a suit and tie was cool and very professional. It was a sort of guarantee for us being successful in the future.' Zai screamed at Udatny while the others looked on. Finally,

Udatny rose from the table and said, 'Zai's an idiot. I'm off!' leaving the others to continue as if nothing had happened. Making Udatny the scapegoat for the group's lack of direction left them with conflicting emotions of relief and shock. On the night train home, Kubli vomited from stress and remorse.

Some time later, Zai and Brainhard knocked on Udatny's door in Vienna and asked him to return his beloved Toshiba laptop, bought for him by etoy. Brainhard remembers: 'It was like a punitive expedition. I felt really filthy, but I was caught up in the system and couldn't get out.' And so Udatny found himself completely isolated from his old friends, with no computer, no money and no job: 'It was the lowest point in my life ever. There was nothing left; I could not rely on etoy any more. I did not even have clothes, apart from the etoy uniform.'

5
Young, Fun and Full of Creative Juices

'Somewhere between the hallucinations of senior management and the cold reality of the market lies something called a business plan.'

Scott Adams, *The Dilbert Principle*, 1996

Meet Toby! In official documents he was properly addressed as Edward C. Lenk, but he was never introduced by anything other than his childhood nickname. Stepping into Toby's tiny, disorganised shared office in the early days of his company, potential new recruits often met a charming man who seemed just as interested in joking about as in asking them tricky questions. His scene-by-scene re-enactments of *Fargo* became legendary in the business; others joined him in golfing balls around the office; and none forgot his inspiring and often foul-mouthed gung-ho spirit. He 'does a pretty good Bill Murray', a former colleague remembered of Toby's *Caddyshack* phase. Loyal and devoted colleagues and friends tend to play up his funny, film-obsessed side, as testimony to his rounded character. Struggling for more evidence to counter his workaholic reputation, they also mention Amos and Tucker, the two Labradors with whom he shares his modest Santa Monica home.

The comic-book, cuddly first impression hides a much more clever and intense soul – brilliantly insightful, wickedly smart and with an edge. His employees described him as 'stubborn', convinced of the rightness of his ideas, and 'arrogant of his ability to succeed'. Also a little suspicious, he was careful not to share too many details. When one journalist asked for his birthdate, Toby said, 'I usually don't give the exact details out. It's such a key piece of information. I'm a little paranoid about it.' At six foot three inches tall, he stoops slightly. With his shoulders usually hunched, his bald head pulled down a little into his neck, he more resembles an old-fashioned European intellectual than the poster star of American corporate locker-rooms that he became.

Toby was born and brought up in the epitome of middle-class suburban Boston by his parents, Edward Snr, a banker, and Marilyn, a housewife. Like many great tycoons – Bill Gross among them – Toby had his own entrepreneurial-creation story: aged nineteen, as a caddy master at a golf course in Hyannisport, Massachusetts, he wrote a business plan, a work schedule and an incentive programme for the caddies. 'It was five or six pages on what he thought we needed to build a successful programme and what our weaknesses and strengths were,' recalled Rick Johnson, the club's head professional at the time. 'It was a beautiful package.'

Toby gained his first degree – in economics – from Bowdoin, a small, liberal arts school tucked away in the Maine pinewoods. After two years as a health-policy wonk in Washington he returned to study, arriving at the Harvard Business School just as business education and theory was in the middle of a revolution. Management doctrines, gurus and consultants were now playing an ever more important role in business, and Harvard had reorganised itself to keep up. A team of 'star' professors had been recruited to focus on the emerging 'hot' fields of entrepreneurship and technology & operations management.

After two years at Harvard, Toby graduated with a distinction in his Masters in Business Administration and went to work for a strategic-management consultancy called the LEK Partnership. In 1991, he was poached by Disney.

Of all American mega-corporations, Disney was then one of the most determinedly hierarchical, authoritarian and aggressive

corporate environments. At the pinnacle of this regime was Corporate Strategic Planning (Strat Planning) and it was here that
Toby would focus his talents. This division's corporate commandos parachuted into troublespots to analyse deals and squeeze
value from them rather like in-house management consultants.
They were responsible for EuroDisney, and it was they, not TV
executives, who swooped into ABC/Capital Cities in 1995 when
Disney acquired the company for $19 billion.

After five years of edging up the Disney hierarchy by 1996
Toby was Vice President of Strategic Planning for the Attraction
Division and responsible for advising on investments of more
than $8 billion. He was handsomely rewarded; later he would
often remind journalists that he'd made 'a lot of money' there –
more than he ever did once he'd left to launch his new career.
According to Toby, Strat Planning was a good education: 'Disney
was a great training ground . . . and there's nothing more fun
than theme parks at Disney.'

In 1996, though, Disney was not the happiest of places. Michael
Ovitz had been brought in from the Creative Artists Agency to
be second-in-command to the Chairman and Chief Executive
Michael Eisner, but they had fallen out. According to Eisner,
Ovitz was more interested in chasing deals than in fine-tuning
the operational engine. As he wrote: 'Disney wasn't mired in the
usual corporate politics. This was a full-blown crisis and it was
tearing the company apart.'

Besides the glitz of the theme parks, for Toby the divided,
huge and lumbering Disney was proving less than fulfilling.
'Theme parks are such capital-intensive projects. I would have
to spend eight or nine years working to have one accomplishment
under my belt. That's a bit slow,' he later explained. Wanting to
be more sprightly, he hankered after a smaller environment and
to start his own business. He resigned, and promised to strike
out on his own. His colleagues were amazed that he should leave
his lucrative job, asking him what he was going to do. Toby said
he didn't know.

Through the autumn of 1996 he pondered various ideas for

businesses. 'I had some crazy personal passions that I thought I could turn into businesses. I'm a keen golfer and there were no places that you could practise if you weren't a member of a private club, no place to putt. I was going to try to create high-quality practice greens for the public.'

It was about this time that Bill Gross was busy publicising idealab!. PeopleLink had been formally hatched and Gross was featured in *Time* magazine as the 'Billion-Dollar Brain'. By November he had completed the sale of Knowledge Adventure and secured finance from his high-profile investors. Confident that he could create a flock of tiny companies, he hoped that some might turn out to be blockbusters. With the promise of his New Math of Ownership he seduced Toby into becoming one of the first idealab! entrepreneurs, giving him the opportunity to direct his own destiny.

When Toby started work at idealab! he quickly recruited thirty-three-year-old Frank Han, who had been recommended to him by an old friend. A Yale mathematics graduate with an MBA from the Stanford Business School, Han loved New Wave 1980s music and movies and was cultured, clever and straight-speaking – though not always an easy man to get on with. Like Toby, he often swore and could be a demanding and testing man. He put up a poster on his office wall, from John Woo's movie *Hard-Boiled*, that depicted the actor Chow Yun-Fat all beat up and holding a gun in one hand and a baby in the other. The movie's tag-line ran underneath: 'As a cop, he has the brains, the brawn and the instincts to kill.'

Frank was recruited from the Union Bank of California, where he had created what later became the most popular online bank in the state. 'I am a huge believer in the Internet,' he had proclaimed, at a time when most people weren't.

Toby and Frank were just two members of Gross's group of entrepreneurs at idealab!, all busy starting their own small companies – including the bridal-planning site weddingchannel.com, Ideamarket for intellectual property and e-ticket, which promised the tabloid scandals of the *National Enquirer* online. But those inside the hothouse were just a small cohort of the legions of business-school graduates, investment bankers and lawyers in the start-up revolution that by 1997 was sweeping across America. In their own version of the hacker ethic, they dreamt of controlling their own fates while benefiting from the 'castles in the air' exuberance of the financial markets.

In the rhetoric of the day, these agitators were creating businesses with the magnanimous motive of the betterment of society. In his book *Startup: A Silicon Valley Adventure*, about burning through $75 million to create a pen-computer company, Jerry Kaplan wrote: 'The startup game is designed to motivate our brightest, most creative and hardest-working individuals to improve the use of society's resources, increase employment, and provide a broader range of quality goods and services.' Indeed the entrepreneurs were basking in a culture where they were soon to be canonised. The grandest of libertarian visionaries, George Gilder, seemed to compare them to prophets: 'It is the entrepreneurs who know the rules of the world and the laws of God.'

For Toby, too, the reasons for starting a business were no less extraordinary; they were almost sublime: 'I've got an MBA degree. To be creative as a writer you write, as a painter you paint. As an MBA holder you set up a business: that's how you get your creative juices flowing.' Running a start-up had apparently become a kind of vocation in itself. As said in *Fast Company* magazine: 'The thousands of . . . start-ups aren't just building companies or executing business plans. They're creating their own reality. They're not in it for the money. They're in it for the freedom.'

Companies and their staff were forging a new business culture in America which promised to be truly different. Start-ups brought with them a fresh set of operational values in which work and play were all but indistinguishable. Offices were decked out with table-football machines and styled after childhood play rooms. Like many revolutionaries, the entrepreneurs distinguished themselves with a uniform: casual trousers and tie-less shirts. Later, as Silicon Valley began to seem even more powerful than the banking community, newspapers ran features on Wall Street executives proudly wearing powerful casuals and giving their fancy suits to charities in poor neighbourhoods. Surnames and titles were out; first names and nicknames were in. Nobody ever addressed Toby Lenk and Frank Han as anything other than Toby and Frank.

These revolutionaries were storming the offices and neatly manicured hierarchies of the old ideal, the command-and-control corporation. As Toby himself said, 'For my father's generation, the whole thing was to put on a blue suit and climb a company ladder. But for me, I prefer smaller companies that are more dynamic. We take chances. We have an entrepreneurial streak. I think it's in the DNA of all the Internet folks.' Start-ups were the vanguard of a movement that would topple the existing blue-blooded establishment. As Frank said, 'You don't have to be a Choate Princeton grad who's a Rockefeller and dating a blonde débutante to succeed. It's about talent and hunger.'

Start-ups were cheered on as the new engines of capitalism. Management buzz now held that bigness had had its day; giant corporations would be out-manoeuvred and replaced by smaller, nimbler organisations. In one book subtitled *Crazy Times Call for Crazy Organizations*, prototypical nineties management guru Tom Peters insisted that managers must 'abandon everything' – meaning all corporate structures and ideas – and prepare to enter a world which he characterised as the 'Age of the Pygmies', dominated by herds of tiny fleet-footed firms.

No single management book captured the moment better than Clayton Christensen's *The Innovator's Dilemma: When New Technologies Cause Great Firms to Fall*, published just as Toby and Frank were getting started at idealab!. Christensen's message to managers was simple: old companies couldn't cope with change. So profound an influence did Christensen become, one critic later wrote that 'it's as if he'd chosen the autumn of 1913 to publish a survival guide to trench warfare'. Christensen's argument was that in an emerging market, where there can be no market history to diligently research, large companies were incapable of responding. In his war-like rhetoric, 'attacking entrant firms' would 'topple the incumbent industry leaders' and the riches would flow to those first into the market, because 'there are such strong first-mover advantages'. In thousands of meetings between investors and entrepreneurs and in hundreds of newspaper articles in the following years, these ideas, reduced to the simplest of formulations, were repeated like a mantra.

In the consumer-retail market, this new orthodoxy maintained that the Internet was the 'disruptive technology' that could attack land-based stores and create a new and direct relationship between corporations and customers. By the end of 1996, amazon.com seemed to have demonstrated this. Having capitalised on its 'first-mover advantage' and spent more than $6 million on advertising, amazon.com had leaped ahead of its high-street rival Barnes & Noble by selling $16 million worth of books online and was about to stage its IPO, the Initial Public Offering. *Fortune* proclaimed amazon.com 'one of a crew of young entrepreneurs using cyberspace technology to steal real-world customers from traditional businesses'. This was a model that everyone wanted to follow.

During this time, Toby was investigating a number of possibilities for online commerce. 'It was critical that we enter a market where we could have first-mover advantage,' he remembered. He considered setting up a real estate service, but found that real estate agents were already giving away their listings and he couldn't find a way to generate value in this free market. He also contemplated selling the top-ten items in every retail category, but then realised that his potential competitors would discount such bestsellers as 'loss-leaders' in order to drive customers to their own Web sites – thus killing his potential for profit.

Down the road from idealab! in Pasadena, another entrepreneur, Greg McLemore, had already stumbled on a first-mover idea: toys. This twenty-nine-year-old Web developer had made much of his money speculating on domain names – buying names like events.com and selling them on to those keen on a unique address. Among the names he had registered was toys.com. In November 1996, he had begun trading online, running a toy shop from his house and storing his stock in the garage. Looking for investors he soon approached Bill Gross, but was not prepared to agree to the tough terms that were offered. His project, however, had struck a chord at idealab!.

In February 1997, Toby and Frank began their toy business at the Toy Fair in New York City, the most important event in the toy industry's calendar, where thousands of vendors meet the media, analysts and retailers in efforts to second-guess what might be the 'hot' toys for the next Christmas. Toby and Frank hoped to discover gaps in the business that they might profitably exploit on the Internet.

What they found was a market that was as hit-driven as the movie or music businesses. Every year, the fickle attention of the developed world's children switches to the latest fad – such as Furbies, Pokémons or Tamagotchis. Toy manufacturers rely on these, and on other blockbuster toys – those which are heavily advertised on television and marketed through fast-food restaurants or co-branded products like children's yoghurts and movies. The biggest of these are Barbie dolls and *Star Wars* figurines. The story of Mr Potato Head illustrates how toys have changed, from being rather cute and haphazardly marketed products to becoming recognisable global brands. Mr Potato Head was launched in 1952, just bits of plastic to stick into vegetables. Eight years later it was modified to include a plastic body, as real vegetables were *passé*. By 1995, it had become a supporting actor in the hit film *Toy Story*, and later became the 'spoke-spud' for Burger King. By early 1997, Mr Potato Head and other blockbusters dominated the toy market; other bestsellers that year included the Happy Holiday Barbie, a *Star Wars* figurine and *Sesame Street*'s Tickle-Me Elmo.

By 1997, just as Mr Potato Head and his friends had been re-styled for the modern, media-obsessed world, so the toy stores through which these toy armies marched had been transformed. Because manufacturers spent so much on marketing the blockbusters, retailers were offered only very thin profit margins. To remain competitive, the retail market was forced to consolidate; neighbourhood toy shops were being replaced by out-of-town consumer cathedrals, discount stores such as Wal-Mart and national toy retailers like Toys'Я'Us. The big chains could demand greater discounts from the manufacturers and therefore could offer lower prices – so customers were flocking to buy cheaper Barbies and the like from the chains. In the face of this competition, local and speciality toy shops, though often offering a more varied and worthy toy selection – including such things as Brio Train Sets, Rokenbok construction kits and educational books – were facing a much tougher marketplace. A few months before the 1997 Toy Fair, one of the US's largest speciality toy chains, Imaginarium, had gone bust; among the hard-pressed toy manufacturers was a hunger for an alternative distribution-channel to that of the fiercely contested shelf-space of the multiple retailers.

In this market Toby and Frank thought they might be able to create a profitable edge that would sneak under the sights of the lumbering giants. Upon returning to California they conducted some market research. They found that people hated the experience of toy shopping at the big chains, seeing it only, as Toby put it, as 'a necessary evil'. Frank elaborated: 'When you take kids to toy stores, their eyes light up; they become uncontrollable and you end up coming away with more than you went in for.' Toby recalled his own experience as the devoted uncle of his sister's three children and his hateful annual pilgrimage into the toy market. Dropping into his favoured quasi-militaristic jargon, he would often describe to journalists his 'typical death-march': scurrying from one store where he'd bought the blockbuster toys to another for more educational ones, in a desperate and exhausting attempt to become the conquering 'hero' of his sister's family Christmas. Much like that of his time as a caddy-master, this story became his company's founding myth and was endlessly repeated in almost every media profile.

Toby promised that his online toy shop would soon replace this sort of 'miserable experience'. No longer would parents have to drag crying kids out of toy stores, suffer the huge weekend crowds or even stand in line. Instead they could enjoy the idyllic experience of shopping with their feet up after the children had gone to bed, participating in a cosy online toy community that provided gift registries, birthday reminders and children's wish-lists. His management would soon adopt this vision with an intense, almost evangelical zeal, as if they really believed that they were making the world a better place.

Beneath the utopianism, however, was a business angle as tough as that of any market trader. Toby thought that a Web toy shop could squeeze profit from a unique and peculiar characteristic of the toy market. He and Frank had realised that the mass-market retailers' top-selling, TV-advertised toys had slim retail-profit margins of two to ten per cent, whereas speciality toys – Playmobil Characters, Gummy Gum Kits, wooden trains, etc. – were sold at a mark-up as high as fifty per cent. They made it their mission to persuade their customers to buy speciality toys; in other words, as one of their suppliers later boasted, the challenge was to 'Expand the horizons of adult buyers of toys by exposing them to the more creative, educational and developmentally-nurturing toy products generally found only in speciality stores.'

This left Toby and Frank wondering whether they should bother to offer the low-margin Barbies and *Star Wars* figurines at all. Following an investigative trip to a speciality toy shop in La Crescenta, Los Angeles, they formulated the question: 'To Barbie or not to Barbie?' Frank was no advocate of Barbie and the like, and had a high-brow vision for their shop. 'How do you out-Barbie Wal-Mart?' he reasoned. Toby, however, argued that if they didn't stock Barbie then the company could not hope to help harassed toy shoppers, who inevitably had to buy mass-market toys as well as speciality ones. 'You can't afford not to Barbie,' he said.

The strategy they agreed upon was to mix the mass-market toys with the more profitable speciality toys. They thought that under one virtual roof they could provide 'infinite shelf-space' to meet toy buyers' every need. Roughly it would work as a business because customers would be drawn in by the blockbuster toys and the profit would be taken from the niche products. With this combination, Toby initially told potential investors that he could generate profit margins of up to an impressive thirty-five per cent.

By late February 1997, Toby and Frank had written a modest business plan and throughout the early spring they continued to hone their ideas. Sometimes Bill Gross would come up with a suggestion, a contact or a tweak to the concept. Toby would go to Gross's lunches for CEOs and get into debates about whether or not he should undercut other retailers and whether he should invest in his own warehouse. They also had to come up with a name for their project. Toby liked pinata.com – after the hollow cardboard figures from Mexican fiestas, which are filled with sweets, hung up and ceremoniously opened. Frank convinced him that the name was 'too ethnic', though, and 'too hard to spell' – he preferred LittleRedWagon.com Finally they settled on eToys.com

The domain name had, however, been registered a few years previously, by Lauren Elliott, the co-writer in the mid-1980s of one of the most successful games for the Apple Macintosh, *Where in the World is Carmen Sandiego*. Elliott ran a computer-games company, and had thought that ETOYS would be a good name for an inter-active-games site on the Web. In the first days of March 1997, he was approached by idealab!'s Chief Operating Officer, Marcia Goodstein, with the proposal that he sell etoys.com and e-toys.com to them. 'It was a quick decision,' Elliott recalls. 'We were a small company that made our life on intellectual ideas, not on the com-mercialisation of ideas. A name for us didn't mean anything.' He sold the name to idealab! on 12 March, for less than $10,000. He almost certainly did not drive a hard enough bargain; that summer, the domain name business.com was sold for $150,000.

After completing the legal details, idealab! asked Network Sol-utions (NSI), the only registrar of dot-com domain names, to change the entry for the eToys.com domain in the master list of dot-coms. Now Web page requests and emails to eToys.com were accurately directed by first inquiring of this master list. The precise location of this dot-com list – like all other top-level domain names including the country codes – was specified in the A-Root, the key Internet document.

At the time the A-Root, as well as dot-com registrations, the two most important elements of the Domain Name System, were controlled by Network Solutions. However, just as they were performing the administrative task for Frank and Toby they were in the midst of a chaotic campaign to emasculate the company's power. The domain name corporation was being forced to defend its shareholders' interests from attacks – not just from hackers, but also from the Internet Old Guard, entrepreneurs, libertarians and ultimately the US Government. To everybody who owned a domain name – including etoy and eToys – this rarefied political drama had real relevance, for what was at stake was both the quality of the service provided to them by Network Solutions and the robustness of the system itself. Most importantly, the outcome of the battle would determine how disputes between big-brand, trademarked corporations and individuals or organisations who owned near identical domain names would be resolved.

More generally, this was a fight that threatened the stability and integrity of the entire Internet. As said in *The Wall Street Journal*: 'The Internet is fraying. For years, the global computer network has operated fairly smoothly even though no central authority oversees it and few rules govern it. But now a disagreement over who assigns new Internet addresses threatens to crumble the fragile ties binding the computer networks that make up the Internet's backbone.' Just as Toby and Frank were imagining their commercial future, others doubted that the Internet could sustain itself or the name they had just registered.

Defending Network Solutions in 1997 was its President, Don Telage, a man who had accepted the role four years earlier when Science Applications International (SAIC) – the secretive defence contractor for whom he worked – had bought Network Solutions. Telage had been able to see the potential of the domain-registration business when it was an insignificant, fixed-cost government contract. It was Telage, a bald, raspy-voiced man with a doctorate in theoretical mathematics, who had in 1995 stewarded the changes to the contract between Network Solutions and the National Science Foundation, introducing user-fees.

Two years after that, the Internet community was painting Telage as a villain and regarding his employer SAIC with great suspicion. Very little was known about the company, despite its revenue of more than a billion dollars, and rumours began to circulate about its close relationship with the CIA – its name spelled backwards was seen as a pointer. On the SAIC board were Bobby Inman, former Chief of the National Security Agency, former Defense Secretary Melvin Laird, and the former Head of Research and Development for the Pentagon, Donald Hicks. Ex-CIA Director Robert Gates, Secretary of Defense William Perry and outgoing CIA Director John Deutch were past board-members. Even though concrete evidence was lacking, it didn't take much imagination to characterise Telage, who had been security cleared to run secret laboratories, as a spook.

Network Solutions' reputation became so bad that Telage found it almost impossible to attract engineers on to his staff, and the vitriol that the domain wars sparked was frightening. 'I lived in abject terror that someone was going to bomb us or bomb my car, or shoot me,' Telage recalled. He received abusive emails and was berated at public gatherings. Keeping his calm seemed only to goad his adversaries. His greatest crime, in the eyes of the broader engineering community, was to control the A-Root. Though Network Solutions was the only company able to register and charge for the top-level domains .com, .org and .net, Telage argued that this wasn't strictly a 'monopoly': customers could register domains under 243 country codes, like .uk for Britain. That said, by 1997 more dot-com domains were being registered than any other, and Network Solutions had 800,000 names under their stewardship and were charging $50 a year for the privilege.

Also by 1997 the company had grown so quickly that it was in chaos. The servers could barely handle the traffic and there wasn't even an electronic payment-system. On one visit to the accounts department that year, Telage discovered 'crates, with invoices without enough information on how to apply the payment stacked six foot deep.' Media headlines claimed that half of the dot-com registrants had not paid the company. And at one point, an employee's technical error accidentally shut down whole sections of the Internet. Caught in a tidal wave of applications and re-registrations, Network Solutions' service was often slow; changing the details of domain registrations was often a frustrating process for Web masters.

What caused most anger, however, was Network Solutions' Dispute Policy, which was supposed to deal with conflicts concerning domain-name ownership. Such disputes usually flared up between big-brand corporations – like McDonald's – and individuals who had registered relevant domain names – like mcdonalds.com – in the hope of extracting a ransom. Don Telage's Network Solutions had effectively given into the demands of the big, trademark-owning corporations, because the Dispute Policy meant that a corporation with a trademark could request the temporary removal from the master list of any domain name identical to that trademark. For Don Telage this policy had one fundamental advantage: Network Solutions could not be sued by corporations that owned trademarks. 'It was a business decision. The trademark lobby was way too powerful; there was no way to withstand them,' he remembers.

While the Dispute Policy took Network Solutions out of the legal firing line, it forced the owners of many domain names into bitter and long-running courtroom disputes. Network Solutions was roundly attacked for bowing to the powerful corporations; the Internet-engineering community and hackers alike were particularly angry about the Dispute Policy, because they believed that domains should be allocated on a 'first come, first served' basis. They didn't like kow-towing to trademark owners, didn't want Network Solutions to have dominion over the names that were their homesteads. The strongest attack was from Jon Postel, one of the creators of the Domain Name System. His friend and colleague Bob Raden remembers the authority that Postel held over the Net community: 'He was a conscience for us. And we treated him that way

. . . Those of us who knew him well saw him as a slightly flawed Gandhi-like figure. He had a very distinct spirit. He was a pacifist – not literally, but he believed in letting people alone, in individual empowerment. He was very democratic and a very good man.'

Postel's first idea about how to seize power from Network Solutions came in the summer of 1996 with the proposal that the A-Root be changed. Already it contained pointers to the address books for the seven generic domains – including .com, .edu and .org – and for 243 country codes. Postel's proposal was to add more generic international names, like .web or .info. These new domains would be in the hands of new companies, thus fracturing Network Solutions' monopoly. His idea was taken up by the not-for-profit Internet Society, on whose board Postel sat; the Internet Society then led the charge to create the International Ad Hoc Committee (IAHC), a self-constituted 'coalition of participants from the broad Internet community', most members of which were inevitably in support of Jon Postel. At the end of April 1997 – just as eToys were choosing their own domain name – the Ad Hoc Committee convened a grand international meeting, at the International Conference Centre in Geneva, to solve, as they put it, 'the problems of domain names'.

For three days, the great and the good of the Internet community discussed the niceties of domains. On the final morning, fifty-seven 'entities' – including some of the world's top telecom companies, MCI, Deutsche Telecom and even the State Department of Posts and Telecommunication of Albania – signed a formal Memorandum as if it was the first announcement of a new international organisation. They toasted each other with 'virtual bouquets' of flowers and congratulated each other with having 'changed the history of the Internet'. The Memorandum stated that the management of the Domain Name System ought to be taken away from Network Solutions and put into the hands of the Ad Hoc Committee, on the basis 'that the Internet Top-Level Domain Name space is a public resource and is subject to the public trust'.

The Memorandum also called for the implementation of Jon Postel's idea to launch more top-level domains. Postel admitted that there was much still to be worked out: 'We can't expect to solve the international trademark issues quickly. We're going to do what we have to do. If it's rough around the edges that's the way it has to be.' It seemed like the return to the principles of 'rough consensus and running code' that had created the technology of the Internet in the first place.

In Herndon, Virginia, Don Telage was not about to give in to this un-elected body that was trying to wrench the Domain Name System from his control. A much savvier and more aggressive politician than the engineering folks, his adversaries soon realised that he had his feet firmly on the ground on Capitol Hill. Telage mounted a sophisticated political campaign against the Ad Hoc Committee and their Memorandum. During this time, a Network Solutions spokesman told *The Wall Street Journal*: 'The bigger question is who has authority over the Internet. The Ad Hoc Committee is trying to ramrod a decision by the end of the month [saying that] they are the authority.' Around Congress in Washington, Telage also spread word of a 'frightening' prospect: that the Ad Hoc Committee would allow the Europeans to actually seize control of the all-American Internet. 'The Conservative members of Congress were easy pawns with the help of some lobbying folks,' he remembers. When the Committee members came to Washington to present their arguments to the politicians, they found that Telage had been everywhere before them.

Telage wasn't the only one campaigning against Postel's initiative. PSI Net Inc., a huge, private Internet service provider, felt that the Ad Hoc Committee were muscling in on territory that didn't belong to them. From inside the US Government machine there were murmurs that the Committee seemed not to be accountable to any organisation or constituency. Eventually, succumbing to media and political pressure the Committee Chair, Don Heath, withdrew his own support from the plan, saying: 'I am not going to go down in history as the one that screwed up.'

The Ad Hoc Committee were not the only ones to launch an assault on Network Solutions. A number of others were also planning to wrest control of the Domain Name System with a battery of weapons.

One of the most telling attacks came from Paul Garrin, a successful video-installation artist who by 1997 had become putative domain-name entrepreneur. On 20 March that year, eight days after eToys had bought their domain name, Garrin's PGP Media served papers on Network Solutions through a New York court. He demanded that they open up the A-Root and allow him to add to it 350 top-level domains – .shop and .space among them.

Garrin's lawsuit exposed the chaos and exacerbated the fissures at the heart of the Domain Name System's governance. According to Network Solutions' contract with the National Science Foundation, the wider policy about the future of the A-Root was to be determined by the Internet Assigned Numbers Authority (IANA), an organisation that was little more than a letterhead run by Jon Postel.

After Network Solutions received Garrin's legal complaint, they wrote to the IANA for advice. IANA's response – effectively Postel's – was to deny that they had any authority. An observer of the time described this as the 'silver bullet' that destroyed the legitimacy and power of Postel's IANA. Postel had effectively declared himself impotent; now nobody was in control of the A-Root governance. Garrin's lawsuit rumbled unsuccessfully on for years, but its legacy was most significant. As Telage remembers: 'It was Jon Postel ducking the bullet; it was an intelligent but disingenuous thing to do.'

With the failure to establish an alternative institution and the legal challenge, the Internet community became more irate at the power of the monopoly domain registrar. So began more aggressive attempts to seize control. One particular adversary was domain entrepreneur Eugene Kashpureff, who had sought to establish a substitute and independent Domain Name System, Alternic. Angered by Network Solutions' increasing authority, Kashpureff hacked their Web site, diverting all its traffic to his own on which he placed an open letter of protest. Kashpureff's digital hijack was a political gesture that landed him in Toronto's Metro West

Detention Center for fifty-five days and saw him forced to apologise to Network Solutions.

Perhaps the strangest assault on the supremacy of Telage and Network Solutions came from Jon Postel himself. Having failed to find institutional legitimacy, Postel decided to act alone in asserting his power over Network Solutions by exploiting a particular vulnerability of the Domain Name System. The information contained within the A-Root cascades to users through a series of other computers, known as the B-Servers. While the A-Root is the ultimate authority, the twelve B-Servers located around the world are its apostles. Every twenty-four hours or so, the B-Servers copy the information from the A-Root; these copies are in turn replicated by domain-name servers accessed by users in homes or offices, every time they access the Web or send an email.

Postel's plan, as the IANA incarnate, was to write to the administrators of the twelve B-Servers and instruct them not to copy the A-Root information from Network Solutions. Instead he told them to take the information from his own server – effectively stealing control of the entire Internet. As John Gilmour, a founder of Sun Microsystems and an early member of John Perry Barlow's Electronic Frontier Foundation, explained, 'He attempted to prudently exert [his] authority.'

Postel's coup was quickly brought to the attention of Ira Magaziner, President Clinton's e-commerce czar, as he dined with Hillary Clinton at the World Economic Forum in Davos, Switzerland. Magaziner thought that Postel's wilful act could destroy the stability of the Internet, and he therefore spent that night talking on the phone with Postel, and his university bosses and lawyers, trying to persuade them all to back down. Don Telage remembered Magaziner telling him that he had threatened to declare a National Emergency; Magaziner recalls otherwise: 'I didn't have to go that far.'

The following day, Magaziner flew from Switzerland to meet Postel in Marina del Rey, California, to restore order to the Internet naming system. Postel eventually gave in. Many people within the Internet community could not excuse him for this –

John Gilmour among them. 'Postel didn't have the backbone to stand up to powerful blowhards like Ira Magaziner and he backed down, agreeing to announce that he was "testing" the infra-structure.'

Amid the chaos of a divided opposition, Network Solutions had been solidifying its hold on the domain-name space. In September 1997, they raised almost $50 million in their IPO. On the first day of trading, the shares rose a respectable thirty per cent. 'We flew up and took a limousine into town. It was a thrilling day for me. I had never taken a company on to the public markets,' remembers Telage. 'We were ebullient.'

But Network Solutions' monopoly had yet to face its greatest threat. There were Congressional committees, and an investigation by the US Department of Justice. Eventually, the US Government would intervene in full force in an attempt to persuade Network Solutions to yield control of the A-Root and change the Dispute Policy. In the meantime, the pawns of the domain wars continued to be the domain-name owners. And, as the wars dragged on through crude dispute procedures and court hearings, finding an agreement about the future of the system continued to be delayed. To both etoy and eToys, this proved precisely relevant.

In Pasadena, in the early summer of 1997, Toby and Frank were busy putting together their start-up. Their challenge was to launch their online toy shop in time for the hectic Christmas, Hannukah and Thanksgiving season, when the majority of toys are sold. To do this they needed, among other things, to order toys, build a Web site, set up a distribution system and sign marketing agreements. They knew they had to launch in the next few months and catch the season: in the speedy world of Internet business, there would be no second chance.

One of the first things on their list was to trademark the eToys name. On 19 May 1997, idealab! filed such an application in the commercial area of 'online retail services for toys and games'.

The next move was to begin playing the start-up game proper.

Toby Lenk, Chief Executive of eToys.

For entrepreneur and author Jerry Kaplan, this is played rather like Monopoly, with a defined set of rules. 'It begins with an aspiring entrepreneur who is willing to step right up and be tested. As in many other games, the player starts with artificial currency – in this case stock, the stock of the new venture. The goal is simple: increase the value of the entrepreneur's shares, because when the game is over they can be cashed in for real money. The trick is to swap some of the stock for three resources – ideas, money and people – then to use these resources to increase the value of the remaining stock.'

First off, Toby and Frank began recruiting. They needed a gang to complement their skills; whoever joined them would be offered a small salary and the enticement of shares. Through mutual friends they were introduced to Phil Polishook, a marketer from Disney; over dinner on Wilshire Boulevard, he, Toby and Frank pitched their respective credentials. Polishook recalls: 'Toby really impressed me with his ability to sell me the vision. I got really excited. All you saw was upside. I saw risk, but didn't see any downside.' Soon Polishook signed on as their Marketing Vice President.

Toby hired the talented graphic designer Christel Leung to design the Web site. The fifth eToys member had an expertise that no one there could match: Kathy Hernandez was a mother with two young children, a perfect example of eToys' target market. Having never run a shop before, Toby also searched for an expert in retail and found Peter Hart, who had spent years looking after the tricky problems of distribution for a San Francisco department store. Jane Saltzman, a toy buyer from the bankrupt Imaginarium, also soon joined the team.

To manage the technology, Robert Ferber was brought on board. Ferber was a graduate of the California Institute of Technology who was working in idealab! hoping to attach himself fully to one of the start-ups. He was sitting at his computer when 'all of a sudden I was being pelted with bean bags'. They were not aimed at him, but he was caught in Toby's crossfire. The pair were formally introduced, and Ferber remembers that 'Toby immediately launched into his sales pitch. Frank and him were balls of energy. They said, "We are going to go out and kill Toys'Я'Us!" It was raw energy. It was fantastically foul-mouthed – "Fuck, fuck, fuck" – not necessarily in a crass or a crude manner. Just the choice of words didn't fit [the toy business].'

Frank and Toby took their team public with a press release that trumpeted: 'eToys is Driven by a Visionary Management Team'. Bill Gross joined in the praise: 'The group that is making eToys a reality is experienced, intuitive and driven to success. These men and women represent the very best in merchandising, marketing, fulfilment and operations; they play to win.'

On 27 June 1997, eToys Inc. was finally incorporated as a legal entity. With a business plan, a small staff and a winning idea this embryonic company had a value which, based on hunches rather than figures, was crudely calculated to be about $155,000. Bill Gross bought 62 per cent of the company for $97,000, and loaned a further $100,000. Toby invested $37,500 for 24 per cent – half in cash, the rest as a loan from eToys. Frank stumped up $6,250 plus the same again in debt to eToys, purchasing 8 per cent. The other seven founders shared out the remaining 5.5 per cent. Under Gross's New Math of Ownership, eToys remained his company; Toby's shares were an incentive, but not the controlling stake.

Throughout the summer, eToys worked out of CitySearch's corporate offices. It was a typically informal New Economy space, with sports equipment scattered across the floor and ludicrous motivational banners strung up on the walls – 'Where is the Love?' one of them asked.

Even with cheap offices and only a handful of people, the rate at which eToys was spending – its 'burn rate' – was growing rapidly; the cash in the bank would barely cover the salaries to Christmas. In order to keep playing the start-up game, Toby needed to swap company equity for more cash. He approached Silicon Valley's venture-capitalist community, a bunch of money managers and entrepreneurs centred in Sand Hill Road, Palo Alto. These people made a business of providing money at a greater risk for greater returns than any other place on the capital-markets feeding tree. Typically, a venture-capitalist rule of thumb is that one of every ten investments should make back more than ten times the initial stake, while some of the others will go bust. But even with this battle-scarred community Toby found it difficult to book meetings.

It was not the easiest of times on the capital markets, and many people thought that the Internet boom was already over. Though Netscape's IPO two years before had been a prelude to a series of enormously successful Internet-company IPOs, even the most excitable parts of the business press had almost immediately proclaimed the speculative bubble burst. From the middle of 1996 until Toby went looking for venture-capital money a year later, the markets had see-sawed as investors tried to calculate whether the Internet was the next big thing or an over-hyped, over-valued technology.

Toby found the venture capitalists unwilling to risk their money on him. 'In the summer of 1997, venture capitalists were saying amazon.com was a fluke,' he explained. Brad Jones, a member of the large Los Angeles firm Brentwood Capital, elaborated on this: 'We were not convinced at the time that toys would sell over the Internet as well as books do.' Jonathan Funk, of another local firm, Media Technology Ventures, was similarly concerned: 'At the time we were not sure that the toy industry was ready for this business model. And we felt that Toby Lenk was unproven as a manager.'

So Toby was forced to find wealthy individuals who were prepared to invest a small amount each. On the ladder of cash for new ventures, these so-called Business Angels are the lowest rung. Unlike powerful venture-capital companies, they often bring no great connections to their projects. Ken Deemer met Toby and Frank at a venture-capital conference in Los Angeles and understood perfectly what they were talking about. 'It was a concept that immediately grabbed me. As a father with young kids, shopping for toys in the real world is one of the most unpleasant experiences of life. It's horrible.' He spent time analysing the company, talking to Toby to 'confirm his gut reaction'. One thing really appealed to him: 'I liked the people a lot, especially the CEO Toby Lenk.'

Despite some enthusiasm from Deemer and other Business Angels, it remained tough for Toby to get all the money he needed. His employees saw a progression of potential investors troop into the company's conference rooms. 'It was a source of stress for Toby and Frank. We were running out of money. They didn't say it to the team but we knew what it was. It was obvious what was going on,' remembers eToys' Rob Ferber. Toby turned to his friends, his ex-colleagues from Disney and LEK Partnership, his brother-in-law and his father. 'We cobbled together $900,000 from friends and family, but it was hard,' he said. While he was optimistic about his prospects, he also knew how risky a new company could be: 'It is hard to ask for money that in all probability you are going to lose.'

As Toby continued to formulate and raise money for his business, he became increasingly strong-willed and resentful of Bill Gross, and the majority stake in eToys that idealab! owned. Throughout the summer, animosity bubbled up between them and soon the time came when eToys had to find a place of their own. Toby was, as Rob Ferber put it, 'adamant about getting us out of the idealab! office'; he needed to move out from under Gross's shadow. In the coming months, although Bill Gross remained on the eToys board, his relationship with Toby deteriorated. Toby the visionary and Gross the hacker genius could no longer inhabit the same space. Gross eventually left the board.

Moving away from idealab! was like a divorce. Senior executives rented a Ryder truck and drove between idealab! and their new offices on 5th Street in Santa Monica. Toby and Frank moved the filing cabinets and together they put up the whiteboards. Creating a new beginning, Phil Polishook recalls, 'We felt so great about what we were doing. We felt like we were on a mission.'

The office into which Toby and the team moved was a block away from the freeway and had been designed as an apartment. Their main space had once been a living room, and the shabby wallpaper and balding carpets remained. Even while they were moving in, Toby knew that this was not going to be enough space for eToys as it grew.

At the time, it was generally thought that Internet retailers did not need warehouses; the virtual company was simply a link between customer and manufacturer, trading in information, branding and customer loyalty. Retailers could save money by not buying stock before anything had been sold. Indeed, the messy business of product distribution could be avoided completely by just taking the customers' money and passing relevant shipping details to manufacturers.

To Toby, these ideas seemed misguided. Having an eToys warehouse was central to his plan – so they procured a 4,000 square foot space in Fremont, California. Comparing his company to Toys'Я'Us, which at the time had something like $5 billion of capital wrapped up in its stores, Toby proudly announced, 'I can serve the world with one store.' To him, owning both the warehouse and the inventory was important, because he wanted eToys to wrap, gift-tag and send multiple gifts to single households. Controlling the warehouse, he thought, would guarantee customers their idyllic experience with his toy shop.

With money, people and property in place, the next most important task was for eToys to set up their Web site. This would display information about the products for sale, take the credit-card orders, send them to the warehouse and keep track of the stock inventory. However, creating it was fraught with problems. In the haste to build the company and because there was not much useful software available, the various eToys players had started using almost incompatible information systems. The main Web server could process credit-card transactions but for some reason could not display the designed pages showing the available toys. So the toy pages had to be coded by hand and married separately into the credit-card processing. Also, the toy pages could not be updated automatically when toys went out of stock in the warehouse; this information would also need to be laboriously and slowly manually updated.

On 30 September 1997, eToys invited their friends and families to test the Web site. It included about 1,000 products, and all agreed that it wasn't pretty but it sort of worked. Toby was happy just to get it launched: 'It's crazy. If a 747 isn't ready to fly, it crashes. But with the Internet, if I waited until everything was perfect . . . I'd be waiting a long time. We're scrambling. There are going to be a lot of nuances to work out after the launch. But that's OK. All Internet sites are works in progress.'

The press were eager for Internet stories. 'The week we launched, it seemed so easy,' remembers Polishook. 'It seemed like shooting fish in a barrel; people just wanted to write about us.' Toby was compelling and persuasive, the journalists lapping up this latest tale from the Internet frontier. *Newsweek*'s response was positive – 'Good news, kids: no more underwear for your birthday' – while London's *Financial Times* spread Toby's gospel with their piece headlined 'Shopping for toys can be fun', explaining that 'Buying on the Web in the quiet of the house after the children have gone to bed seems positively civilised'. Polishook said in *News.com*: 'We honestly think we're going to change the way people buy toys.'

Despite the warm welcome from the press, there were problems for eToys. So determined were they to launch quickly, they were almost too premature. 'Within a week of launching we knew the Web site wasn't going to survive,' remembers Rob Ferber. He had a Plan B, though – which initially had been his Plan A but had been rejected by Toby, who was wary of using untested software. The plan required the help of two twenty-one-year-old final-year students from the California Institute of Technology: Rob Johnson and Shay.

Rob and Shay – who were soon known to Toby and everyone else simply as the Boys – became an essential and remarkable part of eToys. Shay, who considers his first name distinctive enough for there to be no reason to reveal his second, is a fleshy Asian kid with a bowl-cut and a precise, determined manner. Rob is sweet-natured with a goatee beard and a skate-kid fashion sense. Together they are classic 'buddy movie' characters, finishing each other's sentences and laughing at each other's jokes.

In the middle of October 1997, they were hired by Rob Ferber and started building an alternative system. They were brilliant and speedy coders, and within a couple of weeks had developed their first attempt. Remembers Rob: 'I had a bunch of servers next to my bed. We had little tiny dorm rooms – they were fifteen by ten foot – that's where we built the original server. It had a Caltech Web address.' At the beginning of November, eToys stopped using the old Web site and began using the one built by the Boys. The new site included Real-Time Inventory Management, meaning that the toys displayed on the site really existed in the warehouse.

The Boys also created a compelling little application that

allowed Toby and Frank to watch the orders coming in. Soon everybody was glued to their screens, pressing reload, seeing how many people had spent money on the site. 'I remember the first $1,000 day; it was so exciting,' says Kathy Hernandez. By Thanksgiving that year, eToys had already had a $6,000 day. The day after Thanksgiving, they thought they might sell a few thousand dollars' worth of Barbies and Pokémons. 'I didn't think it would be a big day,' remembers Polishook. 'It turned out it doubled our previous best day. We went from $6,000 to $12,000. That was really exciting.' The warehouse staff were barely able to keep up with the pace of toy wrapping, so most of the executives went over to Fremont to help them pick and pack.

Toby and Frank's diligent determination was beginning to pay off. As Frank said, 'In the early days, we sweated over every customer like it was going to be our last.' *USA Today* ran a poll and rated eToys the best online toy shop. By Christmas, Toby could announce that in the previous three months eToys had sold $500,000 worth of goods. At the peak of the holiday season, the site was attracting 30,000 visitors a day. Toby had spent heavily through Christmas; as Kathy Hernandez remembered, the goal was 'to blow through all of our money. At the end of Christmas Toby didn't want to have any money left because he wanted to show the venture capitalists that we had done a good job. If we had left any money sitting around, that was money we hadn't invested in doing a good job.'

At the very least, Toby had proved that the concept worked. At last investors began to phone, book meetings and listen. Tony Hung had been in Strategic Planning at Disney together with Toby, and then had moved to a new venture-capital company called DynaFund. At a time when many investors were still a little sceptical of the Internet, he understood the premise of eToys, as did people from the venture-capital arm of Intel, which was determined to make investments that would continue to boost the market for its Pentium chips. And Moore Capital, one of the largest hedge funds in the world, associated with idealab!, also invested. On the day before Christmas Eve, the deal was closed in the offices of the Venture Law Group on Sand Hill Road in Palo Alto. 'E-commerce is something we believe is taking off now,' declared Tony Hung. 'The toy market is pretty large. If eToys can get out there, build a name for itself, and get even a small piece of the pie, it could be pretty profitable.' Each of the three parties put in $1 million, for roughly ten per cent of the shares each.

eToys was now worth $10 million. The shares that had cost Bill Gross and Toby 1½ cents a piece were now worth more than sixty cents. To celebrate, Toby invited his staff to a restaurant on Los Angeles' La Brea Avenue, where he handed out toys in appreciation of their tireless efforts to execute his dream. Shay was given the Wart Hog, Rob a lion from *The Lion King* and Frank got Woody from *Toy Story*. In turn, Frank gave Toby Buzz Lightyear from the same film, whose favourite motto is 'To infinity . . . and beyond'.

One nagging annoyance was the continued existence of Greg McLemore's toys.com. While Toby and the bright sparks of eToys didn't think the company's young management were much competition, they were worried that a venture-capital firm might finance a new and more experienced management team – making toys.com a serious adversary. But, in the spring of 1998, having taken out substantial advertising contracts with Internet search engines in a bid to compete with eToys, McLemore realised that he no longer had the cash to keep up. His clock was ticking. 'It was a very painful process. We had an overhead of between $50–100,000 a month,' he explains. The money was coming from his own pocket and was running out. He put toys.com on the market and held talks with Wal-Mart, FAO Schwartz and eToys. In the middle of March 1998, eToys bought him out. McLemore was given $270,000 – about the same as his estimated loss in the course of setting up the company. He and his team also received 780,000 eToys shares between them. Inside eToys there was a sense of relief at getting the deal done. The domain name toys.com was transferred to eToys, but the management team did not join Toby and his group. Eva Woodsmall, McLemore's business partner, had met Toby at a party the previous autumn and found him arrogant and unsympathetic – she wasn't about to work for him.

In the new year, Toby set about assessing the Christmas results. He commissioned an audit to understand how the business plan was working in practice. The previous year, on the basis of his ideas about extra margins on speciality toys, Toby had pitched to investors that he could generate a 30 to 35 per cent gross margin. However, Jordan Posell, eToys' new Vice President of Finance, now did the accounting and found that the margin was closer to 17 per cent – half of what Toby had initially predicted.

'People were shocked,' Posell remembers. 'That was because we weren't passing through all the shipping costs. We weren't estimating breakage and theft and obsolescence and just account-ing staff. So that was an interesting wake-up.' It wasn't cata-strophic, but it was slowly scratching away at the core of the eToys idea. It would force the company to increase their volume of sales so that the fixed costs of the warehouse, corporate offices and advertising would become a smaller part of the whole expenses. The only real way to make money was, as Buzz Lightyear would say, to go 'to infinity . . . and beyond'.

6
Go West, Young Men

'Welcome to a world where imagination is the source of value in the economy. It's an insane world, and in an insane world sane organizations make no sense.'

Tom Peters, *The Tom Peters Seminar: Crazy Times Call for Crazy Organisations*, 1994

'The people who are crazy enough to think they can change the world, are the ones who do.'

Advertisement for Apple Computers, 1997

The early spring of 1997 was a miserable time for Zai and the etoy gang. The Digital Hijack had been a stunning success. They had bought new computers but now had little use for them. They were bereft of ideas and their debts were mounting. Even the person whose talents were at the heart of their triumph – Udatny – had been forced from the group, in what Zai described as a 'psycho-winter'. In April, Zai rationalised the trauma: 'The commercial pressure has become much bigger compared to last year. Udatny would not have the capacity to deal with it. This has become clear. He became victim of the growth and the professionalisation.'

In a bid to get etoy to take the next step as a corporation, Zai produced a collection of management documents which outlined a new company structure with a new name: etoy.COMPANY 2.05.

The first thing he did was to rid the boys of any sense of equality. The new etoy.MANAGEMENT made him the Chief Executive Officer. In this new role, Zai would be supported by a Board of Directors consisting of the older, intellectual Gramazio and the poet and spokesman Brainhard. Although Zai was now clearly in control, he gave the impression of democracy or at least corporate empowerment: etoy was to be refashioned into 'departments' which would have some limited budgetary and creative autonomy. (What these departments were actually supposed to do was in some doubt.) The restructure would give etoy's members 'enormous freedom', but at the same time they would benefit from 'synergy as a result of the union'.

Zai was employing the same linguistic sleight of hand of the period's management theory. In the rhetoric of gurus, like the best-selling author and MIT professor Peter Senge, the traditional corporation was an 'authoritarian hierarchy'. Its leaders stifled initiative, suffocated the individual, and didn't understand the changes that were going on in the marketplace. Within the new corporation, iconic status was given to workers who had been empowered. These ideas reached their height in places such as *WIRED*, which in May 1997 ran an eight-page article headlined 'Corporate Rebels'. Iconoclasts and the corporate misfits were lionised; the piece argued that the role of a smart manager was to turn 'the steam of a rebel into the fuel that drives a business'. The business revolution, in its pursuit of change, was following the antagonist philosophy of the likes of etoy and the sixties revolutionaries; and Zai's satirical take on the situation was fortuitously word-perfect. For Zai, COMPANY 2.05 was only the beginning. He was seduced by the language of permanent business revolution. As he wrote: 'We have to get used to reworking the company structure constantly.'

The next stage was for etoy to register the etoy name as trademarks, each agent would own one in a different territory as a talisman of personal identity. For Zai, though, there was also a straightforward competitive objective: 'If we can block these markets, it will be very difficult for another company to establish the name,' he wrote. 'If another company uses our name in a big style, I'll probably shoot myself. And that would not be cool. If we want to make big money, we have to make this step.' Kubli, as the law student, was instructed to research and implement this policy. He discovered that it would cost thousands of dollars in lawyers' fees and filing charges to properly register a set of global trademarks. etoy did not have the resources, and Kubli quietly shelved the project.

In June, Zai's fears were proved correct: a player in another market was interested in using the etoy name. With eToys still connected to idealab!, their Chief Operating Officer, Marcia Goodstein wrote the boys an email with the subject heading: 'domain name "etoy.com"'. In it she asked if etoy.com was for sale and suggested they would be willing to offer a 'reasonable sum'. When Zai read this, he was alarmed, and immediately sent out a message to all the etoy agents: 'FUCK FUCK FUCK!!!! what the hell is this!!!!! goldstein is this you????? marcia goodstein? . . . I don't think this is funny but incredibly threatening . . . hahaha. if someone is making a joke stop it immediately!!!! this kind of jokes is too heavy for my nerves . . .'

Brainhard studied idealab!'s Web site and was convinced the mail was genuine. Goldstein denied any family ties with Marcia Goodstein, and urged etoy lawyer Kubli to take action: 'it's about time that you get into practice. we should register [the trademark] tonight, worldwide, I think :->:-<:-/ maybe we should ask Bill Gross whether he is interested in buying a beer for some artists . . .'

Zai flew to Copenhagen to participate in a conference but continued the discussion from there, determined to persuade the crew not to sell out: 'damn americans, they think they can take our hunting grounds for a handful of glass pearls. I see big danger, if someone in the actual situation is keen for our domain name . . . I say RED ALERT!'

Meanwhile Brainhard researched trademarks and domains and found out that their previous use of the domain name was probably protection enough. In trademark law it is possible to be the owner of a common-law trademark that has been used but not registered.

The common-law-trademark owner can defend himself against newcomers by claiming that a mark was in 'use' prior to any dispute about it. As a precaution, at the end of June etoy applied to register their trademark in the US. Kubli also wanted to register it in Switzerland, but discovered there to be a village near Geneva called Etoy – and Swiss law prevents the registering of any trademarks that share the name of a place.

Since etoy were not interested in selling their domain, they never replied to Marcia Goodstein's mail and heard no more from idealab! – although later, at various interviews and conference speeches, they bragged about the approach. It wasn't the last time that eToys would offer to buy their name.

The request from idealab! spurred Zai to stretch etoy's territorial ambition, as he'd always been convinced that the way for etoy to become 'a strong and secure enterprise' was for it to colonise the world. So, in the summer of 1997, he created the management initiative etoy.INTERNATIONAL – an umbrella term for the various attempts to exploit the etoy brand abroad. The boys' first opportunity to travel was in June 1997 when they were invited to C3, a media-arts gallery in Budapest funded by the benevolent currency speculator George Soros. C3's curator, Suzy Meszoly, wanted them to spend a month in the center creating an exhibition.

The event was called 'protected by etoy'. Long-standing concerns about security on the Internet were its focus and the boys intended it to both coddle and disturb its visitors. The point was that while the Internet might have given citizens unparalleled access to information, it also gave governments and criminals unprecedented opportunity to snoop on or steal from its users. In their show, etoy tried to tread a provocative line between comfortable security and malevolent 'Big Brother' surveillance. As gallery-goers stepped from the cobbled streets of the medieval part of the town into C3's huge white space, they were greeted by a stern doorman sitting in a cubicle. This tall, square-faced man, sporting a bright-orange jacket and a shaved head, was Kubli; he logged visitors into an etoy database and gave them an identity card with a magnetic strip. In the centre of the gallery was a transparent plastic tent. In this, two uniformed etoy agents wearing rubber gloves stood over hundreds of laughing-gas cartridges illuminated with an eerie fluorescent light. On video screens around the space, each visitor was represented by an image of a large eye gently gazing from side to side. Each guest's intake of laughing gas was monitored by etoy; as the intake increased so did the size of the eyes. By the end of the evening, the screens displayed shoals of various-sized eyes slowly swirling to a loop of etoy music.

For etoy, the show was a small part of their activities in Budapest. C3 had given them a grant in the hope that they would produce a media-art exhibit of some sophistication. But etoy had decided that the majority of the cash should be spent on a corporate brochure to be used as promotional material. The booklet had a matt, acid-orange cover, on which the word etoy was picked out in sparkling glossy black ink. Just to the right and a little above the logo were the two small letters 'TM' – signifying the assertion of the etoy name as a trademark. Underneath the logo was their favourite slogan, 'leaving reality behind'. Inside were portraits of the seven skinheads – including Udatny – dressed in orange jackets, bathed in strange purple light, coldly staring straight into the camera. The agents each had a different 'job description' – Powermodel, Legal Affairs, Logistics, Promotion. For himself, Zai had taken responsibility for that most important task, Corporate Identity. The back of the brochure featured a made-up quote from the Icelandic pop star Björk, 'etoy, immature priests from another world . . .' The booklet effortlessly mimicked a significant cultural icon of the Internet boom: the documents that dropped on to the tables of venture-capital royalty, designed to inspire investment with flimsy rhetoric, pretty pictures and a lot of front.

The prospectus was first distributed in Budapest, which etoy considered to be their starting point in getting the etoy message on to a global stage; from there they could build an empire, open new markets and find new investors. They flirted with the idea of going to India next, or possibly New York. But there the art crowd seemed too traditional. So instead etoy set course for California. As Zai wrote in a business report: 'A new time is approaching. Many things will be new. The US will be conquered. Departure is imminent. An ocean forces itself between us.' Brainhard was keen to follow: 'I always liked to identify with Zai's megalomania when he told us how we would conquer the world.' Through contacts that Brainhard had made at the international computer-graphics trade fair, Siggraph, and with help from their professor Peter Weibel in Vienna, Zai and Brainhard procured an invitation to both study and create new projects from the Art Center College in Design in Pasadena, California, just a few miles from where Toby and Frank were nurturing eToys. Not all the etoy members were enthusiastic: Gramazio refused to join in, saying that the trip 'was doomed to failure'; and Kubli didn't want to interrupt his legal studies. Goldstein and Esposto intended to join Zai and Brainhard in due course.

Throughout the summer, Zai and Brainhard planned their trip. They thought of themselves as the advance guard landing in enemy territory with Goldstein and Esposto following later as ground troops. The excursion was going to be decisive. 'We were under huge pressure,' Zai recalls. 'We knew that it was either going to be a big success or a terrible failure. At last we had to prove that we were worth something.'

While preparing for their departure, etoy received a request from the Artothek, the official art collection of Austria's Chancellor, Viktor Klima. The Artothek wanted to procure some etoy art; while the young men were delighted with such recognition, they had a tricky problem – they had nothing to sell. An Artothek curator suggested that the lengths of orange wastepipe from etoy's Ars Electronica installation would be suitable. But Gramazio was horrified, fearful that this might not be sufficiently avant-garde.

Instead, Zai took inspiration from his favourite musician and rock icon, David Bowie, and his song 'The Man Who Sold the World'. At about this time, Bowie was preparing to launch himself on the Web with a portal, and was even dabbling in the financial markets with the issuing of the 'first ever rock'n'roll bond'. These bonds were designed to raise capital in the now, which was set against future revenues from his back-catalogue of albums and songwriting royalties. The scheme was an instant hit, with Prudential Insurance picking up the securities and Bowie pocketing $55 million. As ever, he had proved himself to be very much of the moment; he was an artist using the complicated financial instruments of Wall Street.

etoy did not have a back-catalogue to securitise, but Zai felt sure that their art would be valuable in the glorious future. Besides, he thought that there ought to be etoy.SHARES to further their corporate satire. Artothek agreed to buy shares to the value of almost $10,000 as soon as they became available. After a number of raucous goodbye parties, Zai and Brainhard set off for Los Angeles.

The symbiotic relationship that Zai and Brainhard had developed in Basel and Vienna became all the more intense in California. In some practical ways Zai was dependent on Brainhard who had been born in America, spoke better English and could drive. But their co-dependency was all the more evident in their work for etoy. They would sit next to each other and write documents and manifestos. Both seemed to believe that the other was virtually incapable of doing anything constructive without his own intervention, goading and support. But as they came closer together, their competing egos were reaching an explosive critical mass.

For them, California was the perfect place and the late autumn of 1997 the perfect moment to further develop the concept of etoy shares. They were very aware of the bubbling dot-com craze. As Zai remembers, 'Everybody was talking about it.' They started research into stocks, shares, start-ups, Business Angels and venture capital. From Zürich, Kubli advised them on the language of the law. On the Internet, Zai found a business plan for a company that made light-bulbs and thought he'd use its rhetoric for his own purposes.

They drew on the recent meteoric IPOs of Netscape and the like, which sustained 'castles in the air' valuations. For Zai, the lesson was clear: in the financial markets, 'Buyers literally create value by being willing to buy. If there is demand, it is worth something!' What he wanted to do was create a corporation that sold nothing but itself, just as the Internet companies that had no earnings and often no profits spun themselves a 'value'. Zai and Brainhard also learned a new word, 'vapourware'. In the argot of Silicon Valley, this describes products that are announced – by way of warding off competition, or because of over-extended ambition – but never completed or released. Nonetheless the phantom products can gain real publicity and real investment. Zai's intention was to create a company specialising in vapourware. As he wrote, 'the etoy.CREW will not sell art-work, pop-sound and software as most of their competitors do. etoy has no products – etoy is the product.'

For Zai, the purpose of etoy shares was also to poke fun at the absurdity of the art market, in which savvy collectors buy young artists' work in the hope that it will become better known and thus more valuable. The shares were to be a 'radical transformation of art ownership in the digital age'. Instead of collectors buying physical masterpieces, they would buy etoy share-units. Like real masterpieces, these promised collectors increasing value with the rising notoriety and success of the artists. But they also offered collectors a stake in the corporation of etoy. Shareholders would have the right to vote on key decisions concerning etoy's future, just as they did in real corporations.

The etoy shares were supposed to stand in a long tradition of art history, where money has always been an important subject. Andy Warhol painted sheets of dollars bills in the 1960s; later, American artist J. S. G. Boggs drew perfect replicas of currency, intending to be held up in courts as a counterfeiter; and the British K Foundation supposedly burned £1 million on a Scottish hillside as an art prank. Those who made a performance out of the market itself were particularly indulged: for example Jeff Koons, the famously wealthy former stockbroker who sold cool, ready-made kitsch and consumer products in a high-art context; and Mark Kostabi, who bragged about the amount of money he was making and in various paintings depicted artists making deals, pouring trash over canvases and allowing machines to paint for them. In this market, Zai hoped to find a provocative niche.

Zai and Brainhard spent much of the autumn writing a business plan, which offered 640,000 shares for sale, described the type of market that etoy serviced and outlined the venture's potential risks. The plan declared that the intention was 'to obtain financing in the amount of $640,000 to continue the product development, coding, styling, to set up the immense infrastructure and to implement an aggressive sales and marketing programme for the next level of the etoy.LIFESTYLE.'

Like a genuine corporate document, the plan also bragged about the company's credentials: 'The etoy.CREW raised a high amount of cultural value, recruited fans worldwide and is listed as one of the top 10 media art teams with a potential market of over $350 million over the next 5 years.' Further, it absurdly claimed that by the end of the project's second year etoy would have deals worth $2 million and would be 'self-sustaining' by the end of the fifth year.

The project marked the beginning of the refinement of the etoy philosophy. Now, they were to focus their attention and their art almost exclusively on lampooning the dot-com craze. By masquerading as the most avaricious and greedy entrepreneurs, they hoped to needle the smug satisfaction surrounding the corporate illusionists who conjured value when none existed. Brainhard wrote, 'Let's make money a cult, let's celebrate that for us everything turns around making dough, that venture capitalists and $-deals are the hardcore style and the game to play.' He thought that they could sell etoy by using the rhetoric of the financial community with an additional satirical twist: 'invest in the code of tomorrow . . . play the financial edge-game with the etoy.CORPORATION – you have nothing to lose . . . but your money, your image and your credibility!'

While the group honed their corporate critique, Zai in particular was becoming more serious about etoy's future as a genuine, profitable corporation. The shares might poke fun at the ludicrous excitement of the times, but they might also make etoy some money and therefore enable them to continue with their provocation. As Gramazio remembers, 'we finally had discovered a model of how to make money'. Now the paradox of etoy – that they both loved and hated the idea of corporations – was to take on a new solemnity.

Zai had originally insisted in his plan for COMPANY 2.05 that each group member should have a stake fixed in accordance with their individual commitment and productivity. When etoy became profitable, the gains would be distributed as per this division. Initially the boys had all agreed on a basic stake of 10 per cent each. As time wore on, however, the question of how the rest of the shares should be divided became the subject of a bitter and rancorous dispute. Zai demanded almost half of the remaining 40 per cent, a calculation he'd based on his outstanding performance and devotion to the project. When Brainhard heard this request, he was torn between despair and aggression. It looked as if the American adventure would end even before it had properly begun. Esposto and Goldstein, still in Zürich preparing to sell their sound studio and leave for the US, were concerned. In dozens of mails and phonecalls they discussed Zai's proposal. In the end, Goldstein argued 'that we should give into [Zai's] demand, because he is a maniac, because he is talented, because we need him, because he could bring us world fame, because he keeps the team together.' Eventually, the rest of the group conceded. Zai's stake in etoy was raised to 27.5 per cent of the total. Brainhard and Goldstein owned 18.5 per cent and Esposto 15.5; Kubli and Gramazio, who had continued to pursue their own careers outside of etoy, had to content themselves with the minimum stake of 10 per cent.

For the first sale of their shares, etoy planned to hold an IPO. In December 1997, Gramazio flew to California to help work on the shares. These were to be photographs of Goldstein, Brainhard and Zai which had been taken while they were filming an item for Swiss Television. In the images, the boys are jumping out of a helicopter on to a glacier, wearing their uniforms and holding lengths of their orange wastepipe, and appear to be speaking to each other via headsets. Superimposed on to the pictures would be share-identity numbers, the quantity purchased, the date of issue and some other information which would appear to confer a kind of 'official status'.

In the traditional ritual of IPOs, an entrepreneur's last stop before he rushes to Wall Street is at the offices of venture capitalists who put up a final mezzanine-round of funding which gives the new corporation some credibility and some stability. In much the same way, Zai sought out Joichi Ito, their mentor from Ars Electronica. Late one night, a couple of days before Christmas 1997, Zai met Ito in a Chinese restaurant in San Francisco. 'I hoped that he would give us money,' remembers Zai. 'It was clear to me that Ito should be our angel investor – like Coco, who had been our lifestyle angel.' Joichi Ito gave his support and made a promise – which he kept – to buy shares himself.

etoy set their share price for the IPO at 160 Japanese yen. They were pleased – and a little surprised – to secure the services of the Austrian Chancellor Viktor Klima on behalf of the Artothek as their first buyer. The date was set for 28 January, but there had been some doubt as to whether Chancellor Klima would come good on his promise. Three days before the IPO, Gramazio took a plane to Zürich, where the share certificates were being printed. Chancellor Klima was set to purchase five of these photographs, representing 6,000 shares – almost 1 per cent of the etoy. CORPORATION. These were mounted on two-foot-square pieces of aluminium, they had, as a finishing touch, a silicon chip embedded in each one – like a security device on a credit card.

Gramazio clasping the shares took the night train from Zürich arriving in Vienna in the early morning of 28 January. A press conference was held later that day in the offices of the Federal Chancellor in the heart of the Ringstrasse, Vienna's central district, where a number of neoclassical government buildings are located. Gramazio met the curator of the Artothek, and together they passed through security and made their way to the briefing. It was held in a very large, high-ceilinged room resplendent with chandeliers, gilded furniture and velvet curtains in the style of imperial Austria. To Gramazio, it seemed out of scale – even the doorknobs were placed high up on the doors, as if the place had been built for giants.

Representatives of the press were already in their places, and soon Chancellor Klima arrived with his staff. He told Gramazio that the Austrian Government was enthusiastic about supporting modern art, and that he had a personal interest in the Internet because he had once been a student of computer sciences. Solemnly Klima signed the shares, and then he and Gramazio posed for the cameras. For forty-five minutes the journalists asked questions – about etoy, the shareholding and about a new Government initiative for the media arts. Klima promised that a link to the etoy Web site would be put on the Austrian Government's home page. The following day, pictures of the skinhead in an orange bomber jacket shaking hands with the Chancellor made it into the Austrian newspapers and on to the national television network. Later, the share certificates were exhibited in Austria's Exhibition Hall for Contemporary Art in Vienna. 'It was a great start for the project,' remembers Gramazio. 'It was a real hack.'

In California, Zai changed the etoy Web site to focus on the shares, featuring the business plan and pictures of the share certificates. He also made it appear as if the site constantly tracked the ever-changing share price – when exciting things were happening, it would increase; when etoy ran out of ideas, it would decline. Over time, this peaking and dipping was turned into a graph, a central piece of the etoy oeuvre that plotted the value of their shares. This was just like so many other share-price graphs that new investors could find on the Internet.

Now that the etoy.CORPORATION had a brand and series of shares, the moment had come to extend their corporate irony to fulfil their grandiose dreams. Already they had rejected their juvenile aspirations for a logo-adorned headquarters, and for almost a year had been thinking about creating a global office network. Zai remembered seeing in a trucking magazine pictures of orange cargo containers and imagined that these could house offices, recording studios and living accommodation. They were the perfect module for a global and mobile workforce; they could be packed and shipped, ready to be opened and active on arrival at any troublespot demanding corporate commandos. Zai would create a myth about the containers that there were seventeen etoy.TANKS constantly travelling the world; providing all of their logistical needs as a constantly moving network. In 1997, when Zai was considering the potential of an etoy.TANKS office network, there were 120 million standard size cargo containers transporting almost half the freight across the world's oceans. There was hardly a more potent symbol for globalisation.

etoy's plan was now to buy, fit out and transport one cargo container and use it as if it were a prototype for the whole system. But that would take more money than etoy had. In search of sponsorship, Zai wrote a proposal: 'The idea is to retranslate the etoy.TANKSYSTEM from the data realm back onto the "real space". We construct a meaningful bridge between the mediated and the physical space.' He sent it to Dominik Landwehr, Head of Science and the Future for the Migros Cultural Foundation, connected to Switzerland's largest retail conglomerate. 'I thought that the idea was crap,' Landwehr remembers. 'I told them: "It doesn't make sense that you have emigrated into cyberspace and that now you want to build a heap of scrap metal".' Nonetheless, Zai pushed the idea. Landwehr participated in a video conference between Gramazio in Zürich and Zai in California. Impressed by the energy, determination and the technological sophistication of these trailblazers he ended up sponsoring the etoy.TANK.

By 1998, Zai had investigated the possibility of building the tank in a dockyard, but found it too expensive. He then tried to persuade Peter Lunenfeld, their sponsor at the Art Center College of Design in Pasadena, to find some space but had not succeeded. 'We would have had to give up parking and in California nobody gives up parking,' Lunenfeld recalls. Eventually through a network of artists and academics etoy managed to persuade the Center

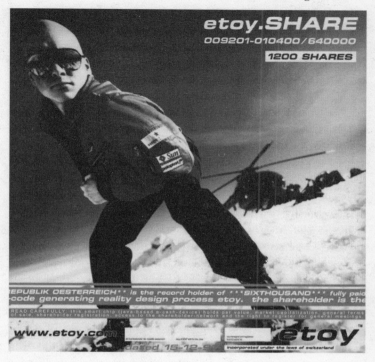

One of the first etoy.SHARES sold to Viktor Klima, the Chancellor of Austria, in January 1998.

for Research in Computing and the Arts at the University of California, San Diego, to lend them some space.

Zai and Brainhard were at last joined by Esposto and Goldstein, and the four of them set up home together in San Diego. From a shipping company in Long Beach, California, Brainhard managed to buy a forty-foot container. Empty, it weighed more than ten tons.

The boys all drove to the harbour to inspect their new purchase. The secondhand container smelled so bad that they had visions of being contaminated by toxic waste or radiation. They refused to buy it and demanded a cleaner one, and commissioned

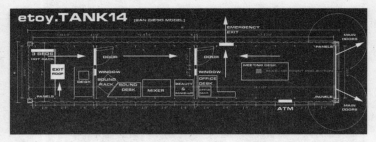

Floorplan of etoy's cargo container.

the company to spray-paint the replacement in etoy orange. It was eventually delivered to them at the University of California, where it was dragged off the flat-bed truck it arrived on and left on a concrete slab at the back of the campus.

Zai oversaw the conversion of this steel box into an office space. It was exhausting work, especially the fitting of heavy sound-insulation into the walls. Technically, the most complex task was puncturing the steel shell to create new doors and windows. Usually, cargo containers have only one set of doors, at the back, to allow the loading and unloading of goods. But the existing doors of etoy's tank were going to reveal a huge video screen covering the back of the tank, with images being projected on to it from inside the tank's belly to viewers outside. The new holes were for an access door and a skylight; and the boys had the idea of installing something like a cash machine in the tank's side.

Inside the tank, they installed two partition walls, each with a door and a glass window as found in more conventional offices. They divided the space into three rooms: a bedroom, with a skylight for ventilation and a three-tiered bunk-bed they welded themselves; a sound studio, with recording and mixing equipment; and a meeting room, which they decked out with shelves, orange steel cupboards and contraptions to lock down their computers.

While Brainhard, Esposto and Goldstein were working relentlessly on the construction, Zai often withdrew into his office in the University building to think, to write and to lead. He wrote screeds of corporate pronouncements and he also started making connections on the West Coast art scene. Travelling to San Francisco he met William Linn, who ran a gallery space called Blasthaus that exhibited digital art and had a lucrative sideline in hosting launch parties for the booming technology and new-media industries. Zai secured an exhibition at the gallery.

In San Francisco, Zai also found a willing guide in the form of an artist, John (the only name he goes by), who ran the art Web site sito.org and whom he had met at Ars Electronica the year before. Together they gatecrashed product launches held by what *WIRED* called the 'digerati' – the glitterati of the technology world. At one *WIRED* party they went to, Zai was delighted to discover that etoy was already known. 'It was so cool; the Internet as a medium had worked out exactly the way we had dreamed it would,' he remembers. 'I knew this theoretically but then I really felt it for the first time.' To his great delight he met Heide Foley, the chief designer of *Mondo 2000*, and was introduced to Jane Metcalfe, one of the founders of *WIRED*.

This was a time when the technology salons of San Francisco were brimming with excitement. *WIRED* celebrated its fifth anniversary with an article headlined 'The Greatest Five Years for Humanity'. It seemed to propose that the arrival of the ubiquitous Internet was better than, say, the discovery of fire or the ability to travel the oceans. By now, especially in America, the Internet had widespread popular appeal. Tens of millions of people used it to gather news. Amazon was selling hundreds of millions of dollars' worth of books annually. The small scene had spread nationwide, and its old-timers were now basking in the glory of being in on it early.

But behind the cheerful façade there was discontent among the inhabitants of the city. Before the Internet boom, San Francisco had been a crucible of liberal radicalism, an old hippy town of eccentric cosmopolitan mores. In *A Heartbreaking Work of Staggering Genius*, Dave Eggers described the time when the city was cool and wealth was not an issue: 'here there is no money, no one is allowed to make money, or spend money, or look like you've spent money, money is suspect, the making of money and caring about money – at least in so far as having more than say $17,000 a year – is archaic.'

However, the boom brought money into the city. The SoMa district – where Eggers's office was – used to be full of derelict warehouses and home to a low-rent artists' community. As the boom took off, SoMa's garrets became populated by incomers: smart and aspiring Internet start-ups. South Park, once inhabited by junkies, became the focus of the new industry and was soon surrounded by bars and chichi restaurants that forced out many of the area's more bohemian residents.

The tension in the city made it fertile ground for the growth of a new, Internet-based political activism. As the powerful forces of venture-funded entrepreneurs were being lionised, so the forces of opposition became more potent and organised. In San Francisco, Zai met a ragtag collection of libertarians and anti-corporate activists determined to use the Internet to campaign against the excesses of governments and corporations. By 1998, the mainstream media were waking to the potential. *The New York Times* claimed that 'the rapid growth of the Internet has transformed what was once a hacker playground into, among other things, a far-reaching political platform.'

The most critical moment in the birth of Internet activism was when the Zapatista Army of National Liberation (EZLN) marched into the town of San Cristóbal des las Casas in Chiapas, Mexico, on 1 January 1994. The rebels were led by the charismatic and self-styled Subcommandante Marcos, a thirty-six-year-old former Marxist professor from the University of Mexico City. Chiapas was the poorest state in Mexico and the EZLN were revolting against the North American Free Trade Agreement that came into force that day, fearful that it would drive down the price of their labour and goods. Within hours, news of the uprising had spread around the world via the Internet. The revolution had come just as the adoption of new technology was hitting critical mass. The protest's instant worldwide support muted the Mexican government's military counter-offensive.

To consolidate his position, Marcos then used the Web as a campaign tool to inspire and cajole his international supporters, uploading communiqués and poetry that were admired and regularly reprinted in the mainstream media. He soon won a special place in the hearts and minds of the Internet community. By the time Zai arrived in San Francisco, Marcos had even made it to the *WIRED* 25, the magazine's list of the twenty-five most significant people in the world. The potency of the movement had sprung from the Internet's ability to place the concerns of the powerless on to the screens and then into the minds of those with wealth, connections and influence. Never before had activists for an indigenous population been able to communicate so directly and immediately right to the heart of the elite.

Shortly before Subcommandante Marcos had arrived on the scene, this process had been accurately predicted by an organisation that was about as close to the centre of power as was possible. Since 1948, the RAND Corporation, based in Santa Monica, had sniffed out a barrage of threats to world peace. RAND were central to Cold War theorising, promoting the dominant Mutually Assured Destruction rationale of the nuclear arms race. In 1993, two RAND researchers wrote a paper entitled 'Cyberwar is coming!' in which they argued that communication networks would empower 'transitory coalitions' to build up around a given issue and be battle-ready for the campaign. The bottom line of this early and shrewd analysis was that the Internet 'diffuses and redistributes power, often to the benefit of what may be considered weaker, smaller actors'.

In the years since then, the Internet had become the principal method of the dissemination and organisation of oppositional political campaigns. Big corporations like McDonald's, Shell and Nike were all dramatically affected by Web-based anti-corporate activism. Tony Juniper of Britain's environmental group Friends of the Earth described the Internet as 'the most potent weapon in the toolbox of resistance'.

In San Francisco Zai also met Ray Thomas of the influential umbrella group ®™ark (pronounced 'Art-Mark'), which posed as an artists' collective but acted like a group of anti-capitalists and anti-corporate campaigners. Thomas (a pseudonym he uses for the press) was one of the group's leaders; he maintained that the group was formed 'to bring to attention the way corporate power erodes public space, in general and in political life'. Despite these rather serious aims, Thomas himself remained a sparkly-eyed, mischievous personality. Though he really wanted to destroy corporate culture he often had to make do by lampooning it.

One of ®™ark's first gestures, in 1993, had been to bankroll the Barbie Liberation Organization. This group swapped the voice boxes of hundreds of talking Barbie and G. I. Joe dolls on toy shop shelves so that Joe henceforth asked, in a sugar-sweet voice, 'Will we ever have enough clothes?' while Barbie threatened, 'Vengeance is mine.' As the Liberation Front had declared, 'The goal of the action was to reveal and correct the problem of gender-based stereotyping in children's toys'. The demonstration perfectly met the ®™ark's 'bottom-line criterion', Ray Thomas says, of being 'an anti-corporate critique or attack, and not causing physical injury'.

By 1998, ®™ark had become a wide-ranging support network for a variety of anti-corporate campaigns. The group's Web site – rtmark.com – stated that they had a collection of 'mutual funds', a joke on the popular American consumer-investment vehicle in which a basket of shares are managed by professionals. For ®™ark, each of these mutual funds promoted an idea that would 'raise consciousness about corporate abuse' and collect money to support projects in line with its 'investment strategy'. The Internet was the perfect tool to bring the different parties together and to allow ®™ark to become 'essentially a matchmaker and bank, helping groups or individuals fund sabotage projects'.

etoy cut a deal with Ray Thomas to share their email lists. By then, etoy had collected 10,000 email addresses and thought that they could use the 3,000 anti-capitalists' addresses that Thomas could provide. Zai was a little uncomfortable with the ®™ark activists, because they reminded him of the pious bickering squatters of Zürich. He certainly saw no further use for them, and could not imagine that he would one day rely on their support, skills and determination.

At the same time that etoy was in San Francisco, the most dramatic force of Internet activism was being developed. This rejected the idea of the Internet as a medium for organising protests by sending of emails and the creation of Web sites. Instead the idea was to use the technology to attack transgressing governments and corporations in wilful and aggressive electronic protest. One of the prime movers in this innovation was a member of ®™ark's network, Ricardo Dominguez. A seemingly peculiar kind of activist – a trained actor, with Rat Pack-style slicked black hair and a caramel voice – he was nonetheless a hardened and passionate agitator. Together with his colleagues in the Critical Art Ensemble, Dominguez developed a language and a set of tools for campaigning and used the Internet as a stage. Significantly, they coined the idiom 'Electronic Civil Disobedience' and wrote a manifesto, the core idea of which was that physical demonstrations – outside airforce bases, embassies or corporate headquarters – were outdated as methods of protest. It said that 'as far as power is concerned, the streets are dead capital! Nothing of value to the power elite can be found on the streets'. In a world of global electronic communication, 'new methods of disruption' had to be invented in order to protest 'on the electronic level'.

When paramilitaries associated with the Mexican Government killed forty-five seemingly innocent peasants, Dominguez declared 1998 as the 'year of war'. Emails and Web sites urged 'all netsurfers with ideals of justice, freedom, solidarity and liberty within their hearts' to show support. Dominguez found financing from an ®™ark mutual fund to put his ideas of Electronic Civil Disobedience into action, the plan being to take advantage of a specific characteristic of the Internet.

While television broadcasting requires a single powerful transmitter and many receivers, a Web server must make an individual and unique connection with each computer it sends information to. This is demanding and time-consuming computer work. It means that some Web sites can be easily overloaded with as few as a couple of hundred connections from Web users around the world. At the beginning of 1998, activists began targeting just this vulnerability of the Mexican Government's Web site and those of its supporters. By email, a 'virtual sit-in' would be called for a specific time. Then activists across the globe would simultaneously log on to the target Web site. For the duration of the demonstration, these activists would press the reload button of their Web browsers; as thousands of people did this the Web site would slow down, and sometimes collapse.

The Electronic Disturbance Theater sought to perfect this idea. Dominguez found two coders, Carmin Karasic and Brett Stalbaum, who automated the process and thus created the Zapatista FloodNet. This was a computer program that, once loaded into a Web browser, would repeatedly and continuously ask for information from the target Web server. For Dominguez, when the Zapatista FloodNet was put to work even on thousands of browsers, it was not intended to have the power to close down a Web site. 'The point of a protest is to register disquiet, not to destroy the organisation,' he said. As with a physical protest, the power of a virtual sit-in should be greater in accordance with the number of participants. Dominguez also insisted that the protest should be done with wit and theatrical staging. In advance of the demonstrations, he would interrogate the target Web servers by typing 'justice' from his machine. The server's automatic response would be, 'Justice is not found on this server'. He would then ask, 'liberty'? Again, the server would reply, 'Liberty is not found on this server'.

The most dramatic virtual sit-in came when Dominguez travelled to Linz to perform at the 1998 Ars Electronica festival. He claims that, before the show, in the small hours of the morning, he was awoken by a telephone call from a speaker with a Mexican accent who said, 'We know who you are. We know where you are at. We know where your family is. We are watching you. Do not go downstairs. Do not make your presentation. Because you know what the situation is! This is not a game.' In spite of the threat, Dominguez took the stage in the Brucknerhaus for the event. It began with his command, 'Commence flooding'; several thousand people logged on around the world then loaded the Zapatista FloodNet into their browsers. On that day, the targets were the Pentagon, Mexico's President and the Frankfurt Stock Exchange, and the attack was supposed to last for eight hours. At its height, Dominguez reckoned it created 600,000 requests for information per minute to each of the three target Web sites.

In the middle of the afternoon, however, the FloodNet program stopped working and Dominguez began receiving emails from frustrated activists. But he couldn't work out why it had suddenly failed. In San Francisco, a reporter from *WIRED* began investigating. Finally he got through to the Pentagon's press office and discovered the remarkable fact that they were retaliating. In a defensive gesture, the Pentagon had launched a program called 'hostileapplet' which neutered Dominguez's FloodNet. 'Our support personnel were aware of this planned Electronic Civil Disobedience attack and were able to take appropriate countermeasures,' Suzan Hansen, a Defense Department spokeswoman, told the journalist. 'Measures were taken to send the countless demands into the great beyond.' This was the first time that the Pentagon officially acknowledged an Internet counter-attack, and it demonstrated how seriously Dominguez's technique was taken.

In the years to come, activists would use Dominguez's technology to protest against Web sites of racists and homophobes, the World Trade Organisation and, particularly, corporations thought to be zealously and aggressively seizing the public space. Zai was not convinced that this antagonistic campaigning technique had any relevance to his sophisticated corporate satire. Though he would later come to rely on them.

The culmination of etoy's American adventure was to be the exhibition and share signing at San Francisco's Blasthaus gallery that Zai had arranged with curator William Linn. To increase etoy's profile in the run up to the exhibition, Linn and his fellow curator, Micha Wyatt, asked them to help with an enormous party for the opening of a Keith Haring retrospective at the San

Francisco Museum of Modern Art. The event was intended to be more of a rave – DJs, dancing and 2,000 guests – than a delicate champagne-and-canapés reception.

etoy were invited to be the event's security – to oversee the queue, check guests' invitations and scrutinise IDs, giving plastic bracelets to those of legal drinking age. They travelled up from San Diego in their collapsing Nissan, Goldstein driving while on the back seat Zai and Esposto prepared 'survival kits', plastic bags with a white pill, a paper clip for picking locks and some etoy publicity material. Brainhard tried to sleep off a hangover.

Micha Wyatt was standing at the museum's back entrance when they arrived: 'They all got out. Their black pants and orange jackets, just like rock stars, like strange rock stars.' Throughout the afternoon, etoy readied themselves for the evening's work and were followed around by a camera crew from a cable-television station. Linn and Wyatt were too busy installing a DJ booth on the grand staircase and hanging banners in the atrium to properly control the orange-clad young men. etoy plastered their own stickers around the gallery; they were prevented from sticking them on to the works but managed to put them across the mirrors in the toilets. Later in the evening, as party-goers washed their hands and stared at their reflections, they would be confronted by the stickers' huge lettering: 'protected by etoy'.

When party time arrived, more people than expected showed up and the queue swelled around the block. '[etoy] did a lot of posturing,' remembers San Francisco artist Eric Paulos. 'They looked [like] sort of *über*-individuals. People didn't know what to do with them. Security is supposed to be invisible and they became the most visible thing there.' etoy began to deliberately subvert the rules, giving drinking permits to the underaged and using the increasing chaos for their own self-promotion. As the evening wore on, the guests' patience began to fray; etoy, though, enjoyed their role more and more. Brainhard started walking up and down the queue, shouting 'Don't panic! Don't panic!' through his megaphone. In an attempt to avert disaster, Jay Finney, the museum's Marketing Director, grabbed him in a bear hug. It was a strange sight, these two men locked in an embrace and spinning around outside the museum. Finney finally told Wyatt, 'I want them out of the museum, and they are never allowed to step foot in [here] again.'

etoy thought the evening went swimmingly.

Back in San Diego, the pressure to finish the cargo container grew more intense. etoy had to meet the deadline of their exhibition's opening. Nineteen-hour workdays became the rule just like in the Internet start-ups they were satirising. Discontent among Brainhard, Goldstein and Esposto bubbled over. As the project's manager, Zai was the one blamed for the situation. As he remembers, 'They reproached me [because] I wanted too much, [because] I wanted everything to be perfect. It is difficult to know how long you can kick people's arses but they have to be kicked. I had to kick mine too.' Under the strain, the etoy family began to fall apart. For Esposto, 'it became obvious how things worked out, how many bad feelings were around, how Zai oppressed us. It was "not allowed" to have fun.'

Zai insisted on the complete dedication of his workers. 'We were not allowed to do anything except work, sometimes not even communicate with our girlfriends,' explains Goldstein, 'let alone go to the beach with other students.' The only expression Brainhard finds to describe the situation is 'pure hell'. In the midst of this, the rivalry between him and Zai was becoming more destructive; their bickering led to grandstanding arguments. Nonetheless, they managed to keep it under control. 'We had a common goal, we knew that we would build the container, take it to San Francisco and that we would conquer the fucking world, there was still no doubt,' recalls Brainhard. 'Each one was convinced of this, otherwise nobody would have continued.'

On 18 June, they finally finished the tank, had it loaded on to another flat-bed truck and drove north. At a petrol station on Route 5, between Los Angeles and San Francisco, they stopped in the early morning. They took a picture of themselves, posing under the petrol station's fluorescent lights, wearing sunglasses despite the sun not yet having risen. Then they drove towards the city. As dawn broke, they crossed San Francisco's Bay Bridge. They were fulfilling their dream; in their excitement, they started cheering and chanting in unison – 'SAN-FRAN-CISCO, SAN-FRAN-CISCO'. They felt they were conquering America.

Upon their arrival at the Blasthaus gallery in SoMa, etoy. TANK 17 was unloaded into the carpark. It was placed at one end of a wall; at the other end, perfectly balancing the TANK in frame and colour, was a blue rubbish skip. To the onlookers, this coincidental juxtaposition looked like beautiful composition.

etoy had just a week to prepare for their opening and they worked determinedly to convert the gallery into their space – even painting the fuse box their characteristic orange. A few days after their arrival, they were featured on the cover of the alternative local newspaper *The San Francisco Weekly*.

For the share signing at the opening, the idea was to have the curator William Linn and one other person doing the honours. Linn managed to get two paternal figures of the San Francisco art scene on board: Renny Pritikin, Chief Curator of the Yerba Buena Center of the Arts, and the *Mondo 2000* veteran R. U. Sirius. Zai had to choose between the two. He remembers the decision being difficult to make: 'One was a cyber legend; the other stood for the art scene. Because the shares were certificates for the art market, we finally chose Pritikin.'

The opening was well attended, by 'artists and eclectics'. Brainhard made a speech announcing to the guests that 'Blasthaus will be acting as official stock-transfer agent for etoy.SHARES'. On the walls were examples of the shares and pictures of various events in etoy's history. There were seven shaven-headed portraits; a picture of them posing at Ars Electronica; and images of Goldstein posturing by the tank. At one end of the gallery were two orange coolers containing liquids. One had the label 'contaminated', the other 'pure'; they held water and vodka respectively. As cameras flashed, William Linn and Renny Pritikin signed their shares.

During the course of the evening, etoy tried to sell shares to the gallery-goers – offering as inducement the privilege of a tour of the cargo container. Zai gave corporate spin, saying that the TANK could be read as a symbol of world trade, a transporter of global labour. He was especially pleased to propose it as metaphor of a 'TCP/IP packet', the Internet protocols that transfer information by breaking it up. Similarly the etoy.TANK 17 would break the modular workforce into groups and then ship them globally.

That night, Esposto had his etoy jacket stolen. 'I did not have an official etoy jacket any more; I had to replace it [with] one without the writing,' he recalls. With hindsight he saw this as 'highly symbolic'. Also that night, etoy's car – now a Pontiac, which they had bought to show off, the doors sporting etoy stickers – was torched; in the morning, they found its windows broken and the motor burned out. They never discovered the perpetrator.

etoy stayed in town while their show remained open. They became a curiosity at local parties and exploited these opportunities for self-promotion. Brainhard, etoy's Publicity Spokesman, garnered the majority of the attention, while the charming Goldstein pouted his way into everyone's affections with his rock-star poses. 'We felt like the Spice Girls,' remembers Goldstein. 'It was the most important moment in the history of etoy. When we walked by a bar, people ran out on the sidewalks to point at us – "Look, there are etoy!".' They all relished what they thought was the beginning of etoy's stardom.

Zai, furiously working in the background, was convinced that his agents' lack of discipline was endangering their success. 'He was very controlling. He was obviously the brain of the operation,' remembers Micha Wyatt. 'He was very authoritative with them. He would have mini-tantrums: "Get in line; you wear the etoy jacket; you do what etoy says, what you are supposed to do."' Behind the happy public front, the group continued to decay. They wondered if they might be like the Sex Pistols and split up in San Francisco.

On American Independence Day, 4 July, etoy held a barbecue on the roof of TANK 17 for their newfound friends. It was the first time in almost six months that they managed to relax. But Esposto began to be irritated by his friend: 'Zai was unable to calm down. He thought that everything was out of control, that it was "unprofessional" to have fun and a laugh.' The atmosphere didn't improve as the evening wore on. William Linn and a local-newspaper reporter suggested that everyone move on to another party.

On the way, etoy stopped at a petrol station where they came across a huge, stainless-steel tanker that they thought would make an appropriate setting for a picture. They balanced on its shiny steel rear. At the moment that the camera's flash went off, Brainhard raised an abusive finger. Zai was annoyed; the gesture didn't suit his new idea of a clean-cut image. There was a cross exchange of words and finally they took the picture again. In the second version, Zai has two fingers up in a sign of victory. This was the last ever photograph taken of the four boys together.

The party was being held on an old house-boat moored in Sausalito. This was the home of Eric Gullichsen, a virtual-reality pioneer. Goldstein went straight in and started talking to *Mondo 2000* designer Heide Foley, who told him that on past occasions Timothy Leary, William Burroughs and John Perry Barlow had all been party-goers on the very same site. Out on the dock in front of the boat, the other members of the etoy gang were in no mood to party. Zai had begun grouching at Esposto. During the previous years Esposto had done his best to avoid all kinds of conflict and had endeavoured to provide the group with both social and technological cohesion. Indeed, as etoy's Human Resource Specialist he had brokered many agreements after disputes between the gang. Now, however, even he could take it no longer. Brainhard witnessed the moment: 'Esposto did something that no one else in our sect would have dared to do; he looked into Zai's eyes and calmly told him, "Shut up!"' An argument exploded. As the young men shouted at each other in Swiss–German, Brainhard tried to convince an English-speaking journalist that it was just a minor incident. But the argument kept raging as months of stress and social isolation poured out. Eventually, etoy had to leave the party in order to avoid further public embarrassment.

The following day, at Esposto's request, the boys gathered in a restaurant in town. Rather than engaging in conversation with Esposto, though, Zai started arguing with his 'rival' Brainhard who had taken sides with Esposto. 'Zai was shouting, crying; he was very aggressive,' Brainhard remembers. 'Esposto and me just did not accept his offers of reconciliation. We both knew that it was not the time for compromising.' Zai was suffering: 'I almost begged to be excused, for bad project-management, for having too-high expectations. I felt guilty; that was my biggest problem. I felt vulnerable because I felt guilty. I was like a wounded animal. They made it too easy for themselves and saw all the mistakes on my side.'

For all of them, the next few days were a time of no sleep, hard drinking and churning arguments. Emotions were eating them up. Goldstein believes that this was the moment where all of them lost touch with reality: 'We did not know any more what was real and what was fake, what we had staged and what was happening just like that.'

Again at Esposto's request, the boys agreed once more to a meeting on neutral ground. This time in the restaurant things got out of control. The closest of friends now became the worst of enemies. The evening wound up with a ferocious crescendo as Zai and Brainhard shouted at each other. Zai remembers: 'I guess I said something like, "I'm going to kill you if you don't stop." These were the last words between Brainhard and me for ever.' Brainhard and Esposto left the restaurant together; Goldstein took care of the desperate Zai.

Gramazio and Kubli were contacted in Zürich for help. To Kubli the stories seemed so at odds that there was no hope of understanding what was going on or of making suggestions for reconciliation. Gramazio came to San Francisco and tried to help: 'I was considering a moratorium – that we should get together again after a month and discuss the issue. I realized quickly that the situation had reached a dead-end.' Brainhard and Esposto were not willing to wait. They met with him in a coffee shop and told him that for them any further cooperation with Zai had become impossible. It was either them or Zai. Gramazio, the ever cool strategist, had tears in his eyes and told them that, in view of Zai's desperation, he could not be responsible for excluding him from etoy for ever. Brainhard and Esposto left, and never returned.

Goldstein and Gramazio reluctantly agreed to supervise the shipping of etoy.TANK 17 to Switzerland. Goldstein drove Zai to the airport. Now, leaving the city, there were no cheers. Both of them were crying.

Back home in Zürich, Zai wrote in the company report: 'For ten months I had been dreaming to bring the tank together with Brainhard down to the harbour and load it onto a ship. I had to let go of the dream and it was tougher than anything before. I boarded the plane as a loser. I had to admit that I was at the end. That's not cool for someone like me. Especially after all my highflying plans.'

Brainhard and Esposto had lost the power struggle. They wrote letters of resignation to the etoy corporation. Goldstein told the remaining crew that he would abandon etoy to pursue a money-making career in Internet consultancy. All of them were deeply wounded by the experience. Brainhard particularly was suffering, because of his special friendship with Zai. 'My pain was enormous. I was sad, desperate and full of doubts,' he says. 'Our relationship had been a passion as well as a fight. It took me a year to realise that I was never going to work with Zai again.'

In Switzerland in the autumn of 1998, etoy's founding members met for the very last time. Coco, the transsexual, etoy's 'lifestyle angel', had committed suicide. To the young men in etoy, she had represented the beginning of the adventure. 'Her attitude towards reality was very similar to ours – "If you are absolutely consistent, reality can be won over,"' Gramazio recalls. 'We had wanted to become a giant corporation; she had done it with her sex.' She had performed at their launch party and now she became the symbol for the end of their dream. With the exception of Udatny, whom they neglected to tell, etoy were to perform at Coco's funeral. So, once more, the six boys put on their black trousers and orange jackets. Some of their skinheads were growing out.

The funeral was two hours from Zürich, in a town called Thun at the foot of the Alps. Without a hope of reconciliation, the boys travelled separately. But Coco's tragic end did allow them to act, albeit briefly, without mutual hostility. Goldstein recalls, 'People that normally could not even look into each other in the eye, *greeted* each other. It was only possible in the face of death.'

The service took place in a large municipal graveyard among rows of uniform, ordered graves. More than a hundred people turned up, half of whom were Coco's family while the others came from the party scene of which she was queen. Her father gave a speech over the grave, where an urn held the ashes of the daughter who had been born his son. For etoy, the sadness of the event was paralleled by their feelings about their own failure. 'It was apocalyptic; everything was fucked up; it was the end of an epoch,' remembers Zai. 'It was very brutal for all of us that someone would say, "things can not continue like this, there is no future", for always and ever. I had dearly loved her.'

At the end of the ceremony, the six etoy members walked up to the open grave to pay their final tribute. On a portable CD player, Goldstein was playing an etoy track, 'Wunderkind', which he and Esposto had dedicated to Coco: 'don't look back, trust us, we leave it all behind . . ./ wunderkind . . . you are our beta-test-pilot, wunderkind . . ./ you are right in the cold, that makes the world go round'. As the song played, Zai stepped forward. He held in his hands the two icons necessary for an etoy agent to live in the hereafter: a microphone/headphone set and an orange jacket. He bent down and paused. Then he carefully placed them next to the ashes of his angel.

7

'To Infinity . . . and Beyond'

'The signal feature of the mass escape from reality that occurred in 1929 and before – and which has characterized every previous speculative outburst from the South Sea bubble to the Florida land boom – was that it carried Authority with it.'

J. K. Galbraith, *The Great Crash 1929*, 1954

'Much has been written about panics and manias, much more than with the most outstretched intellect we are able to follow or conceive; but one thing is certain, that at particular times a great deal of stupid people have a great deal of stupid money.'

Walter Bagehot, *Essay of Edward Gibbon*, 1888

In the spring of 1998, having successfully launched his company, raised some money and bought out the competition, Toby now looked forward to his next important test: eToys' second Christmas-shopping season. Whilst the previous year, he had sold only $500,000 worth of toys, now he planned to sell at least $10 million worth this time round. To expand so speedily, he would need a bigger team, serious advertising and, most significantly, money.

Just a year earlier, investors had barely listened to his story, but now he was part of the e-commerce buzz. As magazines and newspapers keenly reported the online-retail revolution, some even suggested that the little eToys would soon outshine Toys'Я'Us – then worth billions of dollars. The climax of this general excitement came in the summer of 1998, when amazon.com, the barometer of Internet retailing, saw its share price double and then almost double again in little more than one month. When e-commerce made it on to the cover of *Time*, even the shoutline 'Kiss your Mall Goodbye' came close to prophesying the end of all 'actually existing' retail. Inside, the cheer extended from the commercial to the utopian: 'The real promise of all this change is that it will enrich all of us, not just a bunch of kids in Silicon Valley . . . 21st-century Americans will face a radical reshaping of the consumer culture we've been building since the 1950s.'

Toby had been either extraordinarily perceptive or just plain lucky to have started eToys a year before because it was fast becoming a working and easily comprehensible business at just the right time. E-commerce companies were now being ravenously pursued by investors willing to shower millions on tiny start-ups selling anything from pet food to jewels. Throughout the spring and summer of 1998, Toby sold his story to the tough and often arrogant venture-capital community and found its members receptive almost to the point of supplication. 'He was so dynamic and it was clear that he believed in what he was doing. It was very exciting. He was a visionary,' remembers Joanna Strober of Bessemer Venture Partners. Toby was poised to pluck money from the outstretched hands of investors desperate to participate in the goldrush.

At the beginning of June, Toby began closing the second round of venture capital. More than twenty venture firms were now keen to be a part of his business, all of them trying to convince him that their expertise and money were just what he needed to launch eToys into the stratosphere. Unlike the previous year, it was a sellers' market and Toby was able to choose from among the most elite of their cadre.

Mike Moritz, a partner in Sequoia Capital, was one of the stars of Silicon Valley. His Internet pedigree was profound: he had discovered Yahoo!'s Jerry Yang and David Filo and became their first investor and board member, making his firm hundreds of millions of dollars in just a few years. Moritz invested $5 million in eToys and said, 'The premise is that you never have to go to Toys'Я'Us again. That's one of the most compelling investment premises I've ever heard.' The second investor was Daniel Nova, who had a pedigree almost equal to Moritz's – he had been an early investor in the Lycos search engine and sat on their board. His Highland Capital Partners pledged $8 million to eToys and he took a seat on their board too. Bessemer Venture Partners, one of the oldest venture companies, was eToys' third new investor, with a stake of $3 million. In addition, the existing investors poured in more millions.

Toby issued a press release: 'We have just closed a substantial round of venture-capital funding and are welcoming two new board members with superb Internet experience. These, in addition to our other assets, give us great confidence in our ability to continue our online success.' Not everybody was as excited. Bob Kagle at Benchmark Capital, who had been an early investor in the online auctioneer eBay, said, 'We passed based on our view that they were raising too much capital to maintain discipline during their company-building process.'

This batch of funding generated $25 million. The shares that Toby had bought for 1½ cents each just a year before were now worth more than $2 each. A year and half after Toby first went to the Toy Fair, the value of eToys had risen to about $60 million. It was a lot of money for a company that had sold less during the holiday season than a single Toys'Я'Us store sold in an average fortnight. 'It was huge; it was a crazy valuation, and a crazy amount of money,' Joanna Strober recalls.

Three days after closing the funding round, Stephen Paul, a former Disney colleague of Toby's and now eToys' Vice President of Business Development wrote an email to agent Zai with the subject 'Potential Acquisition', asking if he was interested in selling the domain etoy.com. Although eToys.com and etoy.com were not in competition, he said, for the benefit of eToys' customers he wanted to reduce the confusion between the two sites. Like the first message sent to etoy, from idealab! a year earlier, this one was ignored – they were too busy falling out with each other to respond. The toy-shop's management did not press the point for the time being.

With the new money, eToys recruited more people and, by October, they had about a hundred employees – up from thirteen at the beginning of the year. For Toby, marketing was the priority against which 'other costs pale in comparison'. eToys had the lead as the 'first mover' in their chosen field; the money would allow him to advertise aggressively and consolidate the brand. Since their launch, eToys had held prime positions on various search engines' shopping pages pushing customers towards their Web site. For $1 million a year, the site was prominently featured on America Online's Shopping Channel; eToys had also bought a series of search terms from search engines, so that when a user requested a search for 'toys', or 'Brio Trains', for example, an eToys advertising banner would appear onscreen. But, in 1998, Toby decided that it was vital to move the company's marketing off the Internet and instead spend millions on advertising on television and in magazines.

The centrepiece of the campaign was a television commercial that was first aired in mid-October that year. 'We're trying to educate people who currently shop by driving off to stores with kids in tow that there's another option,' Toby said. The commercial ran as follows: the opening shot is of a woman, wearing war-paint, reflected in the rear-view mirror of a car. She drives one of six black Land Cruisers, which manoeuvre into position in a carpark, accompanied – like the malicious helicopters in the movie *Apocalypse Now* – by Wagner's *Ride of the Valkyries*. The woman then strides into a toy shop, Sooper-Dooper Toys, where she finds a scene of devastation. Children fire toy machine-guns, hockey sticks are waved, the woman is splattered with play-do.

From this scene of toy-store Armageddon, it cuts to a quiet house in which there is a computer displaying the eToys logo;

a narrator says, 'Shopping for toys shouldn't be a battle. eToys. com lets you shop online for thousands of toys. eToys.com – we bring the toy store to you.' Then the final shot: the battle-weary woman, her fatigues in tatters, walks away from the war zone. She says, 'I love the smell of play-do in the morning.'

The commercial contained the paradox of eToys. On the one hand, the company was fun, they played with toys and had bean-bag fights in the office corridors. On the other hand, they were pursuing a kind of war, the aggressive and often foul-mouthed seizure of market share and the relentless pursuit of growth. Some within the company thought that Toby's love of war films made it easier for him to agree to the commercial.

It wasn't eToys' own spending that ultimately propelled the little toy shop into the consciousness of America, though; it was one of the most ubiquitous brands in the financial world, Visa. For thirteen years, Visa US had run huge advertising campaigns featuring smaller companies – ranging from Carnival Cruise Lines to a vintage-guitar shop in Tennessee – with the tagline: 'And it doesn't take American Express. Visa: it's everywhere you want to be.' eToys' Vice President of Offline Marketing, Suzanne Rend, had the idea to approach them about featuring eToys.

In an effort to ensure her request was noticed, she persuaded eToys' Engineering Department to change the voice of a speaking-toy character from *Sesame Street*, a Tickle-Me Elmo. When Visa's representatives received it they found an Elmo which instead of 'Tickle me', said, 'Dear everybody at Visa, you should choose eToys for your commercial because we don't take American Express.' For weeks after she sent it off, Rend pestered Visa's Marketing Department. Her persistence eventually paid off when Visa chose eToys for its television campaign.

The commercial opens with a narrator: ' ''Twas the night before Christmas, and all through the house, not a creature was stirring – well, maybe a mouse.' Then a toy is ordered from eToys and a delivery van emblazoned with the eToys logo pulls up outside a snow-covered house, recreated on a Universal Studios set, with gallons of foaming fake snow. The parcels are delivered to happy children. The narrator's final line is, 'eToys eliminates most Christmas duress – unless you try to use American Express.'

In November, the commercial was screened, during breaks in two of the highest-rated shows on American Network television: *Monday Night Football* and the hospital drama *E.R.* These were slots that Toby could only dream of: 'eToys is thrilled to have such extensive support from Visa, not only for what it will do for our business but also for online shopping in general.'

The combined effects of Visa and eToys' advertising saw a growth in orders. The Boys – Rob Johnson and Shay – who, just a year before, had built the site in their dorm room, created a little application that plotted the most recent sales in comparison to those of previous years. The firm's senior management found it compulsive viewing, and would sit in front of their computers 'watching the line' as it rose exponentially upwards.

As the revenues increased, so did Toby's ambition. He wanted eToys to expand beyond toys. 'We fully intend to be a moving target,' he declared to the press. 'If we stand still, we'll get shot.' In June, they stocked 3,000 products, but by Christmas that number had almost doubled. In September they launched 'shops' dedicated to videos, music and software – tabs on the top of the Web site menu bar took the customer into separate pages dedicated to these retail categories. They also started gearing towards bookselling, to take on amazon.com in the children's market. Now, rather than simply having an opportunity in the $23 billion toy market, Toby could say that eToys were a small part of the more than $100 billion market for children's goods.

The year also saw a frenzy of activity towards the improvement of the already easy-to-use Web site. In the office of the Engineering Department there was a white board, about six foot long by five foot wide, upon which were listed some seventy-five small projects that Toby wanted to be completed. His concentration would jump from one priority to another – one manager joked that it was as if he had Attention Deficit Disorder. One such enhancement was that buyers would be notified when the toys they were buying needed batteries and would then have the opportunity to buy them as they passed through the virtual checkout. Another was the facility for children to create a 'wish list' so that their family could know what they wanted.

Throughout the autumn of 1998, eToys was seemingly a wonderful place to work. It was a family, a peer group of like-minded individuals battling against the world. Senior executives remember their sadness at missing working weekends because that was when decisions got made. For one senior manager 'literally half of my friends worked there', while another thought the corporation so perfect that she would work there for the rest of her life. Toys imbued the company with a spirit of fun; even the meeting rooms were named after *Sesame Street* characters. In job interviews, Toby would routinely ask candidates whether they could cope with working in a chaotic environment. One candidate, in his fifties at the time, was asked if he could keep up with the pace of this young company. Like a family, the eToys company members celebrated and cheered together. When Shay and Rob Johnson returned from a European holiday, Toby played Thin Lizzie's 'The Boys are Back in Town' on the tinny stereo in his office.

Like so many companies of the era, eToys trumpeted the rhetoric of a 'flat organisation'. The rigid formalities of the corporate hierarchy were supposedly done away with and in practice many people didn't know to whom they reported. It was, as one manager remembers, 'total creative mayhem'. Less flatteringly, another manager recalls that 'considering they were a bunch of MBAs, they didn't have much strategic idea about structure'.

Beneath this utopian ideal of a circle of friends lay the reality of a more peculiar organisation. Although Toby spent much of the time looking for money or dealing with the board and investors, his personality was stamped on to the company. 'Toby was the heart of the company,' remembers Shay. 'His presence was what drove it.' The company was Toby's fiefdom, and surrounding him was a tight circle of acolytes whose individual success seemed to depend on his patronage and favour.

While many other start-ups hobbled from one funding crisis

to another, at eToys cash was now plentiful; the management disregarded money as a constraint concentrating instead on building their utopian vision of the perfect corporate engine. For example, in their effort to provide their customers with a perfect experience, they created a large and expensive customer-call centre with the capacity to deal with the upper limits of potential customer numbers. And when new computer hardware was needed, the cost was not a point of contention. Frank had a sign, remembered by some of the Engineering Department: he would flick his fingers across his chest, as if his index finger were flicking away a piece of fluff from his shirt. He meant that requests for tens of thousands of dollars for servers or hardware were insignificant compared to the cost of marketing the eToys dream.

In the final months of 1998, the eToys family spent more and more time in their new warehouse – a cathedral-sized ex-bottling plant with 60,000 square feet of floor space. It was buried deep in an industrial neighbourhood in east Los Angeles without so much as a decent restaurant for miles, just a nearby taco stand.

As the Christmas season gathered pace, so many orders were taken through the Web site that every last hand was needed at the warehouse to pick, pack and send parcels to their destinations. All the corporation's core staff took it in turns to sign up for duty amidst the dank and cold shelves; new employees were often surprised at how quickly the rosters, taped up on managers' doors, were filled, as eager business-school graduates rushed to take the graveyard shifts. This was one of the smartest and most overqualified warehousing operations in the history of retail, with many of the workers transported from the corporate offices having an MBA or a second degree. The rest of the warehouse staff was made up of temporary employees from Los Angeles' toughest neighbourhoods, their tattoos and gang allegiances unnerving the bright sparks.

Inside the warehouse, employees were split into teams. Some wheeled supermarket trolleys up and down the aisles of shelves finding the Barbies and Elmos to fulfil the Web site's orders. The toys, software and video games of each order were listed by the bespoke system on a single sheet of paper to enable easy 'picking'. Another team would work as packers, boxing, addressing and stacking the orders for waiting courier vans. Locked away in their warehouse, the eToys employees were developing solidarity. They were fighting the world. 'Everybody bonded because they wanted it to succeed,' one staff member remembers. 'They wanted to prove it to the outside world. There was the exciting sense that there was a lot at stake. Everybody wanted to do everything in their power to make it to another Christmas.'

For many of eToys' employees, this was the high point of their experience at the company. They would read the notes that came in from grandparents who couldn't be with their loved ones, and from divorced fathers who were away from their children, and know that they were touching their customers.

When Christmas was over, their bestselling item was the Happy Holidays Barbie 1998, a low-margin, TV-advertised toy. Half of their top-ten sellers came from the high-margin speciality range. One of these was the Steel Safe with Alarm, made for children to store their valuables.

When the accounts for eToys' second holiday season were done they surpassed most of their own expectations. They'd sold $23 million worth of toys, meaning that the company's revenues had grown more than fortyfold in just one year. If they could continue at that pace, they would conquer the whole of the American toy market in just three years. Clearly, this was a little ambitious; but Amazon's sales growth had shot to almost $500 million in just two years – perhaps eToys would manage that too.

There was, however, a disturbing undercurrent to this hope. With the rise in revenues came a rise in costs. In the three months up to New Year 1998, eToys spent almost $33 million on stock, advertising and running the warehouse: a total loss of almost $10 million in just three months.

In January, the company had a party in a small hall on Main Street, Santa Monica, with an employee band as entertainment. Just a year before, about twenty people had sat around a restaurant table – and that was with a guest-list bulked out by partners. Now there were more than 200 employees. Toby thanked everyone for the huge effort and announced the Christmas bonus of 250 shares each. There was barely a ripple of applause; at the time, his employees didn't really understand the stock market.

Toby's next big challenge was to sell his company's shares on to the public markets, and he could not have chosen a better time to do so than the start of 1999. By then, online shopping was reaching beyond its small audience of technophiles and was about to seduce the investing world. One of the turning points of this transformation began in December 1998, when a little-known investment analyst, Henry Blodget of CIBC Oppenheimer (a small brokerage firm affiliated to a Canadian bank), predicted that the shares in amazon.com then trading at $240 would surpass the $400 mark. To many commentators the prediction seemed extraordinary; it would make this retailing minnow more valuable than some of the market leaders. That Amazon made no profit compounded the disbelief but did not bother Blodget. 'They are investing money, not "losing" money,' he said. As Jeff Bezos, Amazon's Chief Executive, pointed out, focusing on profit in the growth stage would be a 'strategic mistake'. Other influential analysts scoffed, saying that Amazon shares were more likely to drop to $50.

Yet Blodget's prediction did come true, in January 1999, when amazon.com reported its quarterly results to astonished analysts: the company had sold more than $250 million worth of books, compared with the expected $180 million. The share price topped $400 bringing the company's value to $22.1 billion, exceeding the combined value of Kmart and JC Penny. Blodget was crowned by *The Wall Street Journal* as 'King Henry' and given a new job, at Merrill Lynch. Wall Street was now well and truly in the full throes of the boom.

This was an amazing turnaround. Just six months before, in the summer of 1998, the technology markets had looked set to implode as a consequence of wider troubles in the world's economic markets, with both Russia and a huge hedge fund defaulting on loans worth billions of dollars. In the midst of this melancholy sat Lawton Fitt, Head of Technology Equity Capital Markets for Goldman Sachs, one of the grandest Wall Street investment banks. Fitt was a glamorous and sunny-spirited woman who had spent most of her working life in the bank. Sitting in the adrenaline pool of the trading floor, surrounded by screens, one of her principal tasks was to price companies' shares on the day of their IPOs. She was the weather vane of the market, listening to the institutional investors, amassing 'the book' of potential interest and estimating an appropriate debut price for the stock. Having completed more than 200 IPOs, Fitt had one of Wall Street's most finely tuned guts.

In 1998, the Goldman Sachs Technology IPO team of which Fitt was an essential part were having a great year. They'd beaten their biggest rival, Morgan Stanley, to many lucrative deals and were thought by many to be at the pinnacle of their profession. When the markets collapsed, they had just secured a great prize: the mandate to manage the IPO of eBay, the Web's premier auction site. eBay made a brilliant use of Internet technology, bringing together millions of buyers and sellers of everything from arcane collectibles to vehicles. While the company took a cut of every transaction, they never touched the goods or had the headache of delivering them; so, as revenues ballooned, the costs remained quite steady.

Despite this clever idea and having a booming user-base, now it seemed like there might be no buyers for their shares. As whispers of a global financial meltdown spread through Wall Street, through most of September no bankers were prepared to take companies public. The drought lasted twenty-eight days – the longest in a decade – and during this 'financial Chernobyl' one commentator even declared that 'the IPO market is dead'.

To Fitt and the rest of her team, it seemed that investors might have lost interest in the Internet. They were forced to make the difficult decision of whether or not to continue with the eBay IPO. 'The question was, how bad is bad? And could this deal get done anyway?' Fitt recalls. She and her team had to assess whether eBay would buck the market trend or be slaughtered by an unreceptive audience. 'It was our judgement that eBay was significantly different, so much a demonstration of the things the Internet made possible that had never been possible before. It was a really great business model, a tremendous story, so we decided to go for it.' At first investors were a little slow, a little sleepy, but slowly interest picked up. Fitt priced the deal at $18 a share; and, on Wednesday 25 September 1998, the day of the IPO, eBay more than doubled in value.

The nervousness of the market was suddenly neutered by the adrenaline rush of an exploding stock and the desire to make money. 'I think that deal opened the market because it captured people's imaginations again about what was possible,' says Fitt. Although the eBay IPO was a catalyst that pushed the markets, doubts remained and in early October there was another blip. In the first ten days of the month the NASDAQ – the stock exchange that carried most of the high technology companies – crashed. It lost twenty per cent of its value as investors scaled down their inflated expectations. Once again, across Wall Street bankers pulled back.

By early November, Internet IPOs were being made once again; one in particular changed the mood of the market and became an inflection point that further boosted the boom. On Friday 13 November, two twenty-four-year-olds, Todd Krizelman and Stephan Paternot, launched their company, TheGlobe.com – which hosted free Web pages for consumers – on to the stock market. Although the company had never been a big Internet star, the stock, initially priced at $9 per share, surged to $97 per share shortly after trading began. This valued the company at almost $1 billion and meant that Krizelman and Paternot were now worth about $100 million each. As one banker remembered the occasion: 'Suddenly it felt like the institutional investment community, which had been resisting the valuation of Internet stocks, said, "If you can't beat them, join them."'

Fund managers had never had so many riches to funnel into

high-technology companies. In the seventeen years since the stock market bottomed out in 1982, the value of stocks had risen in the longest boom in history. Many Americans were more wealthy than they'd ever been and were rushing to buy investment funds and pensions based on volatile shares, rather than choosing the safer options of bank saving accounts and bonds. As financial writer Joseph Nocera said in his book titled *A Piece of the Action: How the Middle Class Joined the Money Class*, 'The market had become an integral facet of their lives. It held money for their children's college tuition, money to get them through an emergency, money for that great vacation, money that they were saving for retirement.'

The Internet also contributed to the massive influx of cash to the markets. For the first time in history, it was possible for a trader sitting at a computer at home in Kansas, New Jersey or London to place a stock trade and have it executed instantaneously instead of having to phone a stock-broker. Between 1997 and 1999, the number of online brokerage accounts in the United States almost tripled to 9.7 million.

The millions of new traders betting their savings on the market were a different sort than those who had previously invested. Many were 'day traders', who bought and sold stocks in a single day. 'Buying and holding', the old mantra of judicious investment management, was trashed in a frenzy of speculation. As a consequence, the market began to look very different. No longer did stocks rise in gentle increments; they popped and crashed with the fickle interest of the traders. For example, when K-Tel International, well known for selling cheap compilation albums, published a press release announcing a move on to the Internet, their stock doubled in a single day – then doubled and redoubled again in the space of two weeks.

Around the Web, these consumer-investors formed their own distinct community with a proliferation of newsletters. Even New York punk-rocker Joey Ramone wrote a stock-picking newsletter and a Ramones-style ode to a cable-news financial reporter, Maria 'Money Honey' Bartiromo. One of the key methods of communication was the bulletin board. On Yahoo! and financial sites like The Motley Fool and Raging Bull, investors would trade gossip and advice. Such message boards were dismissed by more traditional investors, but did seem to have some effect. In one celebrated case, fourteen-year-old Jonathan Lebed manipulated the market. He chose to invest in small companies, whose volume of tradable shares was small, and repeatedly posted boosting commentaries on a range of investor bulletin boards. As the shares rose in price, he sold his stake – and ultimately made hundreds of thousands of dollars. When he was investigated by the authorities and forced to pay a fine, his defence was, 'If it wasn't for everybody manipulating the market, there wouldn't be a stock market . . .'

The 'easy money' from both Internet stocks and the wider boom also had a wide-ranging cultural effect that was radically changing America. When asked what qualities they'd say made up a 'good life', two thirds of the American public chose 'a lot of money'; this figure was almost double that of twenty years previously. As Yale economist Robert Shiller wrote in his book *Irrational Exuberance*, 'Such feelings have transformed our culture into one that reveres the successful business person as much as or even more than the accomplished scientist, artist or revolutionary.' Now even the bohemian, latte-drinking, educated elite who traditionally disdained the capital markets were enthralled by them. In *Bobos in Paradise: The New Upper Class and How They Got There*, David Brooks argued that sixties individualism meshed with eighties enterprise culture had 'legitimized capitalism among the very people who were its ardent critics, and it has legitimized countercultural posses amongst business elites.'

Lest anyone think that investors were just in it for the money, a collection of commentators were happy to cheer them on as the foot soldiers of an ideological revolution, heralding the triumph of liberty and the breaking down of old Wall Street hierarchies. 'Thanks to online communication, it is now the little-guy investors – not huge brokerage firms – who hold the most valuable cards,' wrote David and Tom Gardner, the brothers who founded the financial Web site The Motley Fool, a bible for this movement. And, as the commercial to promote one of the largest online brokers, E*Trade, proclaimed, 'Now the power is in your hands.'

According to a set of almost utopian writings, the new markets were also going to have the much broader effect of creating a new climate that promised almost eternal good times. *WIRED*'s cover story 'The Long Boom' trumpeted in its standfirst, 'We're facing 25 years of prosperity, freedom and a better environment for the whole world. You got a problem with that?' The piece argued that the growth of both freedom and technology would necessarily lead to greater productivity, better distribution systems and increasing personal wealth. The excited markets also lapped up the ideas promoted in an article in *Foreign Affairs*; 'The End of the Business Cycle' maintained that this boom wasn't going to be followed by a bust – this was a new set of rules. 'For both empirical and theoretical reasons,' it stated, 'in advanced industrial economies the waves of the business cycle may be becoming more like ripples.'

In March 1999, the Dow Jones Industrial Average, the most famous stock market index in the world, passed through the 10,000 mark, having been worth less than half that figure just five years previously. This only boosted the optimism. Merrill Lynch took out a full-page newspaper ad with the headline, 'Even those with a disciplined long-term approach like ours have to sit back and say, "wow".' On the page was a graph which ended up at 10,000; next to it were the words 'HUMAN ACHIEVEMENT'. But even this astonishing event was not seen as a limit. In one influential piece in *The Wall Street Journal*, headlined 'Stock Prices are Still Far Too Low', two pundits predicted that by 2005 'if not sooner' the Dow Jones would have reached 36,000.

Toby seemed to be perfectly positioned to benefit from this jittery excitement – particularly if he could take his company on to the public markets while they were still bubbling and frothing. For the three and a half years since the Netscape IPO some companies had proved themselves to be almost fatally unlucky, announcing their IPOs and then being prevented by 'market conditions' from going through with the event; their competitors, meanwhile, were grabbing tens of millions of dollars from investors and launching themselves into orbit. For Toby, the challenge was to bank the winnings of the market while the opportunity was still there, or suffer the ignominy of being an also-ran.

In January 1999, Toby had to navigate through the tortuous and long-winded process of the eToys IPO as quickly as possible. To guide him through, he needed an investment bank; and he subjected those who came calling to a demanding beauty pageant. In the end, he chose the investment bank who seemed to be playing at the very top of their game: Goldman Sachs. They could pick and choose their clients, because companies were desperate to use Goldman's reputation to bolster their own, and Goldman considered eToys as one of the best of the bunch. They would, it was hoped, be an enduring client.

In the carefully determined hierarchy of Wall Street, the Goldman Sachs name would appear on the far left of the front cover of the IPO prospectus. This signified that they were the lead underwriter, in control of the pricing and timetable of the IPO and in a position to sell the largest portion of shares to their clients. Across the rest of the front cover of the document were to be the names of other firms who had been brought in to add authority, for their specialist knowledge and their existing special customers. Among those to make it to the cover were Merrill Lynch, Donaldson, Lufkin & Jenrette, and BancBoston Robertson Stephens from San Francisco.

Like Amazon's Jeff Bezos, Toby didn't believe that profit was the immediate priority. Spending money, building brand and exploiting his 'first-mover advantage' ought to be the company's focus; and for him, it was important that the banks leading the IPO in some way shared this idea. As he toured the bankers' offices, he came across some who were not as enthusiastic as he was about this business rationale. One of these was Sean McGowan at the Gerard Klauer Mattison & Co, an investment bank in New York. McGowan was one of a few banking analysts on Wall Street with a specialised knowledge of the toy industry, and he was worried that eToys would never make a profit. During their meeting, he asked Toby about this. Each time, Toby sidestepped the question by arguing that it was not the most important issue for an early-stage Web business. As he and his colleagues persisted, McGowan remembers the atmosphere turned antagonistic. 'In the end I think we hurt our chances of making it onto the cover [of the prospectus] by having the gall, the audacity to ask how they were going to make a profit.'

By early January, news of eToys' imminent IPO had made it to the media. 'Wall Street loves the next hot thing and for some in the toy industry not even Furby is as hot as Toby Lenk,' trumpeted *The New York Daily News*, which wrote that Wall Street was 'salivating' over the stock.

Meanwhile in Santa Monica, Toby was urgently reshaping his company to make it glisten in the eyes of investors. His greatest task was a thorough management shakeup. All of the senior posts were to be changed – apart from that of Senior Vice President of Product Development which co-founder Frank was to retain. Positions at the heads of the Operations, Engineering, Finance and Marketing departments were up for grabs, and Toby set about filling them with the very best in the field. For example, L. L. Bean, a billion-dollar catalogue company, was widely considered to be the American leader in impeccable customer service; so Toby recruited their Senior Vice President of Creative and Operations, Lou Zambello. He and a collection of others representing some of the very best of American management were seduced by hundreds of thousands of dollars' worth of signing bonuses and shares that might soon be worth millions. Whilst investors would be duly impressed by their pedigree, few seemed to worry that eToys were about to face their toughest year yet under an entirely new management team.

With the arrival of Steve Schoch, the new Chief Financial Officer, the eToys financial team were ready to move into overdrive in preparation for the IPO. Along with teams from Goldman Sachs, their lawyers and accountants, they spent hours going over documents at the financial printers in Los Angeles. They discussed the nuances of words and numbers, perfected their sales pitch and organised the balance sheets for the best reception from the analysts, all while working within the rigorous regulations of the Securities and Exchange Commission (SEC).

As part of this process, eToys attempted to nail down and secure outstanding leases and contracts so that investors would have no doubt as to the stability of the company. This legal and financial housekeeping extended to consolidating eToys' intellectual property, trademarks and domain names; thus, in spring 1999, they registered a whole collection of domains. These included: etoystv.com and etoysbaby.com – to signify their ambitions; etoyssucks.com – to prevent people rubbishing them; and the vainglorious etoby.com. They also bought domain names relating to their suppliers' trademarks, such as BrioTrains.com. Prudently they registered some domain names that might have been useful to that other 'global' corporation with a name similar to theirs. These included etoy.co.uk and etoy.net.

The toy shop's trademark, eToys, had been registered and finally approved towards the end of 1998. But a small New York distributor, ETNA, now claimed that they had the rights to it and wrote to eToys' lawyers demanding that the company cease to use it. ETNA argued that they had been using it since 1990 and had just filed a trademark registration with the United States Patent and Trademark Office. eToys responded aggressively, filing a complaint immediately against ETNA in the Los Angeles Federal Court. By 5 February 1999, the case was settled; Toby bought the trademark from ETNA for an undisclosed sum.

On 17 February, after a month of sleepless work, the first edition of the prospectus, or the S-1, was finalised and sent to the Securities and Exchange Commission. It contained a detailed breakdown of the history of the company and also included substantive legal documents, from office leases to management-employment contracts, and a set of audited accounts. In total, eToys' S-1 ran to 516 pages. It begins:

OUR BUSINESS

We are the leading Web-based retailer focused exclusively on children's products, including toys, video games, software, videos and music ... Since launching our Web site in October 1997, we have sold children's products to over 320,000 customers. Our net sales for the quarter ended December 31, 1998 totalled $22.9 million as compared to $0.5 million for the quarter ended December 31, 1997.

Outlined over eleven pages, under thirty-two different sub-headings, were the risks that those who chose to invest in eToys would face. Fundamentally this was to point out that, as 'a result of our limited operating history, it is difficult to accurately forecast our net sales and we have limited meaningful historical financial data upon which to base planned operating expenses'. The S-1 warned that eToys had thus far accumulated a $17.5 million debt, and stated that the company's future was very dependent on its management's ability to execute the business plan and to build and staff warehouses big enough to cope with 'a significant increase in customer orders'.

Though etoy.com was not explicitly mentioned, the S-1 also asserted that eToys might not be able to prevent other people from infringing the trademarks of their domain names, because the 'relationship between regulations governing domain names and laws protecting trademarks ... is unclear'.

While Toby concentrated on dealing with his board, the IPO and the demands of external organisations, his management team set about gearing the company towards the demands of the next Christmas season, in which they hoped sales might explode by a factor of ten to $200 million worth of goods – the equivalent of about ten million Barbie dolls. Between January and May, the company's workforce almost doubled to 400. Most of these employees were in Operations, ready to deal with the anticipated demands of the warehouses and customer-call centres. But John

Hnanicek, the new Chief Information Officer, had also recruited a team to spring-clean eToys' technology. The Boys had built the firm's Web site on the foundation of free software released by informal communities for the public good. But Hnanicek now dismissed this as typical 'Gen X Internet start-up stuff'; he reckoned that, while it was cheap to run, it was an accident waiting to happen. He replaced it with software and hardware bought for millions.

During the first three months of 1999, eToys lost another $13 million. So Toby raised another round of $20 million, a sum which Daniel Nova's Highland Capital and Michael Moritz's Sequoia Capital were happy to provide between them. In the previous two and half years, Toby had collected $49 million for his company and sold only $30 million worth of goods.

By early April, the new management team was in place and a new round of funding had been secured; the financial markets, meanwhile, continued to explode – but for how long? eToys aimed to launch themselves on to the markets towards the end of the month. On 5 April, Lawton Fitt at Goldman Sachs tentatively priced the shares at $10–12 each. The final price would be set the day before the offering, but this estimate valued the company at about $1 billion. The press eagerly lapped up this latest event on the digital frontier; *The Wall Street Journal* noted that 'almost anything with an "e" prefix, or a "dot-com" suffix is getting a standing ovation from investors'.

Along with the share-price estimate, eToys announced that the existing company shares would be split; one old share equalled three new ones. Each batch of 250 shares that Toby had given out at the post-Christmas party now amounted to 750 shares, worth more than $7,500. And Toby's millions of shares, effectively bought for half a cent each, had risen in value by more than 2,000 times in just two years. He was now worth tens of millions of dollars.

The pricing announcement inspired legions of small investors. The online message-board service Raging Bull opened up a message service specifically relating to eToys. A user calling herself

'StockMom', who was new to IPOs, was one of the first to post a notice: 'I did all of my girls' Christmas shopping at eToys. The easiest Christmas shopping I have ever done. I will never go to a toy store again. I have no doubt that this will be a great IPO!'

The small shareholders using the service were particularly keen to join in the party and buy some eToys shares. Despite the rhetoric in the media of 'empowerment' and 'democracy', though, they were to be mostly disappointed. Someone named 'Bobbart' wrote, 'I have called Goldman Sachs this week ... They said that they deal with customers that have $5,000,000 accounts, that puts me out.'

The majority of the eight million shares to be sold at the IPO would go directly to the banks' best customers, the institutions: pension funds of large civic and corporate bodies, university endowments, the money-management funds of wealthy individuals and the mutual-funds bought by consumers but managed by professionals. Fund managers dealt directly with the big banks, while the smaller investors would have the opportunity to sign up for shares only through two new Internet banks. As these services were dealing with less than five per cent of the total shares for sale, there was intense competition from small investors to get on board.

Consumer investors who failed to secure an allocation were at a severe disadvantage. To buy eToys shares on the open market after the IPO would probably mean they would have to spend many times the price they were initially sold for. Even this did not deter many of the amateurs on the Internet message boards. So long as they bought the shares on the first day of trading, they argued, they would make money as the share price continued to rise. 'It has that magical "e" in their name,' someone wrote; another added, 'I can't see eToys trading less than $100 for long.'

Toby spent the weeks leading up to the IPO on the road, taking the eToys dream to the ballrooms of upmarket hotels where he and his team pitched to fund managers and wealthy individuals. Toby was a wonderful, entrancing speaker, with a geeky charisma and a way of gently marshalling the facts that inspired his audiences. He had carefully prepared every word of his speech in rehearsals in his Santa Monica offices. After each meeting on the road, representatives from Goldman Sachs would phone members of the audience to find out which parts of the presentation they'd found the most appealing.

Chris Vroom, an Internet analyst at the boutique investment bank Thomas Weisel Partners, attended shows in San Francisco and New York. 'The eToys roadshows were real spectacles, because of the enthusiasm generated by this new online channel of distribution. It was a feeding frenzy. And the management team came in and were loving the attention. It's tough to imagine a more aloof group of executives.' In San Francisco, Joanna Strober, who had invested on behalf of Bessemer Venture Partners, was thrilled that her first professional investment was about to pay off. 'It was great, it was pretty exciting. This was the hottest company around. You know, you look back and you think people were crazy. But at the time, it was pretty damn exciting. It was amazing.'

Others were not quite so caught up in the emotion. Andrew Fishman, of the Internet Fund, remembers the pressure to take part in the offering. 'The investment professionals who attended seemed somewhat sceptical. I don't know if they all bought the story but they were buying the momentum.'

It was the story, more than anything, that Toby was selling. With barely two years of operating history and no profits behind him, he at least had a wonderful narrative that investors seemed desperate to hear. When analysts discussed eToys' prospects in the press, they chose not to discuss the haemorrhaging finances. Instead, again and again, they judged what they described as the quality of its 'story'. As a yarn, when well spun, it seemed to have all the necessary elements: unlike the more arcane technology companies, eToys had a simple, high-concept premise that could be understood in a second; it was perfectly cast, with the brilliant Toby getting top billing, ably supported by his team of bright executives and heavyweight board members; and it nicely chimed with the spirit of the times.

eToys was not the only corporation to be judged in this way. Indeed, at the time it was as if the power of an idea, the assertiveness of the brand, the wonder of the event had become the overwhelming reasons to buy stock. The audited accounts in the back of prospectuses seemed to have less relevance to a valuation than the determined evangelism of heroic chief executives. Investors were buying the promise of a company, in the same way that those who purchase conceptual art from white-cube galleries sometimes speculate on future value.

Repeating the same presentation again and again was a gruelling process for Toby and his team, but nothing was to prevent the shares going on sale towards the end of April. During this time Toby even rebutted an approach from Toys'Я'Us in the belief that eToys could triumph alone. Halfway through the roadshows, though, he suddenly found out that amazon.com was about to move into his territory by buying BabyCenter.com for about $100 million. With more than half a million users, this was considered the best baby-orientated site on the Web.

Toby faced a choice: one option was proceed with the IPO, which would be completed within a couple of weeks; as the markets were still rising, this strategy seemed likely to guarantee eToys the money they needed. Alternatively, eToys could try to steal BabyCenter.com from under Amazon's nose and deny them a foothold in the children's market. However, this would delay the IPO and meant running the risk of the markets collapsing in the meantime. In the end, Toby decided that he could not allow amazon.com the opportunity to get to parents through their babies in case their loyalties became locked in for the long term. So, on Sunday 11 April, Toby phoned BabyCenter.com's founders, Matt Glickman and Mark Selcow, and offered to buy their company. Three days later, they agreed on a price of about fifteen per cent of the eToys shares, valuing BabyCenter.com at more than $150 million. Over piles of Chinese food, Selcow, Glickman and Toby's team then spent three sleepless days and nights negotiating a deal. It was signed exactly a week after Toby's approach.

The next day, the employees of eToys' corporate office were

called to a meeting in their new additional office space in their business park on Ocean Park Boulevard, Santa Monica. Because the company was growing so quickly this was their third new office building in three months. The interiors were unfinished and rolls of carpet were stacked ready to be fitted. Toby announced to the mass gathering that he had just bought BabyCenter and the IPO was going to be postponed so that the purchase could be integrated into the documents. Some of the employees were concerned that the delay might jeopardise the IPO. But Toby reassured them that the purchase made strategic sense and that the prize was well within the company's grasp.

By the end of the week, eToys had filed a new intention to go public: a month later than originally planned, at the end of May.

The company, like the rest of the investing world, revved itself into IPO fever. In the Customer Care Department, the phone operators were retrained. They weren't allowed to talk to customers about the share offering but were instructed to refer enquirers about it to the S-1. The online stock brokers E*Trade came in and conducted one-hour sessions with employees about their own shares and options packages and the Securities Exchange Commission that regulated them. New arrivals to the company were told that they were going to be millionaires.

On the investor message boards, excitement brimmed over. Financial Web sites reported that pages dedicated to eToys were receiving heavy traffic. The nearer the IPO, the greater the expectation. The general belief was that ETYS – the ticker symbol for eToys on NASDAQ – would 'skyrocket'. An investor with the handle of 'elevatorup' wrote, 'The name alone is going to drive the traders nuts.' Even the cynical explained, 'It's all about brand name and hype. The only reason I am interested in getting eToys is because some greater fool will be buying it from me at a higher price.'

The week beginning 17 May 1999 was the perfect week for a toy shop to sell its first shares in the public market. That Friday, George Lucas's prequel to the *Star Wars* trilogy, *The Phantom*

Menace, was scheduled to open. As a consequence, shares in Toys'Я'Us, having already spent weeks on the up, rose further on expectation of the huge sales of the film's tie-in figurines.

Toby and his team were in New York on the evening before the IPO, Wednesday 19 May. Lawton Fitt from Goldman Sachs had amassed 'the book' of interested investors and was to determine a price. In the previous weeks, sale traders at Goldman Sachs and the other participating banks had been nagged by fund managers and institutional investors wanting an allocation. Demand had been strong. Fitt and her team agreed they would price the eToys shares at $20, almost double the figure they had given just a month and a half before. eToys was now going to hit the public markets with a valuation of $2 billion; if Fitt's estimates were accurate, the next day Toby would be worth $162 million. On the Goldman Sachs trading floor, Toby and the eToys management received the news with elation. That night, Toby and Frank and their venture-capital investors celebrated with a luxurious dinner.

The consumer share allocations were only parcelled out that evening. At home at their computers, dozens and dozens of small investors hoped that they would be the lucky winners in the big eToys lottery. Retail-investors' prospects were not good and many were anxiously waiting. When one message-poster, 'Kericraig', received an email from a broker, Wit Capital, announcing his allocation, he considered himself to be in a lucky minority: 'HAAAHAAAAA, Gotcha :)'. When 'InternetAnalyst' received his own good news, he too joined in the frolicking, 'Yipee!!! Go eToys!!!'

Others were not so lucky. They were left staring at their screens waiting for the arrival of an email that would make them rich. They encouraged each other not to lose hope. 'I am still waiting for the confirmation email to come but its exciting,' wrote 'ladybrand' at around 9 p.m. 'Now if my newborn twins will stay asleep so I can be on the computer!' Some waited and wondered if they would have to stay up all night.

As the night drew on, the postings became more desperate. At

10 p.m. someone complained, 'This is taking quite a long time and it's making me edgy.' At 11.24 p.m. 'Luckliz' asked, 'How long are y' all going to sit in front of your screens? I've given up hope on this one.' Still waiting at 11.47 p.m., 'ts'' hopes were slowly vanishing and he took consolation from other members of the message board who were also still waiting. Midnight came and went, and those on the message boards heaved a collective groan. One of the last postings came from 'suem46' at 1.09 a.m. 'Well goodnight just got my confirmation from Wit of a nay on ETYS. Good luck to the rest of you. I'll probably buy in when the frenzy dies back.' Slowly the fire calmed to nothing.

Unlike the New York Stock Exchange (NYSE), which has a physical floor where traders make deals, the NASDAQ stock exchange, where the ETYS shares were to be sold, is just a computer network that brings share buyers and sellers together. But the managers of this cyberspace-based exchange decided not to forgo the opportunities for real-world burlesque that the rolling cable-news channels demand. So, partly for the purpose of melo-drama, a location was found for it in the entertainment heart of New York, across the road from the Disney Store in Times Square. There is even a visitor centre as a focus for tourists. Above it stands a four-storey television screen with stock-ticker symbols rushing across it. The traditional Coke sign that domi-nated Times Square for most of the twentieth century now stood across the street from the real icon of the moment.

Despite all this, it is hard for NASDAQ to match the theatrical-ity of the New York Stock Exchange, where Chief Executives of companies coming on to the market often ring the bell that marks the beginning of the day's trading. Nonetheless, at 8.30 on the morning of 20 May 1999, Frank and Toby were supposed to press the button that starts the markets at NASDAQ. Toby was too tired, though, after the roadshows and the previous night's celebrations, so Frank alone went up to the building's second floor and did the honours.

It was a somewhat symbolic gesture, since the eToys stock

was not set to trade until 12.30 p.m. Throughout the morning, Lawton Fitt on the Goldman trading floor watched the orders coming in. 'I do remember watching the interest build before trading began. There was interest not just from our institutional investors, but from all over the Street. And there was heavy retail interest; there were a lot of small orders.'

Also in New York was Chris Vroom from Thomas Weisel Partners, who was in the CNBC television studio. During that morning, he boosted the eToys stock by predicting that within ten years eToys would be a $10 billion corporation. He was broadcast into the trading floors of Wall Street and into the homes of the little investors wanting a part of it. For hours this cable-news speculation continued as everybody waited for the shares to trade for the first time.

In Santa Monica, three hours behind New York, little work was being done in eToys' corporate offices. In the conference room a crowd sat transfixed by Chris Vroom on the television. Many others were hitting reload on their Web browsers, waiting for ragingbull.com to give word of the eToys debut. These employees later struggled to describe that day, using words like 'exciting', 'surreal' and 'amazing'; often as they recalled the events, their diction stumbled and they shook their heads as if words couldn't begin to capture the sheer drama of the moment.

On the other side of Los Angeles in the offices of WebMagic, the company that had started the first online toy retailer – toys.com – Greg McLemore and his team were on the edge of their seats. For McLemore's company, eToys had paid money and the equivalent of about two million shares, which now looked impossibly valuable.

At 12.25 p.m., the ETYS symbol went across the wire. 'Free ride baby!' exulted 'Moneymaker' at 12.26 on ragingbull.com A couple of seconds later 'Hanaha's' followed, 'Here WE GO!!!!!!!' to which 'Paul Keffer' added, 'TO THE MOON!!!!!!'

eToys had successfully sold 8,320,000 shares on to the market, raising $166 million: $11 million for the bankers; the rest for the company. They had received $20 a share, but the institutions

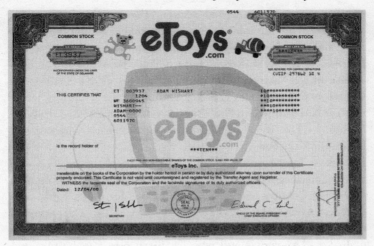

eToys share certificate.

and the few lucky retail investors who had bought them could sell them on for $78 on the open market.

Within the first minute of trading, the share price rose to $79 and then to $80. Three minutes later, it was at $82. By 12.35, five minutes after trading began, the price hit $81. At 12.36, the price reached $85. Bankers shook their heads in amazement.

Inside the eToys offices, the employees were busy with complicated calculations. Many had bought a package of 1,300 'friends and family directed shares' that could be sold on the day, and some had the 750-share bonus that Toby had given out at Christmas. Some sold. Others did not, as they thought the share price would rise to $100.

But most of the wealth was wrapped up in share options that could not be sold for six months because of financial regulations. How valuable these were was a conundrum dependent on two variables: first, how long an employee stayed with the company, as the options were not all given at once but were slowly 'vested' every month; second, what happened to the share price over time. Despite the impossibility of making accurate predictions, a number of employees started deluding themselves with complex calculations and fantasies resting on untenable assumptions. The Boys thought they might be worth $30 million; and that day Louis Zambello was asked what it felt like to be worth $66 million.

Just fifteen minutes after the debut, the eToys share price started to sink. At 12.39 it was $82.31; a minute later, $81.50. At 12.45, it had dropped to $80. By 13.13 p.m. the value had dropped further, to $79. By 13.19, the price had stabilised where it had begun the day: $78.

Back in Los Angeles, it had been arranged that everyone in the Engineering Department should go and see *The Phantom Menace* in Century City. This wasn't a day for doing work. The company's employees, and specifically those in this department, were exactly the generation of young men who had watched the first *Star Wars* movie and who had been obsessed by toys and technology ever since. Despite their interest, it was difficult for them to concentrate. Throughout the film, individuals crept out of the cinema to phone their brokers and find out the stock price. As they skulked back in, there were ripples of whispers and excitement as the rest of the team learned of the developments.

At 13.23, the price of the stock sunk to $77. Perhaps the 'pop' had burst?

In the Commerce warehouse on the outskirts of Los Angeles there was jubilation. Throughout the day, the stock price was written on bits of cardboard and posted on the walls. The pickers and packers on $12 an hour had been allowed to buy the 'directed shares'. Some of these were making $50,000 or more that day.

Through the early afternoon, the price fell further. By 14.35, it was down to $71.8125.

For the eToys employees, these small movements had a real effect. Had they sold their 1,300 directed shares (which they had bought for $26,000) at the peak of trading, they would have been worth $110,000. But by mid-afternoon that was down to $93,000. Toby's wealth varied that day by $100 million or so; at its highest, it reached $636 million. His co-founder Frank was possibly worth about $211 million.

By 3 p.m. the stock was back up to $77.

Finally, the share price settled to close at $76.56. It was the end of a remarkable day which saw the creation of the world's most valuable toy shop.

At its height, eToys was worth $8.65 billion that day. Toby's company had amazing growth characteristics, and he and his team had great vision, but they had just $30 million in turnover and they were losing money. At that time, Toys'Я'Us, their greatest rival, had 1,156 stores around the world and their previous year's revenue had been $11.2 billion with profits of $376 million. And yet eToys was worth almost fifty per cent more than the incumbent retailer.

Toby had brilliant timing. Five days after the IPO, the NASDAQ slid by ten per cent. The media jumped on this 'correction' as the arrival of a crashing-bear market. As Kate Delhagen, Director of E-commerce Research at Forrester Research, said of eToys: 'They got in before the window of opportunity slammed shut.' Had eToys or their bankers paused in the run up to the IPO, it might never have happened. As it was, they had $155 million sitting in the bank to be spent on their continued growth.

Yale economist Professor Robert Shiller's book *Irrational Exuberance* helped to pop the Internet bubble in March 2000; in it was a section entitled 'Examples of "Obvious" Mispricing'. To illustrate his point he chose just one example: 'The valuation the market places on stocks such as eToys appears absurd to many observers, and yet the influence of these observers on market prices does not seem to correct the mispricing . . . Absurd prices sometimes last a long time.' The stock market appeared to have left reality behind.

On the day of the eToys IPO, *Slate*, Microsoft's online journal, suggested that Toby should get in a flying saucer and land outside the Toys'Я'Us headquarters and say simply, 'Surrender now, earthlings. Resistance is futile.'

8
The Phantom Menace

'Markets are conversations . . . Corporations do not speak
in the same voice as these new networked conversations.
To their intended online audiences, companies sound hollow, flat, literally inhuman.'
Chris Locke, *The Cluetrain Manifesto*, 1999

The absurd value of $8 billion that the markets gave eToys on
the day of its IPO profoundly affected the company's self-image.
No longer was it a tiny start-up; it seemed to have the resources
to become a megalith. In the early months of the summer, analysts
from the finest Wall Street banks cheered eToys on. The reports
that they wrote were more than enthusiastic and the single-phrase
ratings given at the end of them were characteristically positive:
eToys shares were a 'buy', 'market out-perform' or 'buy aggressive'. Toby chimed in with his cerebral analysis. 'The Internet is
like the rail roads in the nineteenth century or communications
in the twentieth, it's going to be a major world transforming
event,' he pronounced. 'Children's retailing in the US is worth
more than $100bn; I don't have a crystal ball for what percentage
will come online but eToys will be a leader and that has significant
long-term potential.'

Many assumed that eToys, using the disruptive technology of
the Internet to re-order the toy industry, would soon be a
behemoth. Internet corporate valuations were calculated with

astonishing methodology: roughly, think of the size of the market; next, think of the possible percentage – say, ten per cent – that the 'category-killing' e-commerce site might be able to steal off the incumbents. Hey presto! Calculating the revenue was as simple as multiplying the percentage by the total market size. So, supposing that eToys could capture ten per cent of the $30 billion US toy market, they would have a revenue of $3 billion a year. In which case, it wouldn't be impossible for them to be worth almost $10 billion, since the valuation of retailers is commonly about three times their annual revenue. This back-of-the-envelope calculation, full of incredible assumptions, was trumpeted by some market observers as having an 'analytic basis'.

Such was the madness of the market, some of these analysts had little expertise in assessing the valuation of eToys. They were technology and Internet-retail specialists with little knowledge of the toy business. Incredibly, in one conference call an analyst asked Toby what Pokémon, the bestselling toy of that year, was. Moreover, given the big fees that banks were making from the Internet-company IPOs and secondary share-offerings, there was an incentive for analysts to champion start-ups like eToys in the hope of winning business in the future. For Toby, the logic of the market meant that nurturing the valuation became a central motivation. If eToys was really worth five, eight, maybe ten or twenty billion dollars, then it was a bet on the future. His company had to grow into the valuation like a child growing into a school uniform.

Being a public company put Toby under enormous pressure. From now on, eToys had to report its earnings and activities to the markets every three months. To begin with it wasn't too onerous because the capital markets would cheer every new announcement that promised growth, an increase in revenues, international expansion or the acquisitions of other companies.

Toby set out to spend the $155 million he'd raised from the IPO. In the following year, the company employed a further 600 people, taking the number of staff to almost 1,000. As the company grew, its culture slowly moved away from the irreverent days of the start-up period. Toby, who had once smashed balls around the office, became less approachable. The culture of the employees was also changing, as increasing numbers came from blue-chip corporations and were not imbued with the start-up ethic. Previously decisions had been made by go-getting employees who barely knew who their line manager was. Now they had to pass a circus of meetings and committees in a self-serving bureaucracy. eToys was gradually becoming more like a Big Corporation.

On the lips of eToys employees were smug, self-satisfied smiles. They had done it, created a company and sold it on the markets. Though the majority of staff-owned shares could not be sold until six months after the IPO, there were astonishing winnings ahead. Their millions would soon be liquid and tradable – and these became a central and important part of the eToys belief system. Jonathan Thorpe, who joined eToys at this time to run their British branch, remembers how, during his introductory tour, many of his meetings in the Californian offices and the warehouse would begin with his colleagues speculating about their imminent wealth. The Engineering Department's John Hnanicek is remembered as motivating his team by reminding them that they were going to be millionaires. Money made the employees more ambitious and work harder. Weekends, evenings and early mornings were all part of the rigour of this rapidly growing company.

Toby was featured in *Fortune* as being among the richest Americans under forty. Worth about $600 million, he was placed number thirty-seven on the list. Throughout 1999 the subject of his personal wealth was repeatedly reported by journalists. Toby would try and bat off these intrusions: 'Well, it's a sort of burden to think about these sorts of things and it's a responsibility and what I really like to do is think about keeping our head down, doing a good job for the customer.'

Central to the Big Company was a Big Brand. In the weeks running up to the IPO, Toby had persuaded Janine Bousquette to join

eToys as the Senior Vice President of Marketing. She arrived with
the very best in branding pedigrees. She started her career working
at Procter & Gamble, one of the most reputed training grounds for
would-be marketers. Then as Vice President of Marketing at Pepsi
she had led the crusade to sell the blue tins. Bousquette is a tall and
elegant blonde woman, but behind her smiles and bonhomie is a
determined corporate commando.

In the first few months after her arrival, Bousquette led a
reformulation of what she grandiosely called, 'the core philosophy
of the brand'. Previously eToys had traded under the sobriquet
of 'We bring the toy store to you™', emphasising an end to the
chaos of toy shopping in the real world. Now, however, the Big
Company was in search of a grander, more transcendent theme.
The principal focus of eToys was now, as Bousquette described
it, 'to operate as a parent's ally versus some of the traditional
approaches of nagging and guilt that some people employ when
they're marketing to parents'. This new system of values resulted
in the tagline 'eToys. Where Great Ideas Come to You™'.

To resonate with this updated corporate credo, Bousquette
began commissioning advertising with a gentler tone. 'This is
about creating a lasting bond with parents instead of a sharp poke
in the eye,' she said. She hired the agency Publicis & Hal Riney
in San Francisco and created a set of soft-focus, widely acclaimed
commercials. 'The campaign is about the small epiphanies in
children's lives,' said Alon Shoval, Hal Riney's Creative Director,
'and how when children make a discovery or experience a "first",
parents and kids make a connection.'

In one commercial a mother and son jump across rocks –
accompanied by a Hawaiian folk version of 'Somewhere Over the
Rainbow' – to a coastal tidal pool. There the boy discovers a
school of fish. The advert then cuts to the eToys Web site, where
the mother is typing in the word 'fish'. In the next scene the
child is underwater with a mask and snorkel exploring this new
world. A voiceover asks, 'Where will you find the perfect gift for
your child? eToys. Where great ideas come to you.' Despite
this new cuddly approach, Bousquette launched the campaign in

typically militaristic language saying that its objective was 'to communicate our laser focus on kids and the Internet'.

Janine Bousquette oversaw an astronomical growth in eToys' advertising budgets. In her first year, she spent $55 million, about a third of the revenue of the company. In comparison, Wal-Mart – the world's biggest retailer – spends less than one per cent of its revenues on advertising. As well as buying air-time on the American television networks, eToys consolidated their position in the online world. The summer of 1999 was a boom time for the Internet portals like AOL and Yahoo!. Internet companies were so full of IPO lucre and so desperate to stake their claim in the territory that they were prepared to pay almost anything. The most absurd example of this was drkoop.com, a consumer-health site named after the US Surgeon General. They agreed to an advertising deal with AOL in which they would hand over all but $500,000 from the $89 million raised in their recent IPO in exchange for high-profile banner space.

eToys had struck a $1 million-a-year deal with AOL in 1997 to be the 'anchor tenant' on their shopping page. But with a year of the original contract left to run, AOL persuaded eToys to renegotiate. A new deal was signed, for $6 million a year, which secured them their treasured 'anchor tenancy' in a range of categories, from toys to children's books, on the new shop@aol online-retail zone. In press releases on the subject, Toby was customarily jubilant.

With hindsight, Peter Brine, eToys' Vice President of Online Marketing, thinks eToys paid too much. 'We should never have done the deal but we had to. It was difficult, but if we were the only online company without a deal with AOL, and if we let toysrus.com have that space, the business media would have been all over us. It would have said that we'd run out of cash.' When news of the deal came out the stock market was overjoyed with eToys, even if they had paid over the odds. Their shares climbed nearly six per cent. Toby was pleased at how his new recruit Janine Bousquette was responding to the spendthrift new rules of business. 'It's Internet speed as opposed to regular company speed,' he said. 'She was able to make that transition, and not many traditional company executives are able to make that transition that well.'

In Europe, the remaining members of etoy, Zai, Gramazio and Kubli, were getting on with their lives beyond the group. None of them shaved their heads anymore. Zai, who now often wore his American-bought satin baseball jacket, was preparing to graduate from the Vienna Academy of Applied Arts by completing his final project. The imposing figure of Kubli was about to finish his law studies and start a professional career in a Zürich court. Gramazio was also in Zürich teaching architecture and racing around on his motorbike. They were very pessimistic about the future of etoy. 'It was clear to everybody [that] there was no possibility to earn our living with etoy,' recalls Kubli. 'We dealt with it as if etoy had come to an end. We had a meeting where we talked about the execution of the estate. We decided that etoy should continue to exist as an online archive.'

Once, the idea had been that the etoy agents were roles acted out by living young men; now, they were to be entombed in an online mausoleum. Zai decided to create 'etoy for eternity' for his final diploma. Initially the project was an exploration of the glory years: 'It was an act of coming to terms with the past. We had always pretended that we were on the rise. Now I had to become conscious of the history of etoy, its real ups and downs.' In June, he announced the demise of the corporeal etoy. He shut down the Vienna office and released the etoy agents into their online purgatory. The press release read: 'after 6 years of etoy.RESEARCH & DEVELOP-MENT . . . after 1000 etoy.BETA-TESTS and user behavior studies in Vienna etoy is now ready to prepare for the next level: ZERO GRAVITY / etoy.ETERNITY.' In the last line of the notice, Zai gave his favourite slogan a final twist: 'LEAVING REALITY BEHIND, DEFINITELY!'

While preparing for the final step, Zai at some point remembered about the email received from eToys. It had come in the midst of the bust-up in San Francisco and nobody had responded to it. As he was about to archive etoy, Zai thought that it might be possible to exploit eToys' request and make a little profit. He could not find the original email, so he addressed his reply to admin@etoys.com and asked for it to be forwarded to the appropriate person. He wrote of his experience ever since his online neighbour had set up shop: 'a lot of people visited our site (an art project) looking for your Web site (toy store) since you place a lot of advertisement in television, newspapers etc . . . they send emails with questions we cannot answer as far as they are not related to electronic and media art.' In his slightly stumbling English, he made a proposition: 'are you interested to place a banner on our site?' He hoped that eToys might give him a small amount of money to advertise on the etoy.com home page.

In Santa Monica, eToys considered their position with the renegade Swiss group. One of the key elements of the eToys philosophy was its child-friendly nature. Toby would often remind journalists that this was exactly what distinguished eToys in the marketplace. 'We don't sell Playboy videos,' he explained. 'We don't sell Tupac Shakur rap music. We're child-sensitive, and we get all the special details of the market right.' In contrast, when members of eToys' staff and their security consultants checked out the content of etoy.com they found a universe of dubious irony, aggressive mockery and tasteless self-representation. What was more disturbing was that it was a little unclear what or who etoy were. Janine Bousquette would soon write: 'The etoy Web site presents a serious concern for eToys because of the similarity of their name and Web site address with those of eToys, and because the content of the etoy site is the anti-thesis of the image that eToys is trying to build.' Most threatening, however, was what etoy might become.

Unaware that the corpse of etoy was about to go cold, lawyers representing eToys began to make enquiries as to how they could challenge the artists. In the United States Patent and Trademark database they found that the law offices of Abelman, Frayne & Schwab in New York were listed as representing etoy in their attempts to register a US trademark. In the early summer of 1999,

Abelman received the first letter from eToys, which stated, 'we believe that eToys Inc. clearly has prior rights in the ETOYS® mark that supersede any claim your client, the performance art group etoy, may have in the virtually identical ETOY mark . . . eToys Inc. would like to resolve this matter in as friendly and expeditious a manner as possible.'

In the following months, eToys' lawyers began negotiating with etoy's lawyer, Peter Wild, from the Zürich-based practice Metz & Partners. By the end of June, Peter Juzwiak, eToys' in-house counsel and a Disney alumnus, offered a deal: eToys were willing to buy etoy's domain name for the sum of $30,000. While eToys were prepared to spend more than $50 million on advertising, they appeared to be a little miserly when it came to compensating potential rivals. Peter Wild was not impressed: 'In a continually arrogant way their point of reference was that they had the better rights, that it was a sort of "merciful act" that they were willing to give us a little something.' But etoy were just as wilful as the men and women from Santa Monica. A week after receiving the first offer, Wild sent a fax to Peter Juzwiak. In it he outlined his clients' demand of $750,000 to relinquish the domain name. He argued that etoy felt that this hefty price was needed 'to allow a new start and building up a new brand' and further explained: 'Without such compensation it will not be possible to continue the art work and all related activities at the existing high level and therefore the client would in such case prefer not to change its name and continue to operate as it has until today.'

Later in the summer, eToys' lawyers increased their offer to $100,000. Zai, Gramazio and Kubli again refused; in a telephone call, Peter Wild told Peter Juzwiak that etoy still demanded the $750,000 they'd asked for. Juzwiak retorted that a court case would cost his corporation only a tenth of this sum. Nonetheless, etoy felt duty-bound to remain firm. Wild faxed eToys that his clients were 'just as happy to continue under the status quo'. As Zai remembers: 'We didn't want to lose face by giving away the URL for so little money. It would have been better to die gloriously in a kamikaze act!'

In the midst of this, the front page of etoy.com was changed to feature the words, 'We do not support the old fashioned way . . . get the fucking flash plugin!' This was to warn users that they would have to download an extra piece of software before looking at the site. At eToys, the expletive seemed like provocation.

At the end of August, Thomas A. Cramer, a grandfather and eToys customer from Chantilly, Virginia, was shown the etoy.com Web site by his grandson. Cramer printed off the front page and faxed it to eToys. In his covering letter, which he copied to Channel 7 News, he wrote, 'My grandson was looking for toys for his birthday and brought this to my attention. Are you completely nuts? What an irresponsible thing to show young children. We will never buy from you again.'

Josh Geller, eToys' Director of Quality Control, was passed the letter of complaint by Customer Service. He talked with Peter Juzwiak, who asked him to research etoy and to print out the offending material from the Web site. 'We spent a couple of hours looking at it,' he recalls. 'It was funny stuff. We fired off the print-outs to the Legal Department and that was the last we heard about it.' These papers were added to the growing file about etoy that various security consultants and staff had been gathering over the previous years.

The legal wrangling was a small part of eToys' imperial land-grab. They were trying to seize markets in all directions. Toby was pushing his company towards developing new product categories beyond toys and also into new geographical territories. They opened a baby-products store to exploit the audience gained with the purchase of BabyCenter.com, adding an additional 3,000 items to their inventory, and a bookstore with 80,000 titles. In September, they launched their Idea Center, which a press release declared would 'redefine customer service in the online retail market' by linking editorial content with merchandising. Toby said, 'You have to be a moving target on the Web. If you just stand still somebody's going to copy it and catch up with you. And the trick is continuing to roll out new categories.'

In 1999, eToys went from carrying 8,500 Stock-Keeping Items (SKUs) to carrying more than 80,000. 'The theory at the time,' remembers Lou Zambello, Senior Vice President of Operations, 'was that people are only going to go to the Web site with the most stuff. So that was the strategy.' Every extra SKU, from a Barbie Dream House to a video-cassette, had to be received, stored and despatched through a warehouse. Toys, books, videos, music and baby products came in all different shapes and sizes, and the problem of storing and then despatching them without a glitch, according to Zambello, increased exponentially with each new product category added.

The autumn marked the arrival of very serious competition for eToys. Until then, Toby had his chosen territory very much to himself. Toys'Я'Us had launched an online operation in 1998, but it had been bedevilled with problems. In 1999 their business had continued to suffer; a deal was announced with Benchmark Capital, a respected venture-capital partnership, only for it to collapse a few months later, then toysrus.com lost their Chief Executive. But by early autumn they were doing good business, piggy-backing on the company's well-known stores.

Amazon had also announced a move into the toy market. 'We are embarking on one of the largest expansions ever undertaken in a single year by any company,' declared Jeff Bezos, whose company also bought stakes in online sellers of sporting goods, groceries, medicines and pet supplies. Disney, too, danced into the market by buying the controlling interest in toysmart.com

Newspapers and online news groups reported the battle. 'These guys are in a Claymation death match of a lifetime. Who is going to win?' asked James Cramer in TheStreet.com. 'The War Against eToys is No Game,' headlined *Business Week*. Toby grandly dismissed the opposition, saying it didn't keep him awake at night. He thought his unique proposition would be enough to see him through. 'We were born as an Internet company; we live and breathe the Internet.'

Toby's mission to get eToys growing internationally led his top managers to Japan and Europe throughout 1999. They finally settled on the idea of starting a British version of the world's most valuable toy shop. Toby claimed that he had learned some tough lessons from his experience in Disney: 'We went through all the mistakes at EuroDisney in terms of how you build up a local company in Europe. At eToys, we are absolutely intent on avoiding them. When we launched EuroDisney we were all-American. You can't be successful like that; you need to be local.'

It was at this point that Toby found Jonathan Thorpe, a self-effacing, almost shy Englishman. Compared with the eToys employees on the other side of the Atlantic, he could seem a little uncertain, though he was highly regarded in the toy business because he'd run Playmobil in the US. However, to Thorpe, it looked like eToys were about to make the same mistake as Disney: 'In my opinion, they didn't understand the UK. The market is different; they didn't understand Europe, and they thought they had an endless pot of money. Spend, spend, spend.' Frank went to work for a month in London, as did a number of his colleagues from his MBA class at Stanford Business School. Thorpe didn't have a degree. Having left school at sixteen he had become a business manager by working his way up from the bottom. He was unimpressed by the MBA gang's educational credentials: 'They were really, really clever people, but they just didn't have any common sense.'

When eToys.co.uk launched Toby flew over from Santa Monica and was met by a London taxi in eToys livery. 'International expansion is a cornerstone of our growth strategy and advances our goal of becoming a premier global kids' retail brand in the twenty-first century,' he enthused to the British press. 'Our UK launch will enable us to bring to this market the same combination of superior selection and customer service that has made us the gold standard in kids' retail in the US.'

After the launch, the pragmatic Thorpe and the analytic MBAs continued to clash. Thorpe disagreed with the group's workaholic hours, with how money was being spent and with the off-the-shelf motivational strategies imposed upon the British eToys staff. Within a month, Thorpe had to leave as he was told his job as General Manager would soon no longer exist. He says, 'I think Toby is a very, very clever man, and he had very, very clever people around him, but I think they lost sight of the real world.'

Executives elsewhere in the company were also having doubts about the strategy of spending hundreds of millions of dollars up front in the belief that massive rewards would be reaped in years to come. As Lou Zambello, a man with an excellent old-economy pedigree, recalls, 'People got caught up in an alternate business reality that Internet companies are different. I had a lot of doubts on a lot of this stuff. They said to me, "Lou, you are old economy; you have to embrace the new stuff", and my failing is that I believed that. I thought maybe I would try the new approach and that maybe they were right. I would voice my opinion but I wouldn't stick to it.' Likewise, before he left, Jonathan Thorpe doubted his own business judgements. 'For two months I thought I was stupid.'

Dissent was not greatly tolerated and, in the end, many of the doubters were silenced, steamrollered by the heady evangelism of their colleagues. As one senior manager says off the record, 'They [the eToys management] were overly confident, overly optimistic and overly insular, I felt, in their view of what kind of company they had already built. It was a highly fragile, theoretical enterprise; we had years to prove out if it had any value, and I felt that people were behaving as if it was a *fait accompli*, that we were the winners, and that we had to behave and make these decisions as if we [were] winners.' Wall Street analyst Chris Vroom also remembers the arrogance of the company: 'You know, when you have a ton of people kissing your arse, begging to take their money, that warps your mind.'

The Ars Electronica festival had asked Zai to participate in an event entitled 'And what is it that makes it art?' at the beginning of September 1999. Rather than following the usual procedure of seminars and lectures followed by questions and answers, etoy staged a business presentation during which their mentor Joichi Ito signed the shares that he had bought for $10,000. Zai and

Ito posed for the flashing cameras; then Zai made on behalf of etoy a donation to the ®™ark campaigners, handing Ray Thomas, the group's representative he'd met in San Francisco, $2,000 in small bills.

At this point etoy never really believed that eToys would sue them. The company seemed smart and it wasn't clear what would be gained from a court case. It appeared more likely that a settlement of some kind would be negotiated. During the festival, Zai asked the advice of Ray Thomas and Joichi Ito. Thomas promised to be an ally of the artists should they need his help; he would rally an army of activists who had supported ®™ark's other campaigns to work for etoy's benefit. Ito was busy trying to set up an incubator in Japan, and his help was more business-orientated: he told Zai that the real value of the etoy domain was about $500,000.

On 10 September, the day after the etoy event in Austria, eToys lodged a complaint against them in the Los Angeles Superior Court. They had hired the services of Irell & Manella, a large and well-known Los Angeles law firm that employs more than 200 lawyers and has offices on the glamorously entitled Avenue of the Stars in Century City neighbouring Beverly Hills. The company had represented Hollywood stars and studios, and had a good reputation in litigating about the ownership of such things as trademarks, patents and in other areas of Intellectual Property. Their aggressive litigation methods have been described by one of their Los Angeles colleagues as 'ball breaking'. This was the law firm that Peter Juzwiak had worked within before his move to eToys.

The lead litigating attorney was Bruce Wessel, a short and determined man who specialised in Intellectual Property cases. The initial eToys complaint against etoy comprised fourteen pages of closely and aggressively argued legalese. It was alleged that etoy had infringed and diluted the eToys trademark, had practised unfair competition and had committed 'intentional interference with prospective economic advantage'. At the end of the complaint was a demand for an injunction: that etoy cease using their trademark and cease operation of the Web site at www.etoy.com or at any similar address. The demand also sought to prevent them from selling shares in the United States. To cap it all, eToys wanted punitive damages.

Although previous discussions had been concerned only with the etoy domain name, Wessel took the unusual step of making a more general attack on the etoy boys. He decided to invoke the Unfair Competition Act, §17200 of the Business and Professional Code of California. Under this law, eToys could present themselves as if they were the state's Attorney General protecting citizens from an unfair or fraudulent business. The law had been designed to help consumers defeat false advertising and unscrupulous corporations, but the definition of 'unfair' was, by 1999, very wide-ranging. Wessel cited an Appeals Court Judgement that stated: 'An unfair business practice occurs when the practice offends an established public policy or when the practice is immoral, unethical, oppressive, unscrupulous or substantially injurious to customers.'

The Unfair Competition Act is a controversial piece of legislation. According to a recent study by the Association for California Tort Reform in Sacramento, it was sweeping in scope and application, having 'metamorphosed from an intended equitable "check" on false market economies into a bounty-hunter-type regulatory mechanism of enormous elasticity'. The report continues, 'The law has in itself become a frequent source of unfairness to business and the public.'

By using the Unfair Competition Act, Wessel could include almost everything that etoy had produced as evidence of their dubious business practices. The court papers were like a delicately curated catalogue of their exploits, alongside which he enumerated the reasons that Zai and etoy had been unfair: '(i) infringing the eToys® mark, (ii) tarnishing the eToys® mark, (iii) violating the securities laws by the offers of sales of unregistered "etoy stock"; (iv) conducting the "digital hijack"; and (v) falsely representing that their etoy mark is registered'. In a wonderfully creative piece of lawyering, Wessel outlined the entire conceit of the etoy corporation. What had been built for the intention of art, or at least irony, was now an unfair and unscrupulous business practice used wilfully against the highest-valued toy company on earth.

Bruce Wessel believed that in the new territory of the Internet it was not clear-cut as to what was the correct legal remedy and he was happy to experiment: 'We wanted to present the complete picture to the court of the various things they were doing that caused us concern. [Our case] highlighted, from a legal standpoint, where you draw the line between art and commerce.' eToys were most worried about the confusion that their customers might experience. The Web site was very unclear about whether etoy were artists, hackers or just kids having a laugh, and this uncertainty was a great worry to a company playing at the top of their game. Looming over the case was the possibility that the etoy.com Web site might develop into something nastier and more pernicious at the height of eToys' valuable shopping season, their first as a public company.

At the heart of the complaint was the contention that etoy had infringed the trademark of eToys. During the previous two years, eToys had acquired two trademarks. The first was for 'online retail services for toys and games', filed in May 1997 and registered to eToys in October 1998. The second trademark was for 'importation and distributorship in the area of toys'; it was this trademark that had once been owned by the little New York toy distributor ETNA and had been sold to eToys following a legal tussle at the beginning of 1999.

United States Trademark law is circumscribed by two abiding principles enshrined in the 1946 Lanham Act. The first is that similarly named businesses can co-exist quite happily. The Lanham Act allows for 'concurrent' registrations if they are for different services or goods or in different geographical areas. So, for instance, Yale Locks and Yale University co-exist and have never sued each other for trademark infringement, since they are in different fields of business.

The second principle of the Lanham Act is that the right to own a trademark ultimately comes down to 'use'. Registration is simply an administrative aid that gives corporations the presumption to the rights to a mark; it allows them to warn potential competitors that they already own the trademark and it extends it across the entire United States. However, it does not automatically confer rights if someone else can demonstrate they existed in the same territory and in a related business beforehand. For example, McDonald's Inc. failed in its battle with a man named Ronald McDonald who has run a McDonald's Family Restaurant in a small town in Illinois since 1956.

eToys' claims against etoy rested on the interpretation of the facts with regard to these principles of the Lanham Act. The first argument was that *only* eToys were using that name in the United States when they registered it in 1997. Although etoy were perhaps known in Europe – and were free, even encouraged, to register the domain there – they were not known in the US. Therefore eToys had the right to use their name without confusion in the US. Merely owning a domain, they argued, was not sufficient to meet the 'use' test.

The second argument that eToys used was based on their purchase of a second trademark. This trademark was 'first used in commerce' in 1990, according to the claim, which made eToys' position 'superior' to that of etoy.

In either case, eToys owned the rights to the trademark. The trademark claim was, however, just a small part of the lawsuit. Wessel's use of the Unfair Competition Act meant that the case was an extensive broadside against etoy. By searching for the appropriate legal remedy Wessel had moved the case beyond simply a trademark dispute into one about the rights and responsibilities of neighbours on the Internet and about two different methods of 'doing business' online.

At the end of September, the toy company served further substantive papers of the case. There were declarations from four of eToys' senior executives and a fifteen-page argument from Bruce Wessel. In addition there were marketing reports and a compendium of all their legal citations. Toby did not sign a declaration but he entrusted his closest colleagues with the task:

Leaving Reality Behind

Suzanne Rend, Janine Bousquette, Peter Juzwiak and John Hnanicek.

The package ran to hundreds of pages. In his declaration, Peter Juzwiak wrote, 'etoy at times describes itself as a group of performance artists whose work is self-consciously anti-social and offensive. The etoy site has contained examples of etoy's work including pornography as well as messages and images applauding terrorism.' Wessel quoted etoy's claim to be 'offensive, depraved, insane, obscene, prurient, perverse, destructive, anarchistic, rebellious and antisocial in nature'. The court papers also included images pulled from the Underground tank of etoy's 1995 Web site – one of a woman with spikes sticking out of her breasts; two of men's naked penises; and one of the bombed-out Federal building in Oklahoma with the caption 'Such work needs a lot of training'. There were also images of the Digital Hijack and examples of the rhetoric that etoy used in their 'share offering'.

The marketing surveys claimed that the etoy Web site was benefiting from eToys advertising, while conversely eToys were being harmed by the rebellious young men. As Janine Bousquette said in her declaration: 'The self-consciously antisocial image of etoy is the antithesis of the safe child- and family-orientated reputation that eToys has worked so hard to earn. If etoy is allowed to continue using the name etoy in connection with their offensive conduct, the eToys brand name will inevitably be associated in some customers' minds with etoy's conduct. This harm to eToys' brand name and reputation will be irreparable in that no amount of damages awarded to eToys could truly compensate for the loss of our reputation and our customers' confidence.'

Bousquette's uncompromising statement was even more remarkable because she had been at Pepsi when they had pioneered a relaxed attitude to provocative artists. Back in 1997, the San Francisco-based band Negativland had released an album called *Dispepsi*. They had already been famous for having been sued by U2's record company. This new album was aimed at causing controversy and contained soundbites from Pepsi advertisements mixed with music to pillory the corporation and its advertising. The lyrics were absurd: 'I got fired by my boss – Pepsi! / I nailed Jesus to the cross – Pepsi!'. The *Dispepsi* cover featured a red, white and blue circular logo that bore a striking resemblance to the Pepsi logo. However, when a Pepsi spokesman was asked by *Entertainment Weekly* for a comment, rather than rising to the bait he said it was 'a pretty good listen'. Later, Pepsi's John Harris explained to *Rolling Stone*, 'We constantly laugh at ourselves in our commercials as well as at our competitors, and we feel it's important to have a good sense of humour.'

eToys were not about to play it so cool. When the complaint arrived in the etoy office in Zürich, Zai, Gramazio and Kubli looked at it with amazement and disbelief. 'It literally knocked us out of our shoes,' recalls Kubli. 'We thought it was outrageous . . . total craziness.' Kubli, who had just finished his law degree, was convinced that the documents contained 'pure aggression' intended to intimidate etoy. He believed that they had been filed because Bruce Wessel, Peter Juzwiak and Toby Lenk didn't think that a disorganised bunch of 'European hackers', as they had described etoy, would be ready for a fight.

etoy were indeed frightened. They had no idea how they would pay for lawyers. If they lost the case they would bitterly mourn their domain and they were worried that eToys could sue them for punitive damages. At the same time, the legal papers woke their rebellious spirit. They felt again like the teenage punks they once had been, despising anyone who had tried to make them follow rules. They started to talk about strategies and created a list of arguments in their favour. They weren't about to be bullied.

9
A Conviction or Half a Million Dollars

'Your legal concepts of property, expression, identity, movement, and context do not apply to us. They are based on
matter. There is no matter here.'
John Perry Barlow, 'A Declaration of the Independence of
Cyberspace', 1996

After the complaint and the court papers had been served on etoy,
the boys felt unsure how it would all play out. The ferocious legal
argument, the danger of substantial punitive damages and the
money needed for a protracted legal fight with a multibillion-dollar
corporation made them apprehensive. They were uncertain what
they should do. One option was to try and settle; if the right amount
of money was offered, they weren't going to rule this out as a possibility. Otherwise, they felt obliged to stand up to their adversary
and set about preparing for a full-blown struggle.

To fire up global enthusiasm for their cause, Zai and Gramazio
went to the United States in early October. 'We knew that this
could become a great media topic, so we prepared for the media
battle,' says Zai. 'We collected addresses, talked to journalists
and contacted people who we thought could become soldiers in
the forthcoming battle.'

Wanting to establish a network of support, Zai began contacting
key individuals who might help them. In particular he made an
appointment with Wolfgang Staehle in New York. A soft-spoken

German who always wears black, in his fifties, Staehle had come to the city as a radical young art student in the late 1970s and had set up a bulletin-board system for artists and then an Internet service provider called The Thing. This became the provider to the parts of the New York art scene interested in new technology and soon had affiliates in several European cities. Among many others, The Thing provided Web hosting to nettime, an influential mailing list for Internet cultural theory. Staehle had been a political activist since his youth, and also used his company to support radical organisations such as Ray Thomas's ®™ark and Ricardo Dominguez's Electronic Disturbance Theater – it was from The Thing that Dominguez had launched his attacks against the Mexican Government and the Pentagon.

Zai described for Staehle the problems etoy had with eToys and asked him to register the domain toywar.com. This was to be at arm's length from etoy so that they would not be associated with any of the hacktivist activities that might be promoted there, though its purpose was also to provide a virtual refuge in the event that etoy.com was closed down by the courts. One of Staehle's employees registered toywar.com under the name of a supposed Manhattan resident, Karli Marx. Staehle agreed to host it for free on an old server. He also put Zai in touch with a journalist called Claire Barliant from the *Village Voice*, who was interested in running a story about the conflict.

Back in Zürich, the etoy boys discussed their legal strategy with their lawyer, Peter Wild. They were under some pressure: the preliminary hearing about the injunction was scheduled for 8 October. They contacted Abelman, Frayne & Schwab in New York, the firm who had handled their trademark registration in the US, and hired Marcella Ballard, a specialist in litigation. Ballard, with no licence to practise in the State of California, procured the services of Robert Freimuth from the Los Angeles law firm Isaacman, Kaufman & Painter.

In New York, Ballard set about drafting etoy's defence, by countering each of eToys' trademark arguments in turn. The first concerned the claim that etoy had been neither active nor known in the United States when eToys was founded in 1997. Ballard's response was that etoy had existed since 1994, had properly registered their globally available domain name in 1995 and, to cap it all, had won a prestigious international art prize in 1996. To eToys' second statement of claim – that they had bought a trademark from ETNA that went back to 1990 – Ballard argued that at its inception this trademark was only for the importation and distribution of toys from ETNA's New York base and so had no relevance. In her view, etoy and ETNA could have happily co-existed and the trademark could not simply be extended on to the Internet. As her final argument, Ballard stated that eToys had not sufficiently demonstrated that their customers were being 'confused'. Despite the millions of Web toy-shoppers, few seemed to have noticed the artists' Web site. Only a handful of examples were in the court documents: one complaint letter from a customer, a single email, and a couple of press reports containing misspellings. It seemed, as some eToys insiders later admitted, a little anecdotal.

From the very start, etoy's three lawyers believed this to be primarily a trademark case but because Bruce Wessel had included allegations about the etoy shares, the Digital Hijack and 'antisocial' messages it would be heard in the Superior Court. This body had little experience of trademark disputes and was more likely to be in eToys' favour. They described this sleight of hand as 'a blatant example of forum shopping'.

An Intellectual Property lawyer, Megan Gray, working in Los Angeles, was a fascinated onlooker at the time. 'It was very good lawyering on behalf of the eToys lawyers,' she says. 'It was so blatant what they were trying to do with the litigation. They had a crappy case on the substance. So they did a very good job [of] making the case for everything but the substance.' At the beginning of October, etoy's lawyers reacted by filing a document demanding that the case be heard in the Federal Court, the more usual place for trademark disputes to go.

Whatever the rights and wrongs being argued in the claims and counter-claims, eToys were under increasing pressure to take control of the etoy.com domain before the Christmas toy-shopping rush. Peter Juzwiak was keen to secure it and settle the case, so he called Peter Wild in Zürich and said that he was unable to back down because Toby was digging his heels in. However, he did make another offer: $160,000 in cash and eToys shares.

Zai, Gramazio and Kubli met to discuss the offer in a bar close to their office. Kubli had just begun working in a Zürich court-house and was cautious, studious and simply scared. 'As a lawyer, he was probably more aware of all the consequences and risks,' says Gramazio, remembering how Kubli thought that $160,000 was a sufficient starting point for a successful negotiation. Zai and Gram-azio were prepared to take bigger risks and enjoyed the prospect of a good, proud fight. Zai recalls, 'We did not want to be just the victims; that would have been cheap. We wanted to be giants too.' But, like everyone else, they were also infected with the goldrush spirit and thought they might be able to get their hands on a bigger part of eToys' pile of cash. As Zai remembers, 'My fingers started itching. I knew that this sum could change our life in the two years to come.' Eventually Gramazio and Zai managed to convince Kubli to join them in a unanimous refusal of the offer. The three of them left the bar at the end of the night feeling euphoric.

On 8 November, Robert Freimuth, representing etoy, and Robert Klieger, representing eToys, separately made their way to the Federal Courthouse, a grand Art Deco building situated on the corner of a busy intersection in downtown LA. In front of Judge Edward Rafeedie, Freimuth briefly outlined etoy's prop-osition that the Federal Court was the right place for the case to be heard, based on it being primarily a trademark case. In response, Klieger argued that this complicated Unfair Competition Act suit involving a whole variety of allegations should be properly heard in the more local Superior Court. In a matter of minutes, Judge Rafeedie conceded to eToys' proposal and the case was sent back to the Superior Court. Bruce Wessel's cunning lawyering had succeeded in keeping the trademark case out of the court that was most skilled at dealing with it.

For etoy the decision was a blow, but they were already being overtaken by other events. Zai had just sent out the first mass email informing their fans and supporters of their plight, as a way of 'showing our weapons'.

eToys vs etoy:

> number 16 of the largest US online commerce corporations, eToys.com, is suing etoy.com (without the 's'), the 'digital hijack' artists from the net. eToys Inc. (with the 's') asserts that they are unhappy that US kids could get confused and exposed to those bad guys from europe. family values are at stake; Xmas shopping harmony and american capital against net art.

No sooner was the email sent than their supporters posted it on artists' newsgroups across the Net. People began mailing etoy with messages of support; others added 'Save etoy now!' as the signature to their personal emails. Zai's posting also provoked the first media report about the case, in an influential German Net-culture magazine, *telepolis*. The article outlined the case and painted a romantic view of the old days of the Internet: 'A melancholic longing for the long-lost, open spaces of the frontier is what could soon be the dominant feeling in cyberspace . . . Fences are going up everywhere, moulding what once seemed infinite space into an overcrowded and tightly controlled strip-mall.' etoy were delighted. 'After our mail, the case became public; it was not a private affair any more,' remembers Gramazio. 'Because of the positive response, we lost most of our fears.'

Meanwhile there was a growing sense of desperation inside the eToys camp: time was running out and the holiday shopping season was about to kick in. The problem was that the Superior Court timetable meant they wouldn't get their hearing until 29 November, the Monday after Thanksgiving, which was way too late. In an effort to avoid this delay, eToys filed a motion to 'shorten time'. In an accompanying letter to the court, one of their lawyers outlined the seriousness of the situation: the day after Thanksgiving was the busiest day of the year for the toy industry, a single day that was seen as a 'barometer of the entire holiday shopping season' and enormously significant for a publicly traded company. The plea was unsuccessful.

At much the same time, Marcella Ballard and Kubli completed work on etoy's bundle of court papers, which ran to more than sixty pages. Kubli wrote a declaration in which he described etoy as a 'consortium of artists who sought to group together to creatively "protest" various ideas and to promote its artistic and philosophical viewpoints on the Internet.' He also made a particular effort to explain to the court the concept of the etoy shares, given his lawyers' theory that this was the most dangerous aspect of eToys' case. He wrote that, 'contrary to plaintiff's hyperbolic assertions of securities fraud, etoy Corp's purported "sale" of shares on its Web site is not the equivalent of a stock offering.' In addition, he argued that eToys' barrage of allegations were simply ridiculous. 'Plaintiff's humorless and overly literal reading of etoy's "tongue-in-cheek" estimation of its "stock" value defies common sense. The etoy.com Web site is not about commerce *per se*, it is about artistic and social protest.'

Ballard pointed out that there was no evidence of a 'victim' as no consumers had been misled by etoy offering their shares. She also claimed that the temporary injunction was an 'extraordinary remedy' for a problem that the toy company had been aware of for the previous sixteen months. When she summed up, she hit them with the strongest and the simplest of claims: 'It is the plaintiff's dilatoriness and failure to run a proper name search before it went public that have led to its claims of urgency in this matter, not the upcoming holiday shopping season.'

etoy and their lawyers also chose this moment to strike back. No longer were they to be merely the defendants. Using the same legal weapons as their adversary, they launched a counter-suit in the Federal Court that exactly mirrored eToys' trademark claims. Now etoy argued that it was the toy company who had infringed the artists' commonlaw trademark by arriving late on to the Internet and choosing their name. Were this suit to be successful eToys would be forced to relinquish their trademark and domain name. This was not a great prospect for a company who had just invested millions of dollars in promoting their brand.

The day following the Federal Court hearing, Peter Juzwiak called Peter Wild in Zürich once again. Kubli, who usually listened in on such calls, thought etoy's more aggressive stance seemed to be having some impact. Juzwiak now sounded worried and insisted that eToys were seeking a settlement; he made an extraordinary settlement offer of 7,000 eToys shares and $50,000 in cash in return for the domain – a package which at the time totalled about $400,000, although market volatility in the next few weeks actually pushed this above the $500,000 mark.

Robert Freimuth, etoy's lawyer in Los Angeles, was baffled when he heard the news – normally, those that sue don't also offer to pay: 'The whole case was kind of crazy.' Peter Wild, in Zürich, thought it was 'completely absurd' and 'very weird', but he wrote to etoy: 'I think that we have reached a level at which it would make no sense to refuse the offer reached in the negotiations.' Half a million dollars was a lot of money to pay for a name originally registered in a spirit of exploration and adventure.

Wild invited Zai, Kubli and Gramazio to his office to discuss the offer. He told them, 'Think about it very carefully. This is a lot of money. You will never reach this again.' Wild thought that this might be the end of the matter, but the discussion only became more and more lively. The boys all by now hated the predatory behaviour of the toy company and were not about to give in. Wild remembers, 'It was fascinating for me to see these little guys who definitely did not have loads of money; they just sat there and said, "$500,000? We don't care!" My heart almost stood still.'

eToys' carrot-and-stick negotiation strategy was backfiring. For the members of etoy, the aggressive court manœuvre at one turn and the financial offer at another smacked of their American adversaries' arrogance. Irritated by the different legal culture, Zai and Gramazio both felt their attitude hardening. What they had once thought of as an enjoyable fight was becoming an opportunity that could be exploited for the benefit of etoy's future. 'We felt that this was a tremendous final project for etoy,' explains Gramazio. 'It was a new motivation after everything that had happened in San Francisco. For Zai and me it was an extreme temptation. We realised that this was the best situation we could dream of. eToys were our ideal enemy – we were their worst enemy.'

As Thanksgiving approached, orders through the eToys Web site suddenly picked up. In the space of just a few weeks, customer orders had increased by a factor of twenty, from just a few thousand a day to tens of thousands. This was great news for Toby but it was also creating a crisis. eToys' distribution system couldn't cope with the demand. The step up in volume was so great that the distribution team had had no time to learn the ropes or to fix their problems.

This reality was very different to Toby's optimistic vision. In one exuberant moment, he had even suggested that eToys' service would be better than the very traditional method of Christmas delivery: 'Our expanded distribution system will process more orders in less time . . . Clearly, Santa could use a little help in distributing all those gifts.' But, by the last days of November, it seemed as if eToys could well have done with some help from the man on the sleigh.

Their distribution team was lead by Lou Zambello, whom Toby had once described as 'one of the top direct-to-consumer operations executives in the country'. Even Zambello could not prevent this crisis, though. A year earlier, the expectation had been that the 1999 season could be ten times as big as the previous one. eToys would need enough capacity to shift $200 million worth of toys, books, CDs, software and baby goods, on time and to the correct addresses. When Zambello arrived at eToys at the beginning of the year, he was desperate to accelerate the acquisition of warehouse space. He knew how incredibly difficult this would be and how his career at eToys would hang on the choices he made. Soon he discovered that a previously sleepy catalogue company, Fingerhut, were gearing themselves up to handle contract delivery for e-commerce companies. For Zambello, they came with all the right credentials. They had just been acquired by Federated Stores, the owners of Macy's, one of the premier retail conglomerates in the US, and had also been chosen as the distributor for walmart.com, which seemed like the best of recommendations. With a virtually empty million square feet of warehouse in Provo, Utah, Fingerhut were therefore contracted by eToys to handle the bulk of their deliveries.

Fingerhut's state-of-the-art retail distribution facility was very unlike eToys' own warehouse in Commerce, California. Rather than human 'pickers' collecting individual orders, all orders here were controlled by a sophisticated computer system which sped up the process by amalgamating the collection of orders. In the warehouse, a single item was called an 'each'; if ten orders were being processed for a Special Edition Barbie, then in one robotic journey the ten 'eaches' could be picked and redistributed to the packing stations via a complicated system of conveyor belts. Brilliant and efficient – at least in theory.

The plan was for the warehouse to receive most of the holiday-season goods in the last weeks of August and the first weeks of September. But things soon started to go wrong – how precisely has been the subject of a number of lawsuits. The acrimony between eToys and Fingerhut was so rancorous, it is difficult to discern the splinters of the truth. According to Loren Eggert, General Manager of Fingerhut, eToys had promised new software that would facilitate the warehousing, but it arrived five weeks later than expected; the delay meant that the warehouse was hopelessly incapable of dealing with the hundreds of trucks turning up each day with deliveries of Brio Trains, Pokémon playing packs and *Harry Potter* books. In addition, eToys' management of the inventory was allegedly so chaotic that for many of these loads Eggert had neither a purchase form nor any prior idea of the size, weight or even the number of the products. Without such basic details, the warehouse's complicated computer system was all but useless.

By contrast, eToys claim that Fingerhut's software simply didn't work and that their personnel were not able to help solve the problems. For weeks through the autumn, eToys executives ran around the warehouse with SWAT teams of problem-solving programmers and merchandisers. The Fingerhut and eToys teams would meet daily, sometimes more often, in the cavernous warehouse, to try to figure out a solution to the impending holiday chaos.

By late November – with Thanksgiving and Hanukkah fast approaching – the deluge of orders was handicapping eToys. 'It was a nightmare,' says Zambello, remembering how orders were held up somewhere between the Web site and the warehouse. Although ninety per cent of gifts made their way to the correct destinations, the rest, going wayward, provoked a flood of complaints.

Within eToys it felt like Armageddon. The successes of the previous season receded from memory as many executives took turns working in the warehouse while others answered phones in the call centres. Compared to the joyous and successful camaraderie of a year before, this year felt like a desperate attempt to cope with the tidal wave of demand. All day long, angry customers harangued the call centres' personnel about eToys' failure to deliver items they had ordered. There was little respite. Lou Zambello and Fingerhut were demonised as scapegoats. Company gossip held that it was individual failing that was to be blamed, rather than a more general corporate malaise, or the near impossibility of growing a company so quickly without glitches. The profound inadequacy of the distribution chain during the Christmas season had an enduring effect on eToys' corporate environment; the previously optimistic and utopian culture took a great blow when suddenly confronted with problems. As Lou Zambello remembers, 'These were young people who thought they were in Shangri-La, then they were hit by reality.' Toby found it a hard lesson to learn.

In the run-up to Thanksgiving, eToys haemorrhaged money on advertising, warehouses and technology. Having written in the

May prospectus that no extra money would be required for a whole year, Toby now decided to look for more. However, he and the eToys board did not want to issue new shares: that would dilute their own investments in this company of explosive value. So they found what seemed to be the perfect alternative: eToys took on a debt of $150 million on great terms, returnable at a rate of 6.25 per cent – about $9 million – a year in interest. Given that the company was then valued at almost $8 billion, it seemed unlikely that this would ever become a burden.

Meanwhile, Judge John P. Shook had set a firm date for the etoy/eToys hearing in the Superior Court the Monday after Thanksgiving. However, he hoped to conjure a settlement before then, so called a meeting in his chambers for 19 November. Both Bruce Wessel and Peter Juzwiak turned up for eToys, but it was a source of some frustration to Shook that Robert Freimuth, the local counsel from LA, was the only representative of etoy to show. Also frustrating was that eToys' attorneys simply restated their offer of $50,000 in cash and 7,000 eToys shares. Though Freimuth declared himself in no position to make a decision on behalf of his clients, he did have a counter-proposal from them which would end the case: Zai, Gramazio and Kubli wanted a cool $1 million.

Back in Zürich, Zai on behalf of etoy further raised the stakes by sending out another mass email, entitled 'Toywar, defcon 3', in which he described etoy's predicament at greater length than before and carefully outlined the value of the etoy brand. He acknowledged that 'the eToys business men are not familiar with contemporary art and therefore not aware of the value of the "etoy.BUSINESS".' But Zai imagined that Toby had at least some insight into the value of etoy, as he too had established a famous brand balanced on the precarious foundation of a single domain name. In drawing a parallel between the two 'corporations', Zai reckoned that eToys must have understood that a global brand like etoy was not something easily replaced or 'something you can pick up like a can of coke in a five minute break'.

Zai also tested the community's response to the sale of the domain name, by revealing the $500,000 offer and asking people to vote on whether or not etoy should accept it.

One person who received the email was Stephen Paul, Senior Vice President of Business Development at eToys and an old friend of Toby's. He passed it on to Bruce Wessel, who wrote a letter to Judge Shook complaining that etoy had 'publicly flaunted its disregard for eToys' intellectual property rights – in part by publicizing on the Internet the offers eToys has made and the actions of this Court.'

Most members of the Internet community, as well as friends and family of etoy, advised them to take the money and run. Among them were Douglas Rushkoff, a well-known American writer whom etoy knew, and Heath Bunting, an eccentric British Internet artist. Bunting outlined a politically correct way for them to sell: 'take the money – give half to good causes – eg anti genetics activists or zapatistas – then use the rest to buy and defend: etoy.tm'. Paul Garrin, the artist whose Name.Space project had lost an Anti-Trust battle against Network Solutions, was one of the few to advise etoy to fight on: 'Don't sell! You should counter-sue them for harassment! There is no question that etoy.-com was first, that you had used your name in commerce as well as in art . . . and didn't they approach you before to buy your name and you refused? If so, then the harassment is clear. good luck.'

As Thanksgiving got closer, lawyers on both sides prepared their final court documents. Robert Freimuth and Marcella Ballard for etoy marshalled their defence, restating their claims with some irritation, criticising the plaintiff's tactics in a letter to the court: 'Having failed in its attempt to otherwise acquire etoy, Plaintiff now attempts to use its financial wherewithal, a perceived "home field advantage" and the creative lawyering of a very good firm, to attempt to squelch what it could not buy out cheaply. This litigation is the perfect example of what the etoy site has been about in terms of its social and political protest – the financially powerful using whatever means necessary to achieve further financial gains.' They went on to state once more that etoy would be happy to settle for a figure somewhere in the region of $750,000 to $1 million.

Bruce Wessel's response to the court was riddled with frustrated annoyance. He wrote that 'etoy's primary aim appears to be the disruption of legitimate business activities on the Internet'. He further described the rather bizarre and protracted bidding process over the course of the previous months, in which he felt eToys had been 'bidding against ourselves'. Finally he made a small concession: eToys would offer 'to assist etoy in transitioning to a new name, such as by designing an interim Web page at www.etoy.com that would give visitors the option of visiting either the eToys Web site or defendant's relocated Web site under a different name.'

Wessel was confident that his case was robust and that he had a good chance of winning it. More than this, if it wasn't going to be resolved amicably then he had the most draconian sanction up his sleeve. The huge pile of evidence that he had filed back in September included a copy of Network Solutions' Dispute Policy, which both etoy and eToys had agreed to when they had registered their domains.

Generally speaking, the policy worked in the favour of large corporations in cases where an individual registered a domain name identical to their trademark; in such instances, the domain name in question would usually be closed down. Though eToys did not own a trademark identical to the etoy domain name, they hoped to use the second part of the Dispute Policy. Network Solutions could enforce a court order by putting the etoy domain 'on hold' and in any case were often prepared to err on the side of the more powerful party until a dispute was finally resolved. But whether or not this punishment could be invoked by eToys' lawyers was very dependent on the outcome of a battle between Network Solutions and the full force of the US Government that was reaching its dramatic conclusion at the same time as the court case between eToys and etoy.

*   *   *

The stand-off between the US Government and Network Solutions had begun in earnest at the beginning of 1998. It would determine the future of the Dispute Policy. Although he was no longer their Chief Executive, Don Telage was in charge of leading Network Solutions' campaign. Having spent three years successfully defending the company's monopoly to register dot-com domain names against all and sundry – hackers, professors, disgruntled domain registrants and ad hoc groups – his credentials were impeccable. But his most powerful adversary, Ira Magaziner, President Clinton's e-commerce Czar, began dedicating much of his working week to reducing the power of Network Solutions and making the Internet less dependent on them.

Magaziner began to collect his supporters in the corridors of Washington power to deal with the aspect of the Domain Name System that needed immediate resolution: the contract between Telage's Network Solutions and the US Government's National Science Foundation. This complicated contract, drafted before anyone imagined the enormous commercial implications of the Internet, allowed Network Solutions to register and then charge for domains. The agreement was due to expire in September 1998. Approaching this deadline both sides were involved in dangerous brinkmanship.

Don Telage was fighting to maintain both his company's revenue and what he thought of as the system's overall stability. His greatest bargaining chip was his control of the database, which contained more than a million dot-com registrations. Network Solutions could even claim ownership of this central part of the Internet. Theoretically, at least, they could have told the US Government that they no longer needed a contract and would continue to control the dot-com registration database and the A-Root as a monopoly. They would be answerable to no one but their shareholders.

Ira Magaziner, working inside the US Government with tough Washington lawyer Becky Burr, was determined to keep the Domain Name System in the public realm. But neither he nor Burr were by any means certain that they would be able to force the point. 'There was no document that bound them to do what we said,' Burr remembers. 'There was a chance that Network Solutions would say, "Nice try, see you later" and we might find ourselves up a creek.' The option had in fact crossed Telage's mind and he had even tried to persuade his board to go it alone. 'We were pretty much hated by everybody, so there was not much to lose,' he says. But the possibility of a private company owning the Internet naming system was too much for Commerce Department's Magaziner, who let it be known that he would even contemplate ordering Federal Marshals to recapture the A-Root Server should Network Solutions attempt to hijack it.

Telage and the management of Network Solutions now faced a terrifying decision: to give in to the US Government or to declare open hostility. In the end, it was not the threats that persuaded Network Solutions to negotiate so much as Telage's fear that going it alone would expose his company to a barrage of lawsuits that would damage their reputation, worry their investors and ultimately reduce their share price. Thus Telage and Magaziner sat down and hammered out a deal enshrined in a wide-ranging document, 'Amendment 11'. Fundamentally Telage agreed that he would not alter the A-Root without explicit instructions from the US Government. Although this seemed like a concession, it had the advantage of shielding his company from legal liability since they could now hide behind the cloak of the Government. Magaziner also managed to make Telage agree in principle to the idea that the administration of the Domain Name System would eventually be moved to a non-governmental public body.

Such a public body had been the focus for Jon Postel, the great hippy omnipotent of the Internet, when he had locked himself away with lawyers for most of 1998 to discuss how best to draft its constitution. As a result of 'Amendment 11' and Postel's labours, a rather strange non-governmental international body, the Internet Corporation for Assigned Names and Numbers (ICANN), was created, of which Postel assumed he would become the Chief Technology Officer. The board itself was made up of grandees from the old Internet community carefully chosen from those who hadn't already fought in the Domain Wars. Esther Dyson, a well-known magazine publisher and venture capitalist, became the Chair: 'The Domain Name System frankly had not seemed very interesting to me. Of course for this sin of neglect I was the one that got picked.' At the time, it didn't seem to matter that those on the board lacked intimate knowledge of the debate because Jon Postel would be there to guide them.

On 16 October 1998, however, at precisely the most delicate and crucial moment of the Domain Wars, Jon Postel unexpectedly died of post-operative complications following heart surgery. At his memorial service, Ira Magaziner read out a letter from President Clinton, then added: 'It was Jon and his colleagues who helped create a revolution that will change mankind.'

Responsible for the final negotiations between the profit-seeking Network Solutions, the embryonic public organisation ICANN and the US Government was Becky Burr. For her, Postel's death had an extraordinary impact: 'He had more authority than most anybody else. He could still command loyalty and respect, a kind of generosity of spirit that nobody else could command. So of course at that point there were no more good guys, only bad guys. It was a devastating blow ultimately. Breathtaking in its own way.'

Nonetheless, the US Government began the process of formally recognising ICANN just a week after Postel's death. The broader Internet community greeted the announcement with some suspicion, since they had played no part in its creation and because its constitution initially allowed for no democratic accountability. Don Telage was not impressed either: 'The Old Boys thought they owned the Internet, they honestly thought that it was theirs, and therefore the role of ICANN was just an institutionalisation of something that they felt was theirs anyway.'

Certainly ICANN was a very peculiar hybrid, part international organisation with responsibility for the Internet and part trade body with a membership of domain entrepreneurs and yet also partly under US Government supervision. They had a panoply of committees named with incomprehensible acronyms. Their reputation did not improve when they began to pass controversial policies. Their decision to levy an annual charge of $1 on each domain registrant, for instance, was met with a horrified outcry of 'tax' from the Internet community. That ICANN moreover refused to allow their board meetings to be open and accountable smacked more of a private corporation than of a public body. Many observers were dumbfounded by their stumbling and politically inept behaviour.

In ICANN Becky Burr had a more or less functioning public body and her next step was to try and broker an agreement between them and Network Solutions. However, Don Telage was intent on destabilising ICANN because he was worried that they would become a testing and frustrating regulatory body.

In May 1999, the combatants of the Domain Wars travelled to Berlin for an ICANN public plenary meeting. Don Telage and his team were there with 'a strategy, which was basically to keep our cool, play low key'. In a grand hotel ballroom the ICANN's board gave presentations and answered questions. Domain entrepreneurs and academics from around the world had flown in to participate – that Network Solutions had paid for some of them to travel did not go unnoticed. As Becky Burr remembers, 'There was a lot of Network Solutions-funded insurrection. They were flying very strange people around to go to these meetings and to stir stuff up. Tempers were very hot.' The meeting was arduous and unproductive; ICANN hardly managed to progress through any issues without one or another assault on their integrity. Telage went home with a videotape of a board member threatening to put Network Solutions out of business if they didn't play ball: great ammunition for the political lobbying he was carrying out in Congress in his bid to neuter ICANN.

Becky Burr encouraged ICANN to respond openly to their critics, so they dropped the plan for the $1-a-year charge and opened up their board meetings. But Telage managed to provoke a Congressional Committee to hold a hearing at which he planned to argue that ICANN were unelected and unaccountable and trying to beat down a good, solid American business. Unfortunately for him, he discovered that its date clashed with an important family gathering he had spent months organising, hiring a huge house and flying his relations in from around the country. In his place Network Solutions put forward their Chief Executive, Jim Rutt, for the climax of the battle.

In a committee room on Capitol Hill, the hearing quickly degenerated into catastrophe for Network Solutions. Jim Rutt described himself to the Congressmen as a 'simple old country boy'. Again and again he and his company were accused of stonewalling and delaying the recognition of ICANN in order to continue their near monopoly. Rutt refused to answer many questions by arguing that they were better answered by lawyers. When Congressman Bart Stupak asked him, 'Are [you] saying dot-com belongs to you?' Rutt replied, 'That is a metaphysical question I will leave to lawyers and philosophers.' He lacked a certain finesse and played straight into the hands of the Commerce Department. As Becky Burr recalls, 'I could not have asked for a better performance by Jim Rutt on behalf of Network Solutions. He simply wasn't prepared for those hearings, and as a result he came across as a bumbler. You know, he was just guileless.'

Disaster confronted Don Telage. 'Our credibility had gone down the drain,' he recalls. 'This destroyed our programme.' And so, in the week following the hearing, he held a strategy meeting with his team, saying simply, 'We have to do a deal.'

Through the summer of 1999, just as the etoy/eToys legal suit was getting under way, Telage and Burr were trying to reach a compromise. Eventually, at the beginning of November, a deal was struck in which Telage recognised the authority of ICANN, allowing them to determine the future of the A-Root. He conceded that some parts of the Domain Name System were to be owned by the public. In addition, the largest domain registry, for the top-level domain dot-com, would now be accessible by other commercial registrars. In exchange, Network Solutions managed to extract a fee for every domain registered through this new system. Crucially for the owners of domains and trademarks, the company agreed to abandon the Dispute Policy.

In place of this was to be ICANN's Uniform Dispute Resolution Policy (UDRP), adopted at their board meeting in October 1999. The UDRP meant that both sides of a domain dispute would be subject to extra-judicial arbitration, thus ending the presumption that a trademark registrant was necessarily in the right and that a Web site could be put 'on hold' until this dispute was resolved.

That the negotiations dragged on in this way bore very real relevance to the eToys versus etoy case. ICANN's UDRP was implemented by most other domain-name registrars on 29 November 1999, the very day that etoy and eToys met in court. However, the policy would not be implemented by Network Solutions for another six weeks. For etoy this was bad luck, because the UDRP would have allowed both them and eToys to use a cheaper, non-judicial arbitrator with specialised knowledge; it would also have prevented eToys filing a court order under Network Solutions' Dispute Policy in an attempt to get etoy kicked off the Web. This bizarre twist of fate was to have resounding effects in the Los Angeles courtroom.

Bruce Wessel was able to use Network Solutions' old Dispute Policy. He quoted it in the final 'Reply Memorandum in Support of the Preliminary Injunction', arguing that Network Solutions would look 'to the courts to tell it when particular domain names should be cancelled' and would readily and effectively enforce their decision. All the pieces were now in place for the confrontation in court.

Facing Hill Street, with a plain limestone wall featuring a bas-relief of Justice, the Los Angeles County Courthouse contains more than fifty courtrooms – opening off seven majestic corridors, one on each floor. At 8.30 a.m. on the morning of 29 November, seven attorneys gathered in the court called Department 53 for the strange case of eToys Inc. versus etoy. Marcella Ballard had just flown in from New York to accompany Robert Freimuth. In addition to the six protagonists there was a spectator, Intellectual Property attorney Megan Gray. Gray had been asked to attend the hearing by Claire Barliant, *The Village Voice* journalist to whom Zai had given exclusive access to etoy's story.

Gray immediately noticed eToys' battleforce in the form of Peter Juzwiak, their corporate counsel, and three attorneys from Irell & Manella including Bruce Wessel. She recalled his 'spiffy suit' and that the numbers of lawyers seemed excessive for this short injunction hearing – as it was not a full trial, the judge was unlikely to concentrate on it for more than half an hour and quite possibly for a lot less.

For more than an hour, the attorneys waited at the back of the small, wood-panelled courtroom as Judge John P. Shook, a fourteen-year veteran of the Californian Bar, dealt with other cases: a couple of personal-injury cases and one concerning an independent Hollywood film company. At 9.45 a.m., Shook slicked back his hair, peered over his half spectacles and called the case.

Marcella Ballard who lacked a California legal licence asked whether there were any objections to her representing the case. There were none. Apologising for the absence of the etoy boys, she said they hadn't been able to get a plane because of the Thanksgiving rush. In fact, unknown to her, Peter Wild, their lawyer in Zürich, had advised Zai, Gramazio and Kubli against travelling to the States fearing they might be arrested or served with yet more court papers.

'I think a good place to begin is a company called Network Solutions,' Bruce Wessel began. He then gave a short lesson about how domains were registered. He paraphrased the Dispute Policy, keen to demonstrate to Judge Shook that Network Solutions had ultimate sanction and could release the court of the continuing burden of policing the dispute. As Wessel argued, 'If a court like this one seeks and says, "I think that this domain name should be shut down", then Network Solutions says, "We will listen".'

Marcella Ballard's stern response was to point out that eToys had been forced to go to court because they could not provide the necessary 'identical' trademark to etoy.com that Network Solutions would demand in order to delete the domain. Instead, she said, with a weak case, they were now making an 'emotional appeal'.

Since this was a preliminary injunction hearing, there was need neither to prove the claims nor call witnesses; each side was simply trying to demonstrate that, in a trial, they were likely to prevail. Things quickly moved on to the heart of the case: the various trademark claims. Wessel put his central argument: 'eToys has a registered trademark for eToys. Under trademark law that gives us the presumption that we have the rights to the name.' To the opposing counsel, this statement was so bold and so tendentious as to be somewhat galling; while it wasn't strictly inaccurate, it did imply that eToys had more rights to the name – despite the trump card in trademark law usually being the question of use. But Judge John P. Shook had little experience of this sort of dispute, never having heard a trademark case in his court. So he asked the attorneys for etoy, 'Did etoy ever own a Federal Registration Trademark?' Of course the answer was no, but Marcella Ballard argued that there was no need to: etoy had commonlaw rights as a well-established and famous brand long before eToys came along. Her arguments seemed to fall on deaf ears.

The Judge appeared very impressed by the idea that eToys had a registered trademark; it conferred a certain authority. He asked for confirmation: 'And as I understand it, the plaintiff [eToys] does own a Federal Registration Trademark, eToys, and that goes back to January of 1990, according to your pleadings.' Wessel was only too happy to agree – 'Right, Your Honour' – and went on to explain how eToys had bought the trademark from the New York toy distributor ETNA.

All this was too much for the beleaguered Ballard. She accused Wessel of 'making another emotional appeal' that failed to deal with the letter of the law. She endeavoured to clarify her point: the test, she said, was whether or not, when etoy was founded in 1994, their trademark would have caused confusion with

ETNA, *not* whether it was confusing five years later to the customers of an Internet toy seller.

Ballard then tried to turn the argument to the issue of property rights: 'Are we entitled to have this piece of land on the Internet?' she asked like the cowboy frontiersman of the Internet gone by. 'eToys did not run a title search on this piece of land, and they did not do due diligence on the corporate name when they chose it and created it.' Since trademark rights can be acquired simply by *using* a virgin name, as if planting a stake in an undiscovered land, this was a good argument. But Bruce Wessel was not about to let this go unchallenged: 'I think you can sum up the etoy corporation argument as, we got there first because we registered our domain name first. That is true in many domain-name cases, but who gets there first does not decide the question.' This was a clever claim in so far as it focused not on the rule of use but on the small number of exceptions to it.

Having failed to make much headway, Ballard then tried to explain a little about what etoy actually were – their tongue-in-cheek approach to business, and how eToys had missed the joke. She said, 'They are artists, and this is what they do. This is their baby.' Judge Shook peered over his glasses. 'I have heard that expression before, the name etoy was their baby.' It seemed as if he might be grasping the case, and so Ballard tried to move it on to a different footing by answering the accusations of pornography and support for terrorism. But before she could manoeuvre the argument towards the issue of liberty, she was presumptively cut off by Judge Shook: 'The issue here is not the issue of free speech.'

For half an hour, the two lawyers argued backwards and forwards. Eventually, Judge John P. Shook put an end to the discussion and pronounced his verdict: 'Anyway, it seems to me that there is really enough evidence to grant the preliminary injunction . . . there is a pretty good argument that some of the defendants' conduct in operating their Web site is, indeed, unlawful.' The order was to prevent etoy operating the Web site www.etoy.com, displaying or exploiting the domain name in relation to the Digital Hijack and selling shares in the United States. In his final statement, he pronounced that he especially worried about 'the great danger of children being exposed to profane and hardcore pornographic issues on the computer.'

In front of Judge Shook was the proposal for an injunction submitted by eToys' lawyers. Shook dated and signed it. Robert Klieger, an attorney for eToys, returned to his office and faxed it to Network Solutions.

With it was a request for etoy.com to be shut down.

10
Toywar

'In societies where modern conditions of production prevail, all of life presents itself as an immense accumulation of spectacles. Everything that was directly lived has moved away into a representation.'

Guy Debord, *The Society of the Spectacle*, 1967

Part 1: Shut Down and Gagged

It was long past midnight when the phone rang in etoy's office in Zürich. Zai had been expecting a call from their lawyers with news of the court hearing. Instead, he found himself talking to Claire Barliant from *The Village Voice*. When she asked for Zai's reaction to the judge's ruling, he had no idea which way the hearing had gone. etoy's lawyers had assured them that there was only the slimmest chance of the injunction being granted. So when Barliant told him of the outcome 'it was a major shock.' He recalls, 'We had assumed that the judge would understand that we were right.' Zai pressed Barliant for details, but she didn't have many. All she could really tell him was that Megan Gray, who had attended the hearing at Barliant's request, had said that the case didn't pass 'the giggle test', in as much as eToys should have been ridiculed out of the courtroom rather than winning their plea.

Gramazio and Kubli also took the news badly. That night, Gramazio sorrowfully scrolled through etoy's server log-files, the records of each visitor's IP number, or domain name – their precise location or address on the Internet. Having nothing better to do than wait for the next morning's legal advice, he took the opportunity to pore through the details contained in these files. Soon he realised that a particular visitor was returning to the site every twenty minutes or so throughout the night. The IP number came from within the eToys.com domain.

As a last act of defiance, Gramazio hacked together a Web page that would appear only to this visitor from eToys. It featured the question: 'Do you like to destroy people?' The viewer was asked to tick 'yes' or 'no'. When the visitor answered 'no', Gramazio fired up another page: 'Do you really like your job?' The entertainment provided some solace amid his devastation. 'It was an extremely cool feeling,' Gramazio remembers, 'to know that The Other was out there; that I could talk to him and make him feel insecure, and that I could block out his view of what was really happening at etoy.com.'

The next morning, Peter Wild received a fax from eToys' lawyers, Irell & Manella. He phoned Zai and advised him that etoy should take down their Web site – otherwise they would face substantial penalties. He also explained that to flout American law would make it very difficult for any of the etoy collective ever to return to the US. Included in the fax Wild had received was a copy of the one, sent by Irell & Manella to Network Solutions just hours after the hearing: their request for etoy.com to be put 'on hold'.

This proposal was either audacious or naïve, because it attempted to extend the scope of the court injunction by failing to acknowledge the difference between a Web site (www.etoy.com) and a complete domain (etoy.com). Included in etoy's domain were their other servers, for email (mail.etoy.com) and radio (broadcast.etoy.com). While the injunction drafted by eToys demanded only that etoy cease 'operating a Web site with the domain name www.etoy.com', this request effectively asked Network Solutions for the closure of the entire domain etoy.com. Like a net, this would catch more fish than those court-approved targets.

The request had been hurried to Network Solutions almost immediately after the court hearing, but initially provoked no response; the etoy domain name remained 'live' for the next day without any intervention from eToys or Network Solutions.

On the afternoon of 30 November, Zai, Kubli and Gramazio gathered to discuss their options. At first they considered simply leaving the Web site online, but quickly realised that the stakes were now too high and their resources desperately lacking – they could hardly even pay their lawyers' bills. This was no time for defiance.

To make the 'www' Web site inactive would be as easy as deleting a document from a computer. So Gramazio logged in and typed in the command. Then he rose from his seat and told the others that he could not bring himself to press the 'enter' button to complete the task. Zai also refused, leaving only Kubli. 'He had to do it,' says Zai, 'because it was his world, the world of law and lawyers, that forced us to do such a thing.' And so, at 6.06 p.m. that day, Kubli pressed the button. The computer screen went to '>'; it was all over. 'Our server had been running for over four years with maybe three days on which it was out of order,' recalls Zai. 'It was just too much to stand.' The next time someone typed www.etoy.com into a Web browser, they would simply find an error message informing them that the server could not be found.

When it was all over, Gramazio looked over the server logs for the minutes just prior to the end of www.etoy.com – and found that the last person to view their site was someone from inside eToys.com.

Sad as the day was for etoy, they still had their campaign to focus on. This was consolation at least. The email system still worked – after all, mail.etoy.com wasn't, so far as they knew, affected by the injunction. And it was still possible to view the Web site by typing the full eleven-digit IP number, 146.228.204.72, into a Web browser, dialling directly into the machine that underlay the www.etoy.com address.

* * *

At the same time as etoy were shutting down their Web site, it was morning on the US West Coast. In Seattle, the representatives of more than a thousand Non-Governmental Organisations (NGOs), along with tens of thousands of other individuals, convened to protest outside meetings of the World Trade Organisation (WTO). They were campaigning against global economic liberalisation and the effect that this would have on the world's poor. They carried placards with slogans like 'End Capitalism Now' and 'Down with the WTO'. By 9 a.m., the police had blocked off twenty streets; as the pressure closed in on them, a group of 200 demonstrators occupied an intersection between two main roads and refused to move. Ten minutes later, the police sent tear-gas and plastic bullets into the crowd, providing some with the opportunity to turn the peaceful demonstration into a riot. Just as Kubli completed the etoy shut-down, the first major confrontation kicked off. During the next few hours, police and protestors had running battles. Some demonstrators broke windows of a McDonald's restaurant and a Gap store. Later, the city was put under curfew; the Mayor declared the protest a Civil Emergency and the National Guard took control of the streets.

Because of the unprecedented size and anger of the protest and the violence displayed by both sides, stories of the events were carried on every major global-news outlet. That so many people had actually come to Seattle was proof that a new movement had suddenly come of age – a movement made up of a radical coalition of environmentalists, anti-capitalists, trade unionists and anti-poverty campaigners. More than this, the protest was evidence of the power of the Internet as a force for political organisation, as it had been galvanised and organised via the simplest of technologies: the email list.

Email lists are generally based on communities centred around a common interest – be it sweatshop labour or rainforest preservation. Within any particular group, anyone who writes an email will have it forwarded to all those who have subscribed. In lively communities, hundreds of emails are posted every day; questions are asked, opinions expressed and everything is distributed among the members.

In the months before the Seattle protest, activists had used such lists to mobilise their followers, co-ordinate actions and discuss strategy. 'Everybody clear your calendars,' read an email posted by the Public Citizens' Global Trade Watch, a lead organiser of the anti-WTO protests. 'We're going to Seattle at the end of November.' Every appropriate Internet service was pressed into aiding the cause, from those Web sites offering background political information to others listing accommodation in the houses of sympathetic Seattle locals. During the days of the protests, the Internet was the medium through which the participants communicated and co-ordinated the events happening on the streets and informed the world.

The Web itself became a means to assault the WTO. One group, the British electrohippies, announced a version of Ricardo Dominguez's Zapatista FloodNet. It was used to facilitate virtual sit-ins against the WTO's official Web site which were supported, so the electrohippies claimed, by thousands of activists from around the world. In another attack, Ray Thomas and ®™ark had set up a Web site at GATT.org, satirising the General Agreement on Tariffs and Trade, which is the principal treaty managed by the WTO. The site appeared at first glance to be official as it had the WTO's graphics and colours. Only on closer reading did it become apparent that the texts were anti-capitalist and anti-corporate tracts. ®™ark – for the time being, at least – were too busy to realise that their friends from etoy were in trouble.

As etoy in Zürich tried to come to terms with the demise of their Web site, news of the shut-down was travelling the Internet. In New York, Wolfgang Staehle, from The Thing, the artists' Internet Service Provider and the registrant of toywar.com, was told of the injunction by Claire Barliant. Having already been stoked up by etoy, he promptly fired off an email to all the members of the The Thing's mailing list. He wrote, 'We are all sick and tired of being pushed around by crazed dot-com people and slash and burn casino capitalists and their lawyer dogs. The events in Seattle show that there is growing support for a "World Order" that is not solely based on maximizing corporate profits.'

Staehle's message was soon picked up by a woman called Natalie Bookchin, who ran her own email list, OutOfLine, which, although primarily aimed at her students at the California Institute of Arts, had a much wider readership. Imperceptibly, the news of the etoy injunction began to spread from one list to another.

The next day, on 1 December, *The Village Voice* published the first newspaper article on the subject, 'E-TOY STORY', by Claire Barliant. She quoted an email from Zai about the court decision which, he wrote, 'shows how dangerous it is to take today's perverted financial markets as a topic for an art project . . . as an artist you have to deal with "personal/private" problems . . . and not to jump on things like the stock market etc. you are tolerated as long as you don't disturb!' Bruce Wessel had also been interviewed. He countered, 'If someone has a Web site, the question is whether they have worldwide rights to use the name in all circumstances just because they registered the name first. They were a European-based organisation, and we have no problem with them having a European-based site, such as .ch, which is the Switzerland domain.' This was a somewhat pointless claim, given that etoy.ch was owned by the Swiss village Etoy and eToys had already registered eToys.ch without planning to set up a site there.

Barliant had interviewed Joichi Ito, too, and noted that he had been named as one of the fifty 'cyber elite' by *Time* magazine. By then, Ito was Chairman of Infoseek Japan, a search-engine company that had recently been bought by Disney, and was naturally a little nervous about putting things in print that his new bosses might not have approved of. Nonetheless, he revealed his countercultural roots: 'Basically the Internet is not about capitalism and money. It's about people doing what they want to do,' he told Barliant. 'They [etoy] are the kind of media artists who push back on stuff like this.'

Meanwhile Zai was working feverishly on an etoy press release. Finding the correct tone for his message was proving difficult because, although the aim was to attract the Internet community's attention, his lawyers had advised him to avoid any remarks that could later be exploited in court. He was also being constantly distracted by mails and phonecalls from supporters.

In addition, Joichi Ito was now busy lobbying at the very highest level of the digital elite – making contact with his friends such as John Vasconcellos, the State Senator for Silicon Valley, and Bill Schrader, the Chairman of PSI Net, one of the world's biggest Internet service providers. Ito forwarded Zai an email he had sent to his old friend John Perry Barlow pleading that he and the Electronic Frontier Foundation take up the plight. Finally, in support of their cause, Ito wanted to buy more etoy shares.

The pace at which the details of etoy's case spread around the Net was increasing. Many of those who received the news passed it on to other email lists, and their friends and colleagues. Barliant's *Village Voice* piece served as a catalyst to the waves of emails; soon members of the New York-based digital-art mailing list rhizome.org pledged their support. The core group of activists was swelling.

In Zürich, at 7.21 a.m. on 2 December, a sleepless Zai sent out etoy's official press release. 'now the etoy.CORPORATION will strike back to the maximum extent under american and european law,' it read.

> etoy now prepares for the battle against one of the biggest e-commerce companies in the world, a company which seeks to maximise profit with the take over of the domain etoy.com ostensibly in the name of family values. using their deep pockets and lobbying power to curb choice, dissent and free speech and make the Internet a more colorless and less exciting place.

etoy announced the opening of the toywar.com site, which would be run by one of Wolfgang Staehle's employees at The Thing. To keep their hands clean, they claimed that hackers had stolen material from etoy.com and posted it on the new Web site. 'the etoy.BOARD cannot control or stop the tremendous resistance community from acting,' the press release said. 'it does not know the people involved in this action at this moment and it does not know what the future of toywar.com . . . may be.'

One of the subscribers of Natalie Bookchin's OutOfLine email list was a man called Reinhold Grether in Constance, Germany. Part genius, part madman, with big grey hair and wayward gesticulation, Grether plays the part of an amiable eccentric and likes to claim that having read three books a day for years has made him the 'best-read European'. On finishing his thesis entitled 'Longing for a World-Wide Culture' in 1994, Grether began to study the anthropology of the Internet only to find that the work didn't bring him quite the acclaim he had hoped. Having been denied funding grants, and with his only financial support coming from a programme for unemployed academics at the University of Constance, he found himself in increasingly desperate straits. With a profound contempt for traditional academia he daydreamed of revenge.

When Grether read the etoy message, he was electrified; he says that an inner voice told him that this was a significant moment in his life. He summoned up his resources and whispered to himself, 'Now, Reinhold, jump!' He grabbed a dictionary and in less than twenty minutes carefully composed his first English text, which he posted to the rhizome.org email list: 'Subject: urgently needed. A worldwide campaign to boycott eToys.com – a FLOOD.net action against their Web site – massive individual protests on their Web site.' Later, he would grandiosely refer to his 'famous three-line mail' and, with some overstatement, claim credit for singlehandedly provoking a 'big autonomous revolt'.

By the following day, Grether had received several responses to his mail and was so excited he could not sleep. Instead, using a computer at the end of his bed, he started to research eToys. Quickly he discovered that the toy company was in a financially precarious position; their value was absurd and could only decline. Wouldn't it be amazing, he thought, if activists could sink a billion-dollar corporation?

Straight away, Grether wrote another email to his chosen mailing list headed 'a new toy for you'. It read: 'Here comes a marvellous new toy for you: E*TOY. E*TOY is a toy to destroy eToys.com.' With eToys' share price standing at $55, Grether issued a challenge to the online community: 'All you have to do is TO BRING THIS NUMBER DOWN.'

The methods he suggested included hacker attacks on the eToys site, the creation of anti-eToys Web sites ('Start a Web site "Parents Against Etoys".'), anti-eToys postings on investor bulletin-boards ('Enter a forum and communicate seriously or with a clear disinformation strategy.') and the general spreading of news about eToys' bad behaviour. Still struggling with the English language, Grether managed to outline what was at stake: 'If the electronic vandalism of eToys triumphs, you can forget about netculture and net-art. You will have a totalitarian consumerist anti-culture instead of a protuberant workhouse of ideas.' To further goad potential activists, he wrote, 'Imagine, it's a multi user game and there are thousands of players worldwide.'

On Friday 3 December, four days after the injunction, Slashdot. org – a Web site self-described as 'News for Nerds, Stuff that Matters' – got involved. The site was a key source of information for a million or so hackers who shared information about network technology, computer programming and, most importantly, Linux, the free and enormously powerful operating system that had been collectively and altruistically built by the members of this community.

Jamie McCarthy, a regular Slashdot contributor, wrote a piece entitled 'No etoy for Christmas' describing the case. He commented, 'In the year of the e-tailer, what kind of speech scares corporations more than anything? Disrespect. Artists who don't play by the rules. People who don't understand that business is a serious business.' McCarthy continued by calling for a consumer boycott of eToys, which he would begin by taking his own toy shopping elsewhere. Realising that this was a token protest, he noted that it would at least bring him some brief solace: 'I need everything I can get to help me make sense of the bizarre orgy of spirituality-soaked commerce that serves as the endcap of each year. Ho ho ho.'

In the twenty-four hours following the release of 'No etoy for Christmas', tens of thousands of people read the piece and more than three hundred Slashdotters wrote rejoinders, pouring out their anger, irritation and annoyance at the actions of eToys. It was one of the biggest responses that Slashdot had ever experienced.

Many lamented that the Internet had changed since the days when it was little more than a wilderness. One contributor, 'Dr Caleb', wrote, 'Does anyone remember the good old days? . . . When the Internet was a place for sharing ideas? Who let big business in here anyway? It's all one big commercial now!' Others moaned that the Internet had been co-opted 'in the name of power and money'. What also had annoyed the writers was that many corporations who had ignored the Internet in its early years were trying to seize control of it now that it was valuable.

McCarthy's original piece had been posted in a Slashdot section called 'Your Rights Online'; many responses to it complained that the court case imposed new restrictions on their freedom of expression. Like John Perry Barlow had done five years before, some questioned the jurisdiction of the land-based courts on the regulation of the free lands of cyberspace. One anonymous poster incredulously asked, 'so on Internet-related matters, anyone can sue anyone anywhere on earth using only local rules. How do they expect to enforce the ruling anyway?'

Amid all the impassioned debate, the Slashdot community began to encourage each other to use their consumer power. 'Groucho' wrote, 'eToys is misunderstanding e-market and e-ethics. Having money is not synonym of having reason . . . The e-market are we the people that are on line and work hard for making the net a growing and universal place where justice, fairness and knowledge flow for all.'

In calls for action, many Slashdotters urged their colleagues to phone eToys with complaints. Others composed emails to eToys and posted them on Slashdot to be copied and sent on in numbers. One of these read, 'the Internet is not just a tool to line your own pockets, especially not at the expense of others, others' freedoms, rights, or tolerance, regardless of which nation hosts them. I have no use for you . . . It would be too bad if your own stupidity and greed put you out of business, but those that sow the seed of intolerance should enjoy their bitter harvest.' More aggressive tactics were also suggested, such as taking out the eToys.com Web site or flooding the company's computer system with a virus by email.

For many of the community, this whiff of revolutionary fervour made it a fine moment to be alive. As one anonymous poster wrote, 'I'm feeling like Che Guevara after an ambush . . . THESE PEOPLE NEED TO SUFFER . . . BURN ETOYS!!!'

The most plaintive response actually came from within eToys. One insider posted, 'Actually, the tech team here at eToys all reads Slashdot already.' Rob Johnson and Shay had built the eToys Web site with free software created with the co-operation of many Slashdot community members, 'open source' software that carried with it the utopian dreams of original hacker ethics. As a consequence, eToys' servers ran free Apache software, just as etoy's did, and the eToys Engineering Department had, up to this moment, been the model citizens of the community that was now attacking them.

Email addresses of eToys executives were posted on Slashdot and they too began to receive protest emails. Some were coherent arguments in favour of etoy; others were barrages of abuse and swear-words.

In response, Peter Juzwiak, eToys' in-house counsel, sent an email to the whole company explaining the lawsuit and instructing everybody not to comment. Kathy Hernandez, eToys' employee number five, was bemused; she remembered how she had accidentally logged on to etoy.com two years before, when eToys had just started up. She had thought it was 'no big deal'. She wrote back to Juzwiak, 'You know they were there before us.'

Josh Geller, a Director of Quality Assurance at eToys, says of the period, 'It was uncomfortable to work for a company that was taking advantage, and using traditional corporate business practice to shut out legitimate licence holders.' To him, this miscalculation by Toby and eToys' senior management revealed a more general failure of judgement; he realised for the first time that the management had a 'pretty severe case of self-importance as well as hubris about their business model.'

On the afternoon the Slashdot piece went out, the dispute spilled on to investor message-boards. Someone with the nickname 'busman70' began the campaign against the shareholders, exactly as Reinhold Grether had previously suggested. On fool.-com, a popular bulletin board for investors, 'busman70' politely pointed people towards the Slashdot article: 'I don't now [*sic*] how you feel about the situation but to me is [*sic*] seems very unfair and very foolish! What do you think? Will it have any financial effect coming to Christmas?'

However, 'busman70' and his fellow activists were not welcome voices and their comments proved particularly unpopular with those small investors who had been nervously watching the eToys share price slide downhill over the previous few days. One of the board's opinion leaders, with the moniker 'FoolyFoolFool', tetchily replied, 'Anything coming from slashdot is suspect from the start. I am told eToys offered to purchase the etoy domain, but for some reason the "artists" (pornographers, in my opinion) didn't take it. Probably because they get more press from the fight.' Similar arguments broke out on investor bulletin-boards elsewhere.

At the end of the day, Reinhold Grether checked out the eToys share price and was overjoyed to find that it had gone down to $53.8, having lost just over a dollar in twenty-four hours. He pretended that his game had already proved effective, and congratulated the 'great bunch' of activists, 'Your talent is all the more respectable because the overall Nasdaq market gained 2%. I'm sure you'll bring them down to zero.'

In Century City, eToys' lawyer Bruce Wessel was keen to press on to a full-length trial. In preparation for this, he began the 'discovery' process – where both sides reveal documents to the court. From etoy's lawyer Peter Wild he demanded not only biographies of all the agents but also every document relating to etoy's business contacts and every article that had ever been written about them, as well as all the bank statements, their tax forms, passport copies, the log-files from their server and details of all their US trips and contacts with US citizens. Wessel's request letter listed almost 500 documents to be provided and instructed Wild that every etoy agent, past and present, was to appear in person in one month at Irell & Manella's Los Angeles office where they would be questioned and their answers transcribed.

Zai, Gramazio and Kubli were shocked. 'just insane! they are nuts!!!!!!' Zai ranted in an email to his closest associates, 'just to fuck us and to make us spend millions and lose energy!' He was afraid, but the fear served only to fuel his rebellious spirit. He promised that eToys would soon learn something about the Internet community and the global economy, then he signed off with a final threat: 'We start fighting fire with fire now.'

Toby, meanwhile, was caught up in a round of conference appearances and magazine interviews and was busy glad-handing investors and cheering his management on. Always optimistic he now became positively evangelical about eToys' prospects. 'We want to be the leading children's e-brand in the next century,' he told the *Industry Standard*. 'We don't see anybody who's close to doing that.' While he was often available to boost his company, he never spoke to the press about the etoy case. With masses of coverage in newspapers around the world in the Christmas run-up, eToys were the story of the moment – a cheery, seasonal success story; there was seldom mention of the trademark dispute.

On 7 December 1999, eight days after the hearing, eToys' share price closed down at $51.43.

Zai was invited on to a New York-based radio show, which was supported by the hacker magazine *2600*. He gave an interview down the line, explaining how etoy were not about to get a new domain name, and gave out the original site's numeric IP address. He wanted eToys to know that another domain name wasn't good enough for etoy. He did, however, mutter plaintively, 'America is very powerful.'

In its second week, news of the Toywar campaign began to spread to further levels of the media. As the previous week's papers had been full of news reports, opinion pieces and editorials about the events in Seattle, they were now ready to report another story about a powerful Goliath opposed by a brave David. *Telepolis*, for instance, an influential German culture and technology news site, ran an article, as did a French group called *Multimédium*. And the first mainstream newspaper piece on the case appeared, in *The New York Times*, on 9 December. Its author, Matthew Mirapaul, argued that etoy had a reasonably strong case despite their initial court set-back.

Fuelled by the success of the battle against the WTO, online activists kept the assault alive. Around the Web, momentum was slowly building in the form of individual projects. John Weir, a Berkeley-based artist and graphic designer, created a protest site under the domain name eviltoy.com and several others followed his example, with sites called BoycotteToys, Freetoy and QuiteToys. The sites were as individual as their creators, and ranged from the abusive to the comically satiric. For example, The Cosmic Baseball Association pitched the two sides against each other as if the case were a sport, with team biographies and a score sheet. John Weir also created an email list, edited by Berkeley philosophy student Richard Zach, which became an almost daily update of news from the etoy frontline. By the end of the month, there would be about 1,000 subscribers to this list.

etoy in Zürich were being deluged with supportive emails. It was clear that their campaign was swelling from the ground upwards. Because of the Internet, their supporters did not have to rely on street protests and the traditional media to get their point across. Indeed, by the time the daily newspapers began running stories, there were already hundreds of contributors, activists and campaigners working for the Toywar effort.

On the evening of 9 December, eToys' shares were traded at $48.75.

Matthew Mirapaul's *New York Times* article acted as a media wake-up call and was followed the next day by a story in *The*

Washington Post. In it, a spokeswoman for the Electronic Frontier Foundation declared, 'The etoy injunction is a travesty, and the folks at eToys ought to be ashamed of themselves for misusing the law like this . . . The artists at etoy were not competing with eToys and had their domain name registered years before eToys registered their own.'

At the eToys headquarters, Ken Ross, Vice President of Communications, began spinning their side of the story. As a veteran of public relations for blue-chip corporations, he was more used to carefully placing a few choice pieces in high-profile publications than fighting the many-headed hydra of a Web-based campaign. Rather than trying openly to win the argument on the investor bulletin-boards and the Net-art email lists, he focused his counter-attack on the print media and sent out copies of images from the etoy Web site, including pictures of an almost-naked man in fetish gear. Ross commented, 'It's not our intent in any way, shape or form to comment on what's art and what's not art but I really believe that if the general public were to see this stuff the vast majority would find it offensive.' He also claimed that eToys were trying to resolve the matter amicably; in the event of failure to do so, it was 'responsible and common sense' to ask a court to resolve the dispute. As a competent spin doctor, he added, 'We absolutely respect their freedom and their points of view.'

WIRED jumped on the bandwagon. Steve Kettman, their Berlin correspondent, gave Toywar more importance than any other journalist had so far. 'It's a fight that should have Net-conscious people at least as fired up as the mobs in Seattle were last week, since it could define the rules of engagement between corporations and creative types for years to come.' One of his central concerns echoed that of some Slashdotters – could a US court truly regulate the Internet's international wildernesses?

On the evening of 10 December, eToys share price closed at a new low, $45.12. In the ten days since their injunction against etoy was granted, eToys had lost thirty per cent of their value; whilst NASDAQ's had risen by five per cent.

Meanwhile, eToys' faxed request had been stuck in Network Solutions' bureaucracy for a fortnight. Finally, in Herndon, Virginia, a decision was reached based on the wide-ranging but soon-to-be-outdated Dispute Policy. The court order did not ask for the closure of the etoy.com domain, merely for the closing down of the Web site, but Network Solutions put the entire domain 'on hold'. This included etoy's email server, so effectively extending the scope of the injunction beyond the judge's decision.

On Friday 10 December, Network Solutions removed etoy.com from the complete list of dot-com domains. In the next twenty-four hours, the twelve back-up domain-name servers situated around the world – the B-Servers – updated their files. The new list of dot-com domains, which no longer included etoy.com, was in turn copied by local domain-name servers, those used by consumers in corporate offices and at home. Slowly, anyone who sent an email to etoy.com found their messages sent back – their local servers could find no record of the domain. In Zürich, the volume of incoming etoy emails decreased and Zai thought that they had somehow been 'hacked by the enemy'.

When Zai, Gramazio and Kubli discovered on 12 December that their domain had been erased, they felt desperate. This was a catastrophe; the lifeline to their community had been cut off. They had not imagined that this, the worst of scenarios, could ever be possible. They controlled some other domains including toybomb.com which they had prudently registered in November but it would take days to communicate the new email address to the Internet community. Zai poured out his rage into a press release: 'this is robbery of digital territory. american imperialism, corporate destruction and bulldozing in the way of the 19th century.' In an email to selected supporters he was even more explicit, claiming that this was 'ABUSE OF THE LAW SYSTEM TO DESTROY OUR RIGHTS TO TALK TO PEOPLE'. He ranted against those 'hypocritical bastards' within eToys, 'who tell the press that they have no time to comment because they have to concentrate on the xmas traffic on the eToys servers . . .

what a cynical perspective. and network solutions doesn't pick up the phone. they don't even call back our lawyers.'

Yet this further blow to etoy, ten days after the injunction was granted, meant that the war had taken a turn: what had once been a commercial dispute was now about freedom of speech and Internet liberty and justice. To many commentators in the press, on investor bulletin-boards and on email lists, it seemed clear that a bullying $8 billion corporation was trying to gag a group of almost powerless artists. And it was at this moment that one of the Internet's most effective ambassadors and lobbyists, John Perry Barlow, finally stepped into the fray. With vociferousness, he began to defend etoy: 'This is the point where people begin to realise there is a difference between the Internet industry and the Internet community, and the Internet community needs to bind itself together and find a common voice.' Barlow harked back to a previous age and a recently deceased guiding light: 'If Jon Postel had been alive, he would be in tears.'

Part 2: Fighting Back

News of etoy's plight had spread like a virus through the global Internet community. First it had been posted on to one small-circulation, digital-art mailing list; it had then spilled over to the other parts of the online artistic community. From there, it had jumped across the communal divide into the forums of the hackers and software geeks, who in turn took the issue on to the investor bulletin-boards and into the homes of the investors. The number of people writing and getting involved had steadily increased, demonstrating the Internet's extraordinary power as a means of communication and organisation.

By the time the news bubbled into the mainstream media, thousands of people were already informed and hundreds had contributed to etoy's campaign. These people came from all over the world – from Europe, the US and even Korea – and it was remarkable that this enormous response had been seeded by such a tiny force: Zai, Gramazio and Kubli and just a few sympathetic souls. Never before had such a large conflict been so determinedly of the Internet. Previously battles had been fought between the Internet community and 'outside' forces, such as governments or corporations; in the Toywar, both parties existed online. Ultimately the battlefield was not the courtroom or the press, it was the Internet itself – initially its forums and, later, the very guts of its technology.

The virus had already infected a huge population. Now it was to achieve pandemic proportions, aided by the arrival of the past masters of Internet activism, ®™ark and Ricardo Dominguez.

'We didn't even ask etoy; the issue was ours,' says ®™ark's Ray Thomas, whose mischievous grins and a tendency to giggle make him a kind of Laughing Cavalier of the anti-corporate movement. 'The point was that eToys were attacking this art group, who were using the Internet as it was really meant to be used, as a public space. And this company, for rigorous bottom-line reasons, was trying to squelch them. We went in like bulls. We made it an issue and we focused attention in the ways that we wanted.'

Looking for a way to coalesce the fragmented Internet community Thomas saw this as a perfect opportunity. Of course, ®™ark would also reap their own, non-profit reward, a 'whole lot of name recognition which would help our reputation, and help our "bottom line" of cultural profit,' he recalls.

Thomas and other ®™ark members began to create a unified umbrella of support under which could sit many different campaigns – media, financial and technological. Their first step was to find a figurehead, an Internet celebrity to back their vision. To fill this role, they asked Mark Pauline, who ran Survival Research Laboratories, a group who organised public performances of massive mechanical monsters gnashing their teeth and waving their limbs. For a decade he had been a key figure in the San Francisco digerati and now became the Fund Manager for ®™ark's etoy fund.

®™ark's next task was to establish themselves as co-ordinators of the wide-ranging campaign. On 12 December, two days after the whole domain of etoy.com had ceased to function, they put out a press release in which the rules of corporate spin were strictly observed. It had a catchy title ('NEW INTERNET "GAME" DESIGNED TO DESTROY ETOYS.COM'), authoritative statements in the third person ('®™ark has joined the growing torrent of outrage, sometimes violent in tone, against Internet toy giant eToys'), and of course a corporate spokesperson, Ernesto Lucha (which means 'Ernesto fights' in Spanish), an invented persona of the already pseudonymous Ray Thomas. In the release, Lucha said, 'This game is much more exciting than any other computer game because you have a real-world bad guy to fight. Many of the projects – boycotts, pickets, email campaigns – can be played by anyone, while other projects – countersuing eToys, disturbing the eToys servers, etc. – require specialized work. There's something for everyone and we know we can easily count on 10,000 players to start with.'

®™ark's press release created a new wave of media coverage. An *Inter@ctive Week* headline screamed, 'Protest group out to "destroy" eToys', and *WIRED news* warned 'E-Riots Threaten eToys.com'. For the first time, a syndicated news agency, Associated Press, reported the case: 'Online Toy Store Under Attack'. The news quickly arrived on the screens of countless newspaper offices around the world – even the *Sydney Morning Herald* ran a piece.

This fresh burst of publicity came as a boost to the 'toy warriors' fighting on the frontline of the investor bulletin-boards. Activists posted the latest headlines into the forums. 'I would advise everyone to sell before this boycott – and this stock – gets ugly!' a member of fool.com nicknamed 'dominiquefp' warned. 'Lets say one hacker succeeds and closes down this site . . . what then? Get out, thats my advice . . . these attacks are not drawing favorable publicity and no one wants to shop at an online shop where hackers can get your credit card information!!!' Others threatened eToys, while some explained that their site could easily be brought down; as one person assertively wrote, 'the stock will continue to drop – period.'

On the investor bulletin-board it was not, however, a one-sided argument. The army of small shareholders holding eToys stock were frustrated at the collapse of their share price. Some responded to the activists and nay-sayers on the list with equal aggression. 'Screw the artists,' exclaimed one. 'Why don't you shut up?' asked another. 'People invest their hard earned money into companies like eToys for good reasons. Don't come up here asking us to boycott a company we obviously believe in and have our dollars invested in. That is a sacrifice that will not be made on your behalf, Scum.' Some vented their anger by abusing the campaigners as 'selfish, self-righteous morons' who were hurting the hundreds of consumer investors who had their savings tied up in the toy company's stock. 'Whether or not eToys' stock goes up or down means my life,' pleaded one fool.com regular.

Whatever the cause, many eToys investors were becoming itchy with the situation and thinking of selling. As a bulletin-board member by the nickname of 'vsega72' wrote, 'I don't know guys. This is going nowhere but down. I'm on the verge of selling and taking a huge loss since I bought at $59. Is there anyone that can convince me to hold?' Some lost their nerve and sold despite their losses. One regular contributor since the shares first traded in May wrote, 'Well, guess I'm going to sell out tomorrow morning. Tired of losing sleep over this.'

Nonetheless, on the morning of Monday 13 December, eToys' shares opened at $48.50, almost $3 up from the previous Friday's price. This was perhaps a result of Anthony Noto, Goldman Sachs' star e-commerce analyst, having upgraded his rating for eToys to a 'buy'. He wrote that the forty-two per cent decline in the value of the stock since October was overdone because eToys had an excellent management and one of the best selections of toys on the Web. Among some journalists there was cynicism about Noto's motives for championing the eToys stock; Goldman Sachs were the lead underwriter of eToys' IPO, after all, and it might be better for the bank if eToys' value did not collapse further. Whatever, on the same day, the stock fell from its morning high to trade at $45.93 at closing.

eToys were now facing the few final days of Christmas ordering. Delivery took three or four days, so this week was the last opportunity to meet the Christmas deadline for customers. Now the challenge was do or die; eToys had to bank sufficient orders or face a cruel punishment from Wall Street. It was the culmination of two and a half years of planning by Toby and the management team. On the eToys Web site, tens of thousands of customers were tapping in orders and their credit-card numbers every day. In Sunnyvale, the heart of Silicon Valley, eToys' servers were dealing with their highest traffic ever. The back-up servers in Herndon, Virginia, were on stand-by in case of a power cut or disaster. In Provo, Utah, and in Commerce, California, eToys' warehouses strained at the seams; LEGO kits, Buzz Lightyears and Monopoly games were being picked, wrapped, packed and despatched to happy waiting children everywhere. The operation was being pushed to the limit. eToys' offices were alive with activity. Inside the Los Angeles call centre were 200 employees; above them banners extolled, 'Moms and dads take care of kids. Customer Service takes care of moms and dads.' Many of the phonecalls were complaints as parents chased their missing orders. Although the distribution teams had worked hard to fix most of the problems associated with the Fingerhut warehouse, a lot of packages were still astray; with Christmas fast approaching, purchasers were getting desperate.

Whilst journalists reported an upbeat mood this was hiding real misery. Imperfect performance was damaging company morale and the collapsing share price meant that the anticipated riches from employees' share options were vanishing. Diligent, enthusiastic and loyal as ever, the eToys team were straining every muscle and working every hour, but this was not enough. eToys were not quite hitting the mark for either their customers or their shareholders.

Wednesday 15 December marked an important day in the development of the Toywar. etoy announced the formation of an

Advisory Board to give them strategic counsel concerning their struggle. Joichi Ito signed up, as did John Perry Barlow, who called eToys' behaviour 'extremely predatory and wrong'. For Barlow, the campaign became the test of whether cyberspace would become a tightly patrolled shopping mall. 'This is where the frontlines really come down between traditional business practices and the practices that are born in cyberspace,' he would tell *WIRED news*. 'It's really where we decide if we're going to make cyberspace a better place. I don't think it's idealistic to think we have the opportunity to start afresh – if we don't blow it.' Zai had also corralled Suzy Meszoly, former curator of the C3 gallery in Budapest, and the writer and radio broadcaster Douglas Rushkoff, author of the bestselling book *Cyberia*. The creation of the Advisory Board strengthened etoy's credibility within the traditional Internet community.

That Wednesday also saw the start of the ®™ark etoy 'mutual fund' project, 'The Twelve Days of Christmas'. Its goal was to 'cripple the eToys servers' using the Zapatista FloodNet as demonstrated by Ricardo Dominguez's attack against the Pentagon. Dominguez by this time had released the software on to the Internet for public use, but for this special project he commanded the attack himself. He built a Web site entitled 'The End of the Net as We Know it', where he wrote, 'This hysterical powerplay perfectly demonstrates the intentions of the new net elite; to turn the World Wide Web into their own private home-shopping network.' He called upon the Internet community: 'PLAY WITH US!!'

At 11.45 a.m. Pacific Standard Time, campaigners began loading the FloodNet into their browsers and attacking eToys. Anyone who opened the FloodNet page found campaign information below which were three little windows. The FloodNet script loaded the front page of the eToys.com site into these windows every three seconds; first in the window on the left, then the middle, then the right, and so on, endlessly repeating the process. Within hours, hundreds of people around the Net had uploaded the page. Over the coming days, many more would follow and the demand began to slow down the eToys.com Web servers.

The FloodNet had a surreal, comic aspect to it. A user could click on another window and Dominguez's code would fire off one of the following messages to eToys:

I'm looking for the etoy URL.
Is there any art here?
Do you have the power to take my domain?
Do corporations have too much power?
Does eToys care about their image?
Does eToys care about their shareprice?
Did you know you were in the Washington Post?
How are the Christmas sales?

Around the world, FloodNet scripts were posted on many other sites. Other activist groups soon joined in with their own variations on the FloodNet theme; among these people were the British electrohippies and the French Federation of Random Action. The most sophisticated device was created by an art group called Airworld – they constructed a screensaver that would continuously call up the eToys Web site.

Those inside eToys felt as if they were under attack from the 'entire Internet'. Rob Johnson and Shay were called up for active service in defence of the eToys site, manning the barricades against FloodNet activists and rogue hackers. They faced a difficult question of allegiance. Both were self-described 'technogeeks', aficionados of free, community-built software, and so not natural defenders of eToys' position. As Rob Johnson remembers, 'One thing I would tell my boss is that I felt it was hard fighting this battle, because if I wasn't working for eToys then I would be on the side of the people against eToys. What they [eToys] were doing was wrong. I didn't agree with it. They had no right to it.' At the same time, however, Rob and Shay had, of course, built the eToys Web site so the FloodNet activists and the hackers were attacking something very close to their hearts. 'There was a lot of loyalty, defending our creation. I didn't agree with it politically,' says Rob. But, as Shay adds, 'It's like, "You are attacking my work. And you are not getting away with that".'

The attack continued from noon to midnight on 15 December, every two hours for fifteen minutes each time, and went on in the same fashion for a further two days. For eToys the weight of Web traffic was edging into the danger zone and at times their Web site began to run slower. The Engineering Department treated the alert status as 'Defcon Five, into full defence mode', recalls one insider. It was vital that the site did not crash in this final, crucial stage in the shopping season, when eToys were being so avidly watched by investors around the country. 'It was warfare,' says Shay. 'They brought us really slow for a couple of hours.'

Shay had the brilliant idea to defend by denying access to particularly malevolent computers identified by their IP address. In a determined effort to prevent the collapse of the eToys Web site, he started shutting out whole ranges of IP numbers – effectively stopping great swathes of Internet users from looking at, buying from, or attacking the site. He described the event as if it was a video game: 'Basically, I spent two days non-stop blocking . . . just like Bam, Bam, Bam!' As he proudly remembers: 'They might have almost taken the site down for maybe fifteen minutes before I started blocking.'

To those inside the company, the FloodNet attacks looked like a crude attempt to shut down eToys. Bruce Wessel, picking up on ®™ark's hyperbolic assertion that they were out to destroy eToys.com, drew a distinction that existed in the real world: it was legally acceptable to demonstrate outside a shop but not to prevent customers from accessing it. He explains: 'When you try and stop shoppers getting into an e-commerce site because you don't like them, that is a serious threat. It is denying people access and the police can't come and take you away. It is a very effective tool but it has to be treated as unlawful and improper.'

But, according to Ricardo Dominguez, that wasn't the point; the purpose of the FloodNet attacks was disturbance, not destruction. He and Ray Thomas had considered mounting a Distributed Denial of Service (DDoS). This would have automatically launched more powerful attacks from a number of machines without the need for individual human activists to upload the FloodNet browser window. But Dominguez ruled this out: 'We had a single-bullet script which could have taken down eToys – a tactical nuke, if you will. But we felt this script did not represent the presence of a global group of people gathering to bear witness to a wrong.'

Meanwhile, Zai in Zürich had been told by his lawyers that etoy ought not to be associated with the virtual sit-ins or hacker attacks. Whilst etoy received various offers to damage the eToys site they steered clear of them. As Zai smugly told *WIRED*, 'I immediately delete these emails and send back an email saying we don't want to have anything to do with anything illegal. We want to win this case.'

For the first two nights of the FloodNet battle, Shay and Rob did not sleep but continued to defend their baby. With each rebuff came another attack. Around the world, activists were creating new and more aggressive tools. Alvar Freude, a student at the Merz Academy in Stuttgart and System Administrator for the school's computer lab, had read about Toywar and felt he had to take part: 'I thought that the outcome of this story would determine the meaning of value on the Internet, whether value would only be about money or whether other values would have priority.' He wrote a special computer script called Tschekker, which made random searches in the eToys database as a means to slowing down their server. He started using it himself and also posted it on the Internet for others to download. Soon he noticed that the program had been downloaded three times from a machine inside eToys.

eToys' Engineering Department quickly figured out how to neuter Freude's weapon; in response to their efforts, he changed his code slightly. Once again, eToys countered with their own new code. In this way, the cat-and-mouse battle continued. Over the course of two days, the Engineering Department continuously changed the Web site's workings to counter the attacks; and every time they rewrote their program, they tested it to be certain of its invincibility.

The Engineering team became increasingly frustrated and exhausted. One of them created a pseudonymous email account in the name of 'Big daddE' and sent a message to Alvar Freude saying, 'Hello my little friend. Build [sic] any new scripts lately? I suggest for you to get the hell out of dodge before the neighbors find out.' Freude was a little bemused upon receiving the threat, but soon realised that it had the tell-tale fingerprint of the computer from which it was sent. 'When I realized that it came from eToys I could hardly believe it. I thought that they were totally crazy!' he remembers.

On the evening of 16 December, the eToys shares fell for the first time below the $40 mark. During the first two days of anti-eToys hacktivism their value had decreased by $6, more than fourteen per cent of their value, whilst the NASDAQ Composite Index had gained almost five per cent.

The eToys Engineering Department now started to counter some of the attacks against the company by approaching the universities and businesses whose equipment was being used to facilitate them. Soon, a number of students were hauled up in front of their academic superiors to explain why university resources were being used to assault an online retailer. Shay and Rob also boasts that eToys persuaded one major computer-equipment supplier to escort an employee off the premises after his activities in the Toywar had been exposed.

On the evening of 17 December, Rob and Shay set out to neuter one of the biggest sources of irritation, Wolfgang Staehle's The Thing. Staehle's Internet service provider was of course key to the campaign because it hosted not only the Zapatista FloodNet and Toywar.com but also ®™ark. Rob found out that the Internet backbone company Verio connected The Thing to the rest of the Internet. So he called the company and spoke first to a junior-level operator, then to a more senior supervisor. Eventually he managed to talk to a vice president to whom he explained the malignant role of The Thing's Web site. So in the early hours of Saturday morning, a security executive from Verio left a message of explanation on The Thing's answerphone and then shut off their Internet connection.

In disconnecting The Thing, Verio took more than 200 private Web sites offline. Wolfgang Staehle was unmoved; 'That makes a good headline,' is all he said, according to one of his employees. He did contact Ricardo Dominguez, though, and after a little discussion they decided to take the FloodNet scripts off the server so that all the other Web sites on The Thing could be put online again. Dominguez did not believe that this would mute the effectiveness of the attack, since the FloodNet scripts were already copied on to various Web sites elsewhere. Staehle called Verio who agreed to his deal but when he complained about their behaviour they asked him to secure his data so that the FBI could investigate. Although Staehle never complied, news of the request filtered out on to the Internet and one weary combatant in San Francisco kept his eyes on The Thing's Web cam in the belief that FBI agents were about to arrive. Within eighteen hours of shutting off The Thing, Verio restored the connection – sans FloodNet scripts.

eToys had apparently won another battle. They had prevented their Web site from collapsing during the most crucial holiday week. Shay and Rob were pleased with their achievements. 'Toward the end of the two days we had won. That was the entire Internet; they didn't manage to hack us,' says Shay, while Rob is keen to point out, 'It was never defaced, they never entered the system. The worst they did was slow it down.' As Shay recalls, 'Basically I think we won that exchange with the Internet. It was pretty cool.' Media Metrix, a Web rating agency, would later announce that eToys' availability had slipped during those days from 100 to 98 per cent.

Although eToys had successfully navigated their way through this most critical period, etoy remained determined to get their domain back and so the campaign continued. The Thing being taken off the Web provoked Matthew Mirapaul to write another piece in *The New York Times* and in London the *Financial Times* also ran an article. CNN aired the story, too; their reporter Steve Young began his report by saying: 'At the leading edge of cyberspace, protesters say they have been disrupting the eToys Web site. Supporters of these tactics call this a virtual sit-in. But critics have a different term for it: cybersabotage.'

The extensive and persistent media attention began to try tempers inside eToys. Speaking to *USA Today*, Ken Ross, eToys' Vice President for Communications, refused to comment 'on routine security and maintenance issues' but asked the question, 'Do you think we're a horrible company that gets up every day thinking of ways to go after artists? Our only interest in this matter is making certain that there's no confusion in the marketplace. Period.'

Meanwhile, the hundreds of employees in the warehouse, the call centres and the toy teams had little or no knowledge of what eToys were actually going through, of the conflict and confusion of Internet politics that their company was embroiled in. For these people too, however, this was the worst of times: the share price was collapsing and the legacy of the distribution problems continued to be felt, with customers still calling asking why they'd received a blue Furbie when they'd ordered a green one and so on. Beyond those immediately concerned, there was little communication about the real situation and even among some senior managers there was confusion. Some believed that hackers had managed to close the site and send email viruses to the company, while others believed that fifth-columnists inside the company were betraying security secrets to make eToys more vulnerable. It was also rumoured that office security had been stepped up to guard against rogue real-life protestors.

At the same time the company was confronted with more bad news when a PC Data Online study revealed that toysrus.com had at last edged in front of eToys.com as the leading Internet toy site. To counter the bad news, Toby announced that eToys had managed to pull in more than a million and a half customers in the previous four months.

On Friday 17 December, the eToys share price closed down at $37.56.

In Zürich, Zai and Gramazio in the etoy office were overloaded by campaign work. Kubli, who was working in a Zürich court, stopped by in every free moment that he had, each day after work and at the weekends. After three weeks of combat, the three of them felt on the verge of collapse. etoy received about 300 emaïls a day in support of their cause and, as Gramazio recalls, 'The phone kept ringing, every ten minutes, day and night, because of our international contacts. It helped us keep going. Things were happening all the time; it was like a ticking clock.' The pressure was immense and they never took a day off. 'It was like being on drugs,' explains Zai. According to his girlfriend, Ms Monorom, there were many times when he just slept with his head on the table next to his computer keyboard.

Zai and Gramazio adapted to working within American time zones, which for them meant late into the night. 'It was like being in a submarine,' Gramazio recalls. 'We were totally caught up in this parallel reality.' Their existence comprised the office, themselves and their screens. On many occasions they asked themselves, 'What if all this is only a simulation, one that the enemy has set up in order to distract us from checking outside what is really going on, what is really up?' When Steve Kettman from *WIRED news* turned up in Zürich to interview them and they were forced to go out and see normal people sitting in a restaurant, they were bemused and a little confused.

On Sunday 19 December, a tired etoy crew sent out a mail to their fan community announcing that they had to take a break. 'it's far away from under control. no one can navigate this madness,' they wrote. They needed a little time to think about their moves beyond the judicial and media battle. Elsewhere, the struggle continued on their behalf.

On the morning of 20 December, the eToys shares opened at $38.43. By the time the markets closed that evening, at 4.30 p.m. in New York, they had fallen by a further $4, more than ten per cent. Two hours later, outside the Museum of Modern Art in Midtown Manhattan, more than 200 people gathered in the rain to demonstrate their support of etoy. Among them were ten 'Santas', wearing white beards, false bellies and red hats, some of whom carried placards reading 'Coal for eToys' and 'Ho Ho Ho eToys No'.

The crowd filed into the Museum, led by a marching band who pumped out a cacophonous rendition of 'O Come All Ye Faithful' on their trombones and tubas. One protester carried a cross with a Mickey Mouse nailed to it and was asked by the Museum's security staff to leave it in the cloakroom. The protesters made their way to a lecture theatre inside. Draped across the stage was a huge banner which proclaimed, 'etoy.SHARES, infecting global markets'; the 'Buy and Trade' slogan that once ran across the background had been obscured with red tape – the demonstrators were not about to break the court injunction that forbade the trading of etoy shares. Reverend Billy, a satirist and Minister of the Church of Stop Shopping, in a white jacket and dog collar, opened the proceedings with a sermon. 'We are drowning in a sea of identical details,' he preached. 'Times Square has been blown up by 10,000 smiling stuffed animals . . . Don't shop, children, save your souls!'

For the only time in his life etoy Advisory Board member Douglas Rushkoff read from a written text because he considered the event so significant that he wanted to be precise about what he said. He bemoaned the changing times: 'When commercial interests moved online, many of us were concerned they would change the essential character of this space – that a communications infrastructure would be turned into an electronic strip mall. But *WIRED*, cyber-libertarians, and e-commerce enthusiasts reminded us all of the simple fact that the Internet has infinite real estate. There's room for everyone. Not so . . . etoy's resistance demonstrates that the Bottom Line in our civilisation must not be the bottom line. etoy will not abandon its existing shareholders by taking the money and running away. Unlike almost everyone else in the Internet space, they have no "exit strategy" because they are here to stay. And, unlike eToys, etoy is more than just a URL. The name is not for sale.'

Suzy Meszoly, also a member of the Advisory Board, took the microphone next. Wearing an etoy bomber jacket, she eulogised the 'etoy message', saying that the Toywar was a reminder of the purpose of the etoy project. 'The message has broken through the glass doors of the museum, through the computer monitors and hit the streets, the newspapers, CNN, the business news, the television,' she preached. 'The stocks, the court judges, the activists, the riots, MOMA, the advisors, the netizens, the world has transformed the etoy ideology into a reality. The surreal has become real. Hacking reality?? This is the etoy value.'

On 23 December, the last day of NASDAQ trading until after the Christmas holidays, the eToys shares closed at $30.93. This was less than half of their value on the day of the temporary injunction not even a month ago.

For many concerned, Christmas 1999 was going to be a strange time. Kathy Hernandez of eToys' customer-call centre thought herself lucky not to be working on Christmas Eve. Having left the office on the evening before, she got in her car and wept. 'I have never cried such tears of joy. I remember being on the cellphone to my sister. I said, "I am so happy to be out of there, it was just horrible". I just went home and slept.'

For many eToys employees, that Christmas marked a fundamental change. Once, eToys had been cool, a small, family-like company conjuring value out of nothing, striving for greatness. The fun and friendly eToys had seemed capable of incredible things. Now, it had become a sluggish megalith apparently unable even to deliver some sweet toys to children. The hackers' paradise had been transformed into the poor relation of an old fashioned corporation.

In Zürich, Zai spent Christmas conferring with etoy's lawyer in preparation for the next hearing in the Los Angeles Superior Court, scheduled for 27 December. In San Francisco, Ray Thomas from ®™ark composed his next press release, in which he stated that the outcome of the case would 'set a precedent determining whether the Internet will be governed by the brute force of multinational corporations or by individuals and democratic processes'. Even the investors contributing to the message-board frenzy calmed down to a festive quiet – although the lonely voice of activist 'toplyrics' continued to stir up the community with the advice, 'eToys is bankrupted – Run and sell!'

As the message boards and email lists grew quiet, under Christmas trees children were unwrapping their gifts. More than a million packages had been sent out by eToys in the previous three months, arriving in specially unmarked boxes because Toby thought that branding the packages might ruin the surprise for the children. Such was the diligence of the eToys staff, the boxes contained special biodegradable and child-friendly packing material. Some contained notes with messages from loved ones who had ordered gifts but could not make it home for the festivities. eToys delivered happiness across the world.

Part 3: Turning the Tables

The Toywar seemed already to be a great achievement for the Internet community. Only a month after the court case, the campaign had blossomed from a small and speedy media virus into a mass movement. Many of the activists outside eToys, and even some defenders inside the company, reckoned that the assault had been of unprecedented size in the short history of the Internet; never before had so many risen up to attack a corporation in order to defend the rights of the few.

The Toywar was also cheered on as heralding a new kind of conflict. The future, it was argued, would see battles that would no longer be fought on the streets, the targets no longer being workers, warehouses or corporate office blocks. Direct action would happen only in the realm of information; at stake would be control over Web sites, databases and the news agenda. eToys provided the perfect test-case. Having no 'real-world' presence, their sole public face was their Web site; they had no high-street shops to which they could beat their retreat. The Zapatista FloodNet attack against eToys, unlike that against the Pentagon Web site, targeted the thing most central to the toy company's existence. As such, the assault was cast as a warning: as corporations and governments moved further into the world of trading information, as the new economy became increasingly dominant, the conflict between etoy and eToys would be seen as just the first battle in a new kind of war.

Yet, for all the success in mobilising such a large crowd, the Toywar had not yet achieved its concrete objective; the legal case was far from resolved. But eToys' aggressive tactics had goaded Zai and the others into thinking that a legal resolution was no longer enough – they also wanted to turn the events of the Toywar into a piece of art. For Zai, eToys had 'challenged us to create our masterpiece'. As the New Year approached, their legal and artistic ambitions began to rub against each other; the heat this friction generated pushed etoy into a radically new position.

Their initial artistic plan was to create a Web site that would look like an online game. It would be called the Toywar Platform. Zai and Gramazio would then recruit Toywar Soldiers from among their campaigning supporters and throw them into this new theatre of operations. The soldiers, once logged on, could communicate with each other to plot, plan and push the campaign against eToys. Most importantly, they could use Internet tools to continue the fight. A Toybomb, for example, would send emails to the eToys management and shareholders.

But the Toywar Platform was to be more than a campaign tool. It was to be something like a global theatrical performance, the online, graphical representation of the conflict. Toywar Soldiers would be represented by LEGO-like images of little men with dollar signs in their eyes carrying weapons and wearing gasmasks. With a nod towards etoy's original hope of becoming pop-stars they also planned some soldiers which were DJs standing in front of turntables. To create these malevolent figures, Zai contacted

Alex Fischl, whom he had met at Ars Electronica where Fischl had won a prize for graphics. He was only eighteen and living in a flat with his mum in Vienna, where he began working day and night to shape these icons of the Toywar.

The Toywar Platform was to be a kind of agitprop performance piece, as if it were an online version of political street-theatre which both told a story and inspired its audience to action. On the Web there was no need for a table stacked with leaflets, petitions and pro forma letters, as all these would be included in the spectacle itself. The most ambitious idea was that the participants – the Toy Soldiers logged on to the Web site and the press dragooned into reporting the show – were to be the star performers.

Shortly before Christmas, Zai had written a mail announcing on behalf of etoy that the game would 'leave the etoy.BETA-LABS in a few days'. Gramazio, in charge of the coding and project management, and some helpers spent days and nights slowly and meticulously working on their 'masterpiece'. They were racing to finish because the game would make sense only if there was an injustice for the Toy Soldiers to campaign against. In other words, it had to be played while the dispute between etoy and eToys was still bubbling. The pressure, therefore, was on as the endgame of the legal dispute, the court hearing of 27 December, was fast approaching.

Still believing that etoy's sole ambition was to retain their domain name, Peter Wild sent the boys an admonishing fax: 'I would like to point out once more that the time seems to be right to re-start serious talks with the other party, with the pre-condition that eToys consents to the release of the domain name as well as an end to the legal procedures.' Zai, however, was in no mood to speed ahead with any type of resolution. He felt that the case was strengthening in the light of a startling new piece of evidence.

This evidence concerned the eToys trademark bought from the New York toy distributor ETNA, who had claimed that it had been in use – though they'd never registered it – since 1990.

Half of the eToys trademark case rested upon this claim, but etoy had uncovered the fact that, two weeks before the injunction hearing, the US Patent and Trademark Office had formally refused to register this new eToys trademark. Zai was incensed by the finding and told the press that eToys had still used to try to trample etoy's rights. As his confidence grew he became all the more belligerent.

The arrival of a new lawyer, Chris Truax, added to Zai's determination. When the case had become a *cause célèbre*, Truax from San Diego had written: 'I am an attorney in California specializing in Internet law. I was quite shocked when I heard that E-toys actually got their injunction. I'm sure you are already well-represented by an attorney, however, please let your legal team know that I would be happy to consult with them and provide any assistance I can (free of charge) if they believe it would be of help in preparing your case.' etoy at the time were losing faith in their lawyers – a feeling fuelled by an outstanding legal bill for $16,000. They asked Peter Wild to get in touch with Truax and check out his credentials; it transpired that he was a sole-practitioner who had spent much of the previous three years writing about Intellectual Property law on the Internet.

Zai feared that Truax might be a spy, so he was asked to sign a document assuring them that he had never been in contact with eToys. While thus far etoy's lawyers had worked for a fee, Truax offered to work for expenses and a minimum of ten per cent of any settlement. Joichi Ito was initially worried that this pecuniary interest might predispose him to an early cash settlement, but a phonecall with Truax satisfied him that this wasn't the immediate strategy. Zai also warmed to Truax's approach: 'He was enthusiastic, he had loads of ideas and propositions outside of just the legal frame. He talked to us on the phone, day or night, whenever needed.'

Truax radically changed the tone of the legal confrontation. He convinced etoy to smooth their rough edges and to spin a more conciliatory tone, and he insisted that they no longer describe themselves as a 'virus'. Zai also had to apologise to him for having told a reporter that Judge Shook was 'stupid'. Whilst creating the impression that etoy's surface might be softening, Truax in fact was contributing to the hardening of their position.

Preparing for the imminent court hearing, Truax sent a fax to Zai in which he suggested that eToys should be allowed to buy the etoy domain and their interests in the trademark for the impressive sum of $3.7 million. While this seemed like a lot of money, it was considerably less than the $7.5 million which business.com had been sold for a few weeks earlier, a domain which had none of the advertising that eToys had lavished on their own. Zai scribbled his response by hand, raising the demand to not less than $10 million, and returned it to Truax. The discussion continued.

Next Zai wrote a press release in anticipation of the hearing, in which he said that etoy 'is ready to talk about solutions to stop this insane media war'. However, he chastised eToys for their 'rude way' of doing business and refused to come to the table until they had not only reinstated the domain name and apologised but also appeared genuinely intent on 'fair and violence-free negotiations'. Wryly he added another paragraph: 'The beginning of a new century could be a good moment to think about business, responsibility and society on a larger scale . . . we wish eToys a happy new year and that their share value may recover a bit.'

On 27 December, eToys' shares opened at $30. That morning, despite the case being scheduled in the Superior Court, it was postponed by eToys' lawyers until 10 January.

There was no time to rearrange the press conference already happening on the steps of the Superior Court. Peter Lunenfeld, the professor at the Art Center College of Design who had once worked with Zai and Brainhard, spoke to a small group of maybe fifteen activists. His oration had the conviction of the street speakers of old: 'etoy vs. eToys is more than just the David vs. Goliath cliché that's been covered in the media; it's the opening salvo in the twenty-first century's battle over cyberspace.'

The enthusiasm cloaked a somewhat pathetic and futile demonstration. The protestors were so desperate to find value in their show of strength that they conjured phantoms. At one point they were convinced that they had spotted an eToys spy, a man in a suit with a half-open briefcase that they presumed carried a tape recorder. Before the event was over, he had walked away. As Lunenfeld recalls, 'We realised he was just a guy in a suit. Which is particularly deflating, because a spy would have stayed.' To add to the collective disappointment, the event was covered only by an obscure online newspaper. For Lunenfeld this was typical Los Angeles: 'We would have had to have Jack Nicholson fucking the Olsen twins to get any attention whatsoever.' If nothing else, the demonstration proved the mantra of Electronic Civil Disobedience correct: 'As far as power is concerned, the streets are dead.'

It was also a bad day on Wall Street. eToys' shares tumbled $5, or sixteen per cent, to close at a little less than $26. This was partly as a result of a downgrade from the Robertson Stephens analyst Lauren Cooks Levitan, who now rated eToys' shares as 'long-term attractive' – meaning, in the double-speak of bankers, not really attractive at all. A survey sponsored by Levitan found that twelve per cent of eToys shoppers wouldn't return because they were dissatisfied with the delivery and service. This might not suggest a perfect performance, but eToys were the best-performing toy shop according to the survey and inside the company it was reckoned that they had delivered more than ninety per cent of the orders on time. However, they had been plagued all season by headlines such as this one from *The Wall Street Journal*: 'Some Web Customers Cry: All I Want for Christmas is My Order!'

On 28 December, the shares recovered a little and closed at $29.

With the new hearing almost two weeks away, etoy were feeling ever more confident and determined to press ahead. They faxed Truax a set of new suggestions for deals, ranging from $7.5 million for eToys to buy the domain name to their placing of a permanent advertising banner on etoy.com for the sum of $1.9 million.

Having received the fax, Truax wrote to Bruce Wessel, acting for eToys. 'You suggested that I bring a new pair of eyes to this case: I think that is true and, more to the point, I'm somewhat objective in the sense that I'm not invested in which has gone before. Therefore, I'd like to lay out my view of this case. The primary issue in this case is respect.'

He then outlined a menu of three options. First, eToys could buy the etoy.com domain and any rights to the trademark. However, the price for this had more than doubled, to $20 million. Kubli justifies this rise: 'Our prices rose and rose because through Toywar we had become more and more famous.' The second option and the idea that Zai most favoured was a corporate takeover. For $8 million, eToys Inc. would merge with the etoy.CORPORATION and share the spoils of the subsequent publicity fest. As Truax wrote, 'etoy would be willing to come to Santa Monica to work on this project which would take between two and three months. Moreover, as this would be a collaborative piece, etoy would be willing to give your client a veto over any ideas that eToys' public relations people thought were too far out. At the end of the project, eToys will have solved its intellectual property problem and will be perceived as having acquired both a hipper corporate image and a sense of humor.' The third option was to share the Web sites so that etoy and eToys would together own and operate the front pages of both etoy.com and eToys.com. This would cost eToys $500,000. The simple solution of putting a banner on etoy.com, warning prospective shoppers that they had come to the wrong place and redirecting them to eToys.com, was no longer even suggested.

For the first time, Truax also revealed the aggression that he was going to bring to the case. etoy had already filed a counterclaim which attempted to wrest the trademark and domain of eToys.com from the toy company. Until now, this had not really been a serious proposal. It had been more of a defensive measure that would be withdrawn when the main dispute was settled. But now Truax made it clear that he was willing to pursue eToys for that which they held dearest, their brand, their trademark and their domain name, in just the same way as eToys had gone after etoy. He wrote, 'The bottom line here is that there is a real possibility that etoy will triumph on the merits and that it is eToys who will be thrown off the Internet.'

During these days, Zai, Gramazio and Kubli robustly confronted eToys through their lawyer but in the press and speaking to their public they were careful to tread a little more gingerly. etoy had won the media agenda and cast the conflict as one about art and freedom of speech against money and greedy opportunists. They didn't want to jeopardise their image within the Internet community and end up looking like the bad guys. When asked by a reporter of *The Washington Post* about their demand for $20 million, Zai insisted that money was not an important issue, that etoy just wanted 'respect' and 'equal standing with the e-tail giants that now dominate the Web'.

On 29 December, Wessel replied to Truax: 'EToys will not meet etoy corporation's escalating demands.' Then he unexpectedly raised the white flag. eToys was tired, ready to give in and offered a simple settlement whereby the lawsuits would be dismissed and both sides would sign non-disparagement agreements and return to the days when 'the two companies operated side by side without problem'. There was just one thing that eToys asked for, 'In light of the many children who visit eToys.-com, to give good faith consideration as our neighbour on the Internet, to concentrate the profanity, nudity and violence that is sometimes part of the etoy corporation message to etoy corporation's other web sites.'

At the same time eToys' spokesman, Ken Ross, faxed a statement to media outlets in which he explained, 'We've received over the last several weeks a lot of emails and letters from members of the arts community and Internet community. They've overwhelmingly urged us to find a way to peacefully coexist with the etoy group, and we've decided to do that.' A couple of hours after the statement's release, the news was on the Internet. Yahoo! headlined: 'EToys Backs Down From Bully Stance'. Tara Lemmey, President of the Electronic Frontier Foundation, was quoted,

'This case had very big free speech implications. It's great that the public reaction has helped eToys understand that.'

etoy could now have rightly claimed the victory. They could have celebrated in jubilation. But they were disappointed. The satisfaction of a settlement offer had come too early. Whereas their legal ambition had been mostly fulfilled, their artistic one, to launch the Toywar Platform, was still struggling to come alive. When approached by the press, Truax was circumspect, having by now become centrally involved in plotting the trajectory of the legal case and the spinning of the story. When one journalist asked him if etoy were popping champagne corks he replied, 'Not until I tell them to.'

Now etoy informed some in the activist community that the lawsuit wasn't going to be dropped. Their supporters on email lists started telling each other stories of corporations saying one thing and doing another.

By the end of that day, eToys shares were $26, down from $67 exactly one month before, on the day of the injunction hearing.

On 30 December, Truax revealed his hand igniting the campaign afresh with an interview with *WIRED news*. They ran a piece entitled 'etoy: "The Fight Isn't Over"' in which he pounced on eToys' request to put the profanity, violence and nudity on another Web site, and cast it as a demand to 'cede control over the etoy art project'. He even increased the stakes by threatening the toy company, declaring that eToys 'have every reason to be nervous. We have been fairly passive so far. If we are not able to settle this, we're going to have to take a much, much more aggressive posture.' At the same time, ®™ark launched a letter-writing campaign aimed at eToys' employees, with the slogan 'Quit eToys Now!' and urging eToys' Chief Executive 'Toby step down!' Ray Thomas was pleased when the press release was published on Bloomberg, one of the most important financial-information systems in the world, as if the issuing of a press release was a vital piece of news in itself.

This provoked an irritated response from eToys. To the press, Ken Ross vehemently denied Truax's interpretation of the offer, while Irell & Manella promptly sent a fax to Truax to clarify the situation: 'Our settlement proposal is not contingent upon etoy.CORPORATION agreeing to restrict the content of its Web site in any fashion.' They also offered to pay the artists $25,000 to cover their legal expenses.

For etoy, this very public negotiation became another opportunity that they could milk for their own ends. Zai promoted etoy's online Toywar Platform to *WIRED news*, saying that he was about to launch 'an online game that will mock eToys and the domain-name fight. The game will offer a playful take on the highly public struggle.' Also etoy was about to release a Toywar CD, called *Lullabies*. This included a track by Negativland, the band who made their name by mocking big companies and their brands.

That day, the closing price of the eToys shares was $25.56.

As the old millennium drew to a close, etoy was working with a radical new strategy: to drag their feet during the remaining settlement process to give them time to launch their artwork. As Kubli recalls, 'It is obvious that after a certain moment we did not have any interest in helping to speed things up.'

On Friday 31 December, the Toywar Platform still did not work but etoy could wait no longer and sent out a call for soldiers to register. Over the first weekend of the new year, many campaigners tried to sign up but found that the game crashed their computers. The coding had been too hasty, was a little unstable and still full of bugs. Some, however, managed to get through. Reinhold Grether, the academic from Constance, was thrilled that he managed to be the first to register. He wanted to be the most valiant of all the soldiers and dreamed that one day he would write 'the most famous email in Internet history' – which would declare victory over eToys with the single word 'done'.

As an enticement to players, etoy decided to give away ten per cent of their shares to Toywar Soldiers as compensation for their services. They took care to call the shares 'points', however, for fear of making trouble with the Californian court. Hoping to make the etoy army grow faster, they advertised a 'friends and family program' that would reward Toy Soldiers who recruited new activists. As Zai promised, 'this is the best moment for you to build a huge TOYWAR.empire.'

The trouble was that Gramazio had still not finished the software to allow their new recruits to do anything. The promise of an online game, or a platform from which to continue fighting, remained unfulfilled. etoy still needed some time to get their act together. Luckily for them there was still the opportunity to further draw out the legal wrangling.

On 3 January, Truax wrote to etoy explaining the position of eToys: 'In plain English this appears to mean that eToys is now offering to drop the lawsuit, to agree not to sue etoy in the future and to pay etoy's costs and fees if etoy will drop its lawsuit and agree not to sue eToys in the future.' This was more or less what the campaigners had been fighting for.

For Zai, Gramazio and Kubli, this was something of a dilemma: to settle the court case or to pursue their art work. Now a third motivation came into play: money. Truax still reckoned that etoy might be looking at a lucrative payout if they filed a trademark claim against the toy company with arguments similar to those used against them. But etoy would be unable to do this if they accepted eToys' 'with prejudice' offer in which neither side could sue the other again. 'I would advise you not to accept the money and to keep your right to challenge the eToys trademark later,' Truax counselled them.

Zai, Kubli and Gramazio had started out simply defending their right to stay on the Web, but now decided to act on Truax's advice: they would refuse eToys' deal in order to retain the right to attack the toy company and maybe become rich men. In Truax's opinion, 'total victory for etoy' was close.

When he drafted a counter-proposal the priority was to stall for time to allow Gramazio to fix the bugs in the Toywar Platform. Previously etoy seemed to have all the time in the world to answer questions from journalists. Now, Truax argued, they were unaccountably too busy, and for a whole week would be unable to handle the media interest of a settlement. He also made a concrete offer that etoy was willing to dismiss the case if eToys 'is willing to pay our expenses and legal fees caused by this suit and issue a press release acceptable to etoy.' He added an important condition: that the case be dismissed 'without prejudice'. Indeed this final caveat now became the sole important sticking point in the negotiations.

At the same time, to keep up the pressure within the Internet community, etoy issued a press release: 'we have the strongest impression that the statements [eToys] make to the press and the ones they make to our lawyers are not 100% identical . . . we do not reject talking to eToys but we don't trust them so far. first they try to kill us (by spending maybe half a million dollars on lawyers), and now they try to turn back the clock and say . . . oh this was just a little misunderstanding!? did we miss something?' What the press release did not mention was that eToys had offered to drop the suit.

In Los Angeles, eToys organised a party to celebrate the holiday season. They booked the House of Blues on Sunset Boulevard and invited almost 1,000 people – very different to the few dozen just two years before. By all accounts it was a spirited party, with dancing and drinking and, after the stress of the holiday season, the real pleasure of an alcohol-fuelled collective sigh of relief. Toby thanked eToys' hundreds of employees and the investors. Entertainment was provided by an employee band, The Frank Han Explosion; Frank, the co-founder, got on stage and posed like a rock star. By chance he chose an anthem that could have been the rallying cry for the activists of the Toywar, 'Fight for the Right' by The Beastie Boys. Like a childish rebel, he sang the lyrics and repeated the chorus: 'You gotta fight / for your right / to party.'

On 10 January, the day the two sides were to meet in court, the shares opened at $22.

A few hours before the hearing began Gramazio finally managed to get the Toywar Platform running. Now soldiers would log on, chat to each other and use the campaign tools. Zai sent out an

etoy.SHARE depicting a Toywar Soldier fighting in the Toywar.

email to welcome on behalf of etoy the participants who had already registered: 'the TOYWAR.crisis control-board is proud to invite you to enter the TOYWAR.battlefield as one of the first human Internet agents! TOYWAR.com is a place where all servers and all involved people melt and build a living system. in our eyes it is the best way to express and document what's going on at the moment: people start to think about new ways to fight for their ideas, their lifestyle, contemporary culture and power relations.'

Eventually many Toy Soldiers did manage to register; etoy later claimed that there were 1,600 in their army. Around the world, recruits had to persuade others that they were honest and interested. New recruits were faced with a questionnaire. 'WAR is a hard business,' the screen warned. 'The TOYWAR.board needs to test your performance to make sure you will perform at your best in the most dangerous situations. The following test will expose you to psychological stress in order to determine your mental integrity.' Like a weird corporate human-resources questionnaire, it asked recruits about whether they'd killed anyone, or thought about it, or 'Did you ever wake up at night and realize you had real sick dreams?' Having answered these questions, recruits had to wait until they'd received an email telling them whether their answers were correct. When they were welcomed as Toy Soldiers they could choose a LEGO-like image to represent themselves.

The Web site was adorned with barbed wire and contained links to information about the case. But really it was a glorified chat-room in which most of the talk was of people looking for social interaction with likeminded souls. After the arduous entrance requirements, many soldiers were disappointed that there was not more action. Some logged off to play shoot-'em-up video-games instead.

Some hours after the Toywar Platform launch, in the Los Angeles Superior Court, Truax faced eToys' lawyers. He insisted that eToys' pay the legal expenses, request Network Solutions to restore etoy.com and, most importantly, that the case be dropped without prejudice, which would allow etoy the opportunity to launch another suit in the future. No settlement was reached in the meeting and to the media afterwards no reason was given for the lack of closure.

In the meantime, etoy were busy trying to build their army. They bombarded their community with imploring emails to join the Toywar Platform. Zai also asked for email addresses of other people whom he could 'invite' to become soldiers. Encouraging all supporters, Zai continued, 'don't believe the propaganda! it only looks like there is no war anymore! the etoy.com domain is still on hold. nothing really happened.'

To activists and journalists, a fog of confusion now descended on the battlefield. While eToys had been making overtures, etoy had kept up their story that the fight wasn't over. And yet, behind the scenes, Zai told some people that there was nothing to worry about. etoy had even refused offers of legal support from researchers at Ivy League universities. When an Austrian virtual-reality researcher, Christian Bauer, offered to act as a mediator he was welcomed by eToys spokesman Ken Ross, but was stalled by Zai. Even Steve Kettman from *WIRED news*, the most diligent of reporters, couldn't quite figure out why there was an apparent delay in the courtroom settlement. The only news from the settlement talks that he was able to report was etoy's apparent willingness to give up their demand for an apology.

For almost two weeks, the delay continued. This would later allow Zai to claim that the Toywar Platform was decisive in winning the battle, though he would be unable to provide concrete evidence to support this. Indeed, both Zai and Chris Truax skate around the issue when asked precisely what went on in the crucial two weeks in January 2000 – beyond etoy's own self-promotion.

The last stand orchestrated by etoy from the Toywar Platform was on 24 January, when Zai ordered the Toy Army to send emails to the enemy: 'eToys has to accept our conditions not the other way around.' He also gave a tongue-in-cheek reminder to eToys that this was their 'last chance to avoid toy. harbor'. He also kept asserting that the malevolent Toywar characters were having an effect on the toy company: 'Many hundreds of EMAIL-TOY-BOMBS exploded in the brains of customers, e-shoppers, brokers and nervous business men all over the world.' In Santa Monica, no one remembers receiving them.

The next day, 25 January, the game came to an end. Truax faxed an agreement to Bruce Wessel at Irell & Manella: both parties would dismiss their complaint and cross-complaint without prejudice, leaving open the possibility of further suits. eToys would reimburse the artists $40,000 and immediately contact Network Solutions to ask them to reinstall etoy.com. eToys accepted these terms.

From Zürich etoy excitedly sent out an email:

VICTORY*VICTORY*VICTORY*VICTORY*
VICTORY!
OFFICIAL etoy.PRESS-RELEASE:
IT WAS A PLEASURE TO DO BUSINESS WITH
ONE OF THE BIGGEST E-COMMERCE GIANTS
IN THE WORLD: F*U*C*K*I*N*G* INTENSE &
REALLY EXPENSIVE BUT A KICK FOR ALL OF
US! WE ALL LEARNED A LOT.
WE THANK ALL THE BRAVE AGENTS WHO
LINED UP BEHIND US TO PROTECT THE ART
BRAND "etoy" & FREEDOM ON THE NET!

Wolfgang Staehle from The Thing was triumphant. 'We survived their brutal force. Spirit has defeated money,' he told a reporter. ®™ark also rejoiced. 'eToys thought it could act like corporations typically do, but it had no idea how the Internet works,' Ray Thomas wrote in their press release. 'Now e-commerce corporations have a choice: either obtain a legal stranglehold on the Internet . . . or behave decently towards the humans who use this medium for purposes other than profit.' He optimistically claimed that 'a precedent has now finally been set in stone'.

Chris Truax dryly explained the situation to *WIRED news*: 'It's not a settlement, because it doesn't settle anything. All it does is terminate this lawsuit.' Many other media outlets carried the story. *The Wall Street Journal* even saw it as a lesson to be learned, and wagged a finger at eToys, whose 'fantastic pedigree did not stop it from behaving like any number of stupid companies'. The lesson was, 'if you don't want to get trashed as a dumb, lawyer-infested corporate lummox, don't act like one.'

On a few email lists, some activists berated etoy for their opportunistic exploitation of the cause. Zai responded to one such discussion by writing, 'etoy can not be reproached to have taken advantage of all this for their own cause . . . we are into branding and promoting. The only issue is what we triggered with it . . .'

On the day the lawsuit was put to rest, eToys' share price fell and closed at $19.31. For the first time, the stock was below the price it had been issued at on the day of their IPO eight months before. The company's value was now less than the banks' original estimation of it.

Two days later, Toby issued their quarterly results. He announced that they had sold $107 million worth of toys to 1.7 million customers in the Christmas quarter. eToys had spent $36 million on advertising, which meant that every customer had spent on average $67 but had cost eToys $33 to acquire. The shares shed another twenty per cent of their value, to close at a little above $16. The *Financial Times* noted that Toby claimed his company 'won the holiday'; its influential Lex column commented, 'If that is a victory, what would Mr Lenk classify as defeat?'

Since their most recent peak, two months earlier on the day of the injunction, eToys' shares had lost seventy per cent of their value. Their showing was worse than other Internet stocks in this period. While Yahoo! had gained about fifty per cent in value in the same period, eBay.com lost fifteen per cent and amazon.com, Toby's role model, lost thirty per cent.

In the media and on email lists, there was heated debate about what had caused such a singular and spectacular decline in eToys' fortunes. Roughly three possible scenarios were advanced.

The first was the most orthodox. Essentially this was the 'firm foundation' approach, put forward by financial analysts and many inside the company. They considered that eToys stock had fallen because the intrinsic value of the company had been reduced due to operational failures and spiralling costs. The primary problem was the failure of the warehouse system. Although several surveys of all Internet companies that Christmas said that eToys had ranked first or second in customer satisfaction, inside the company this was generally held to be the single most important reason for the share-price decline.

The second scenario had little or nothing to do with any underlying business. Maverick stock-picker James Cramer, founder of TheStreet.com, argued that one of the things that had affected the company share price was the selling of the stock by insiders. When eToys had gone public they had sold eight million shares; the other ninety-three million shares were owned by insiders – early investors, the founders and their employees. The regulations governing the IPO meant that the insiders were not allowed to sell any of their shares for a period of six months. In the jargon of Wall Street this is called the 'lock-in' period, and for eToys it had ended in the first weeks in November. From then, many early investors and various ex-employees took the opportunity to sell, releasing millions of shares on to the market. For followers of the 'castle in the air' theories of corporate value, who care more about the behaviour of investors than the intrinsic worth of a company, this increase in the supply of shares was the important cause for the decline in their price.

The third scenario was that the stock's decline had been caused by etoy and their supporters, exactly as Reinhold Grether had proposed right after the injunction and ®™ark had taken up in their campaign. The idea was that bad press, the threats of the hacktivists and the commentators on the investor bulletin-boards had affected the share price. Many activists advocated versions of this point of view on email lists and Web sites. John Perry Barlow declared, 'I'm actually surprised that the market would respond in this way but it did. It shows you that the people doing Internet analysis realized there might be some need to take into account the Internet community, and if that's the case, then the Internet community has more influence than I thought we did . . . If we can band together against predatory practices and drive eToys' stock down, then we have a considerable tool.' Joichi Ito commented, 'A lot of people lost money. I think [the Toywar] . . . affected the value to a certain degree. It's unclear by how much. I think you will never be able to prove it but I think the idea that it did affect the stock is a great story.'

Even influential analysts without any ties to etoy gave the idea some credit. As James Cramer wrote, one 'reason for the decline might be some sort of sabotage of the site itself by dissident Web folk – who are apparently enraged about a court battle eToys has had against etoy.com . . . The publicity over this tussle has apparently frightened some holders into selling.'

In the end, perhaps, this perspective overstates the influence of the Toywar. Since the injunction there had been more than 2,000 mentions of eToys in the global press, with only a fraction of these reporting the legal case. Many analysts and professionals on Wall Street and investors at home simply hadn't heard of the Toywar. At its peak, thirteen million shares in eToys were changing hands in a single day, transactions worth $220 million. This was not a small stock ripe for manipulation. As *The Wall Street Journal* suggested, campaigners 'continue to fantasize that an extended plunge in eToys stock price was related to bad publicity'.

The idea that a group of artists could affect a billion dollar corporation is nonetheless intriguing. Whether or not the activists had a direct causal effect on the decline in the share price, their hyperbolic assertions brilliantly reveal much about the value of eToys as a kind of quicksilver which would as easily pass through the fingers as be turned into real cash. In the alchemy of the Internet stock market bubble, where gold seemed to be conjured out of the most unlikely elements, the parable of the Toywar demonstrates that even the most absurd of ideas could in very real ways be less ridiculous and more sensible than the heavily regulated and deeply serious capital markets themselves and the corporations they promoted. Indeed in this topsy-turvy world etoy's claim that the Toywar was 'one of the most expensive performances in art history (4.5 billion dollars)' is much less ludicrous, and certainly more entertaining, than many of the other assertions of an era that had lost touch with reality.

For etoy, the Toywar meant a fillip to their own share-price. Zai meticulously updated the etoy.SHARE graph and claimed that at the end of the battle the shares had risen to almost $6 per unit.

On 14 February, Network Solutions put the etoy.com domain back on to their master list and www.etoy.com went active for the first time in almost three months. On it etoy played a bombastic version of 'Yankee Doodle Dandy'. The accompanying text read: 'Let's give thanks to the Generals and the Heroes and Heroines of Toywar.' Across the bottom of the screen snaked a victory parade, headed by two white stretch-limousines blazing the names of the etoy lawyers Peter Wild and Chris Truax. Behind these marched a never-ending parade of Toy Soldiers, generals driving toy tanks and LEGO men in front of turntables, all celebrating the historic victory.

The parade was followed by a long list of credits scrolling upwards. The beginning of this list read: 'Toywar.com, produced by TOBY LENK & FRIENDS (financed by the eToys shareholders); directed by the etoy.CORPORATION; witnessed by more than 100 million Internet users, television viewers and newspaper readers on planet earth; november 1999–february 2000; starring: 1780 TOYWAR.agents, ca. 38000 NASDAQ shareholders, 250 journalists worldwide, 45 lawyers & one judge'.

11
Game Over

'Nothing sedates rationality like large doses of effortless money.'
   Warren Buffett, *Berkshire Hathaway Annual Report* 2001

'Ever had the feelin' that you've been cheated?'
   Johnny Rotten of the Sex Pistols, at the end of their last
                                                   concert in 1978

The first few months of 2000 were not the happiest for eToys as they grappled with the post-mortems of the Christmas distribution sagas. For many working there the company no longer seemed like a small determined business on the up. Now it was big, faceless and devoid of the previous camaraderie – executives even began to argue about the relative sizes of their offices. And everywhere the air was heavy with the scent of vanished millions as the share price collapse wiped out most of the benefit of employees' share options. Many of the team left. Rob Johnson and Shay – once nicknamed 'The Boys' – felt they had outgrown the company. It was no longer interesting to work for such a bureaucratic organisation; they hungered for the entrepreneurial days of old.

Despite the collapsing share price, Toby continued to feel that eToys could become greater still. The prevailing wisdom of the time was that only one, or possibly two, children's retailers would come to dominate the market, so it was vital to continue to be the frontrunner. As their Web site claimed, 'Vision: To be the pre-eminent online children's brand in the 21st century.' This ambition was heartily cheered by some investment analysts, including Lauren Cooks Levitan of Robertson Stephens, who increased her rating of the company in February to a 'buy' announcing, 'We believe the current valuation offers investors a compelling opportunity to own an important etailing franchise' – words she would later be forced to eat.

With the capital markets still bubbling, money looked almost free. Toby and the eToys management therefore decided to gamble on the future by building some of the biggest and best retail distribution warehouses in the whole of America. On sites in Ontario, California, Danville, Virginia, Blairs, North Carolina and elsewhere they leased more than two million square feet of industrial shedding – equivalent floor area for ten thousand cargo containers. These were to be palaces of the warehouse world, fitted out at the cost of tens of millions of dollars with state-of-the-art pick and pack equipment. They were built on the promise of a capacity of about a billion dollars a year in sales, which predicted an eight-fold increase in turnover. At this scale, it was hoped, the costs of distribution would become a smaller proportion of the out-goings and eToys might even be able to make a profit.

In contrast to eToys' crashing share price, most other technology shares were on the up and up. Shares in Cisco and Intel rose by more than a third between January and March 2000. On 10 March the NASDAQ Composite Index – the value of all the shares in the technology-heavy NASDAQ exchange – having more than doubled in less than a year, pierced an important psychological barrier, the 5,000 mark. To many of the amateur investors it seemed as if the markets would never fall.

On Wall Street bankers and investment professionals muttered to themselves that the intrinsic 'firm foundation' value of corporations did not justify the enormous share prices. Despite the facts, only a few investors were willing to take their money out of the market for fear they would miss its next leap.

Warren Buffett, arguably the greatest investor of his generation, was one of the few who never bought Internet company shares. For much of the previous five years he was laughed at for failing to ride the markets as he stuck to his 'value' philosophy of buying into old economy companies. Reaching for an allegory to describe the heady moment of March 2000, he described it as if it was Cinderella's ball in which investors 'hate to miss a single minute of what is one helluva party. Therefore, the giddy participants all plan to leave just seconds before midnight. There's a problem, though: They are dancing in a room in which the clocks have no hands.'

As March progressed, the ideological and fiscal pillars of the boom were slowly dismantled. First, a Yale economics professor, Robert Shiller, published a book, *Irrational Exuberance*, which was a damning analysis of the boom times and painted a picture in which the valuations of companies had become detached from reality: 'The high valuations in the stock market have come about for no good reasons. The market level does not, as so many imagine, represent the consensus judgement of experts who have carefully weighed the long-term evidence.' He attacked many of the fundamental axioms of the Long Boom belief system describing a foolish media, and an even stupider investing populace who believed in an ever rising market.

Then, on 30 March, *Barrons*, the influential financial weekly, ran a piece headlined 'Burning Up' which surveyed more than 200 Internet companies and found not only were they running out of cash but that a quarter of them were going to burn through all their reserves in the coming year. The article also included a small paragraph about eToys, which said they had 'enough cash on hand to last only 11 more months, so stay tuned.' The hot air and grandiose ideas that had supported the bubble were now rapidly vanishing.

On Tuesday 4 April, the stock market underwent an extraordinary gyration. By 1.18 p.m. Eastern Standard Time, the NASDAQ Composite Index had collapsed by 13.6 per cent. But suddenly the panic selling hit its limit and in just over an hour the index almost recovered. By the end of the day it had fallen by only 1.77 per cent. This was both the biggest single day loss and the biggest single day rise in any major index in history. The expanding bubble had reached bursting point and in the following ten days various pieces of news – including economic indicators and the continuing Anti-Trust suit against Microsoft – further dampened enthusiasm.

Then on 14 April, the market finally snapped; the NASDAQ Composite Index lost almost 10 per cent of its value having already declined by 15 per cent in the course of the previous week. The wider stock market also fell, wiping $2.1 trillion out of US share values in the biggest one-day market loss since money was created. As Dan Rather reported on CBS *Evening News*, 'The closing bell didn't ring, it tolled.' Investors were feeling the pain. One senior Wall Street investor told Rather, 'I sound calm because I'm numb. This is the level after panic. It's like watching a natural disaster.' As the euphoria evaporated the word 'reality' became a standby for journalists and headline writers: *The Industry Standard* screamed, 'Reality is biting hard'; *The Economist* claimed that 'reality has kicked in'; and others spoke of 'a big dose of reality' for the world of the Internet. Everyone was waking up to what had happened.

During the following weeks and months, the world's press went on a determined hunt for scapegoats. With every passing day another newspaper piece spotlighted the sinners of the Great Internet Bubble. Everybody, it seemed, was guilty, from the venture capitalists for pushing their companies too hard, to the brokers for lending investors too much money, to the media that had reported the 'financial markets like a sport', to the fund managers for aggressively investing in companies built on air.

Investment analysts were particularly chastised for not accurately predicting the falling market and for having a conflict of interest: rather than offering independent advice they were in the dock for promoting companies so that their banks could secure the lucrative business of issuing shares and debt. Investment bankers were also berated for throwing out the Old Rules of cautious banking, which demanded corporate endurance, profit and stability before a public offering. Some commentators even suggested that it was as if companies were designed more with an eye to making money *off* investors rather than *for* them.

Even the age's heroes – the small investors – now became the villains. The Internet, by shattering the old cartel of Wall Street, devolving power to hordes of outsiders sitting in the suburbs in America and across the world, had created a new culpable community. According to the press it was they that had formed a 'critical mass of opinion' posting to investor bulletin boards and channel-surfing the twenty-four hour cable financial news hyping the boom. This was a bit rich. Many had lost their savings. But the odds were stacked against them: for all the dreams of truly democratic capital markets, the trading floor was still controlled by the professionals.

Nonetheless in the end everybody who played the market – from stock-picking mother in Utah to the smartest of Wall Street bankers – contributed to the crash. As Warren Buffett said, 'It was as if some virus, racing wildly among investment professionals as well as amateurs, induced hallucinations in which the values of stocks in certain sectors became decoupled from the values of the businesses that underlay them.' There was an irony that Timothy Leary's belief, way back when, that the Net's future lay in tripping into virtual reality had been transformed into the capital markets' journey into a field of dreams.

A few miles from Wall Street and barely a fortnight after the crash, on 29 April, a hundred or so people gathered for a very different event. A fashionable art gallery called The Postmasters in Chelsea was holding the opening of an etoy exhibit. A forty-foot cargo container, 'Tank 7', was parked outside the gallery with the large etoy logo on the side; spidering into its roof were plastic pipes, which seemed to deliver the utilities to the mobile office.

Reinhold Grether – the eccentric academic from Constance

who had first imagined that etoy's supporters could play with share prices – had boarded a plane for the first time in his life to fly in from Germany. Chris Truax – etoy's aggressive lawyer – had had his ticket from San Diego paid for by etoy. Other valiant Toy Soldiers also arrived for the victory celebration to find Zai, Gramazio and Kubli no longer sporting their orange uniforms but mingling with the crowd in white shirts, black ties and black suits with their sponsors' logos embroidered on to their sleeves. Underneath their jackets they were wearing what seemed to be orange bullet-proof vests.

Kubli acted as a master of ceremonies. From behind an orange table in the gallery he handed out share certificates to the most prominent Toywar soldiers. Chris Truax and a man who represented the activist group ®™ark posed for the cameras with their shares. Later DJ Spooky, a star in the esoteric world of digital music, spun tracks, including tunes from the Toywar CD *Lullabies*.

Inside one of the gallery's white cubes visitors were confronted with a full collection of two-feet-high etoy.SHARES portraying a complete history of the group arranged on the walls, including seven staring faces of the original members of the gang, the Digital Hijack, Gramazio shaking hands with the Austrian Chancellor at their first share sale, and then a collection of Toywar images in the form of malevolent LEGO characters. In the gallery's centre stood an orange tent, protected by barbed wire snaking across its peak. Inside there were four plinths on each of which was a keyboard and a mouse. These controlled computers, which projected the 'glorious' history of the Toywar onto the tent's sides.

In another room an orange banner, with a quotation ascribed to 'Joichi Ito, CEO of NEOTENY JAPAN and major etoy. INVESTOR', adorned most of a wall. It read, 'Unlike most Internet stocks, etoy.SHARES have actually paid massive dividends in the form of art and fun. I feel I've already received a return on my principle and everything else is pure upshot. etoy continues to beat analysts' expectations on reach and retention.

Solid products, strong marketing and first mover advantage in the hype management sector have put etoy in the lead. I would rate etoy.SHARES a strong BUY.'

That the show made it into *The New York Times* was thrilling enough for etoy but they were even more delighted to have moved from the Business to the Arts section. The respected art critic Roberta Smith described etoy's visual style as a blend of Devo, a space-age pop group from the 1980s, and Neo Geo, the art movement whose most famous member was Jeff Koons, 'with a dash of James Bond', and concluded, 'The group's anonymity, lack of physical product and combination of explicit parody and implicit idealism seem typically avant-garde, and the "boys just want to have fun" spirit is as old as the hills. What is exceptional, however, is the skill with which etoy melds different spaces – cyber, actual and Conceptual – into genuine, if artistic, liquidity.'

The next day Zai, Gramazio and Kubli met Chris Truax in the unventilated and suffocatingly hot tank. The first item on the agenda was to try and secure the etoy trademark and prevent further questions about the legitimacy of the etoy domain. Also, having fought so hard in January to end the legal case 'without prejudice', the option to sue the toy company was now on the table. Zai was excited about the prospect; it would go some way to satisfy his anger about the original lawsuit and might make them some money. It was also a way of distancing themselves from the pious protestors as they were keen to make etoy's brand

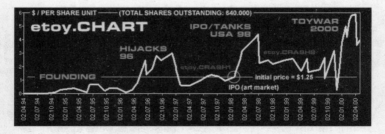

The rise and fall of etoy shares.

more than simply about anti-corporate activism. For them the world that etoy mimicked was one in which everything was mixed and good and bad were extremely close and interchangeable. To make etoy a more ambiguous proposition it was decided that Truax would, if necessary, sue eToys in exactly the same way that they themselves had been sued some eight months before. They were taking the war back to toy town.

Halfway through this meeting the door of the tank was pushed open to reveal two cowboy boots: having wanted to attend the opening John Perry Barlow had inadvertently shown up a day late. The etoy boys, however, were delighted to meet for the first time the writer of the Declaration of the Independence of Cyberspace. 'It's exactly for those situations that we have built the tank,' Zai recalls. 'It is a perfectly absurd environment. Barlow walked around the tank, knocking on the walls and saying over and over, "you are crazy, you guys are insane. You guys have taken too much LSD".' Inevitably they launched into a discussion about Timothy Leary, LSD and the story of how Barlow had met Joichi Ito at Leary's home. They partied on late into the night.

For a week etoy plied their business in New York. They were never out of character – after all they were a serious company doing serious business, so they tried to persuade art lovers to speculatively invest in their cultural corporation.

On the other coast of America at the same time, the end of April 2000, eToys published their year end results, announcing that annual sales had leapt from the $30 million the year before to $151 million. A substantial hike, albeit not the ten-fold increase they had once aimed for. Against this they had spent in total $340 million, of which an astonishing $56 million on advertising alone. The bottom line loss was $189 million. And the results disguised the even sourer news, that it cost far more to distribute the toys than anyone had hoped. Additionally, because their sales were so heavily skewed to the Christmas season, their expensive call centres and warehouses – not to mention the management staff – were wildly underused for the rest of the time. With their share price down to $8.00, the company was also now worth less than a billion dollars. Toby declared to the press, 'We see a clear path to profitability. The largest of the quarterly losses is behind us. We're putting the stake firmly in the ground.'

In May, Toby called investment analysts from Wall Street banks to a meeting in New York at which he assembled his company's executives. His big news was that he thought he could break even by 2002, and to do so eToys would make an annual revenue of between $750 and $900 million. It was an extraordinary promise. This was more than five times the current annual turnover. The company had only been going for three years, and yet it gambled on being able to see three years into the future.

Toby also announced that he was trying to reduce the reliance of the company on toys, and move to less seasonal categories like party supplies and hobby items. The idea was that they should become a one-stop-shop for all things related to children. There was even talk that the name they had so determinedly defended and marketed, eToys, was no longer appropriate for a company with such grand ambitions. Really it should be 'ekids', and they had set about registering ekids.com and the trademark, as well as a collection of other associated names, in the hope of having the time to change their brand.

Sean McGowan, the senior analyst at the boutique bank Gerard Klauer Mattison was present at the analyst meeting. Listening to Toby's speech about future profits he remembered how he had probably squandered the chance to participate in the eToys Initial Public Offering when he had dared to ask Toby about the prospects of profitability. Now he felt that Toby gave 'a pretty good presentation and that he had at least thought it out'. But he was still sceptical as to whether eToys could win. When Toby finally walked out of the room, he seemed as exuberant as ever. McGowan recalls, 'He walks out, and as he goes by he wags his finger at me, and says, "Sean, I have given you the DNA to profitability, do not miss it." I'm thinking, "never mind DNA, what about DNR, Do Not Resuscitate?"'

In August, eToys' two largest competitors amazon.com and Toys'Я'Us forged an alliance which was well received on the capital markets. The toy company agreed to manage the inventory, and pay amazon.com to deal with the warehouses and the Web site. Toby had been approached about the deal earlier but had refused, thinking he could make it on his own. He remained bullishly mocking. 'I'm pleased as punch,' he said. 'They recognize that neither can compete alone against us.' And yet what it did demonstrate was that the real-world retailers were not easily surpassed, nor were they willing to give in to the new arrivals.

With the bubble bursting Toby was having problems raising the cash he needed to pay for warehousing, advertising and office space. One particular piece of company history made things especially difficult, which was that in November 1999 Toby and the board had raised a debt of $150 million, having to pay $9 million a year in interest alone. At the height of the boom it had seemed to be a good deal. Raising money by issuing new shares would have come on easier terms but would have meant giving up more ownership, whereas by taking a debt they retained much more of this incredibly valuable company for the existing shareholders. In the bust, the debt was an albatross. By June 2000, it was worth about a quarter of the value of eToys. New investors were wary of lending money to an already indebted company.

With the options closing all about him Toby swallowed the bitterest financial pill of them all by raising the $100 million he needed in 'convertible notes': as Wall Street figuratively calls it, the 'toxic convertible' is a type of financing which has taken many companies to their graves. The terms were draconian. If the share price rose then the debt could eventually be paid back. But if the share price fell below $3 then the 'poison' would be released onto the market as the overall debt would be converted into new shares created from scratch. The lower the share price, the more shares would be issued, thus diluting the value of all existing shareholders' holdings, flooding the market with millions of unwanted shares which would drive the stock price even lower.

It was an extreme gamble. *Fortune* magazine wrote, 'the honeymoon is over'.

In Zürich Zai was busying himself with other projects. Moving etoy 'off shore' he set up a 'branch' on the Cayman Islands. He also hatched a plan with Joichi Ito to safeguard etoy's precious data on Sealand, an old oil rig in the North Sea, which promised to keep it out of the reach of any national jurisdiction. But at the same time an old wound was re-opening. Brainhard, once the etoy spokesman and Zai's Viennese collaborator, having resigned in San Francisco, had watched the Toywar and etoy's success. Now he was embittered that Zai had emerged from all the power struggles as the heir of the etoy empire. Brainhard had come to believe that it was unfair that he could not use the etoy name for his own purposes.

However he knew of etoy's hidden vulnerability: that they had neglected to register the etoy trademark in the European Union. So he filed for it in Austria. He also started signing emails with 'etoy.Brainhard, reactivated' and registered the domain digitalhijack.org. Once in possession of the Austrian trademark he filed for it across the EU. As he says, 'Zai can't claim etoy just for himself. etoy is a lifestyle that we adopted. It's not about legal matters, it's about identity. Once you are etoy, you are etoy forever.'

When Zai, Gramazio and Kubli learned about Brainhard's coup, they were outraged at his 'unscrupulous' behaviour. Kubli, responsible for legal issues, 'almost went crazy', Zai says. 'He could not sleep anymore at night, he could not participate in our meetings anymore. For the sake of his own sanity he had to stay away from everything that was etoy.' Kubli thought about resignation; even Zai considered giving up his beloved art project. Under the extreme emotional pressure Zai even went as far as telling people: 'I am going to shoot Brainhard in the head if this crazy trademark dispute continues.'

For Zai, Brainhard's behaviour had opened a second front in the war to retain possession of etoy and so he asked etoy's shareholders to declare Brainhard 'persona non grata', threatening that Brainhard and eToys 'should prepare for legal wrestling. the court room will be their stage. as real funky businessmen who love attention they deserve the "full show".' The Chief Executive of etoy felt caught in a Catch 22: 'Either we give in and Brainhard decides the image of the etoy brand, or we defend our rights and end up in court with all the heinous consequences. Everybody will think we are fucked up because we sue an ex-member.' It was a bind not too dissimilar to the one that eToys had faced a year before.

Over the course of that year Zai became more and more obsessed, often unable to sleep as he irritably defended 'his' brand. He spent hours discussing with Chris Truax each and every contact with eToys' lawyers. He found some comfort from the approval and registration of etoy's US trademark after three years of waiting but it could not dampen his rage against Brainhard. He wrote regularly to his advisors to appraise them of the events, although not all of them managed to keep a straight face when he demanded that 'his' brand be aggressively defended. Douglas Rushkoff says, 'I felt that etoy were always the strongest when they understood that they were playing a game. But they started thinking "we have this curatorial value, and our art works are worth this or that". They started talking in the rhetoric of their shareholder value, of the brand they had created over all these years. And that is where Brainhard, to his credit, served up a truth serum to etoy, by being "I am going to fuck with this".'

As Zai ranted and insisted that everyone takes sides he began to annoy some of the Toywar activists. They were even more irritated when etoy seemed to claim exclusive credit for the Toywar victory. For example, Gramazio wrote, 'what they [the audience] saw and understood was not reality but just another fiction, a thrilling and monumental story designed by a bunch of media manipulators.' Some of their supporters applauded their hubris. The loyal academic, Reinhold Grether from Constance, began composing treatises praising the achievement of the Toywar

Platform. In one he wrote, 'The Toywar platform remains a monument to world culture for all times.'

By contrast ®™ark, who were one of etoy's biggest helpers in the Toywar, became one of their biggest critics. Where ®™ark believed that they deserved some credit for the media campaign, Zai insisted that the victory was mostly down to the Toywar Platform, although this had only come online in January. As Frank Guerrero of ®™ark said, 'the "etoy veneer machine" is interested in turning the organic, independent activist response to the eToys suit into a piece of art, seemingly coordinated by etoy . . . which seems in some ways counterproductive for modelling future actions, especially given that etoy now has all these activists enlisted in their toy army, but refuses to send them anywhere to fight. So in the end, it is a digital activist hijack, the toy soldiers forever lodged in an unusable database . . .' In the end these former brothers-in-arms stopped speaking to each other.

As the American holiday season approached October 2000, it became increasingly apparent that eToys would die if it did not pull off a blockbuster quarter. Toby and his board had gambled at every turn, having spent millions on new warehousing, promising to increase the annual turnover to between $750 and $900 million within three years and capping it all by swallowing the poisonous financial pill of toxic convertibles. Now Toby announced that this holiday season would see revenue soar to between $210 and $240 million, trumping previous corporate ambitions with an additional attempt to remodel the company as a catalogue retailer by dropping hundreds of thousands of eToys glossy brochures on to American doorsteps. There couldn't have been a worse time for this attempt as the American retail market was about to suffer its poorest Christmas season for years.

The company also chose that moment to move into a huge bespoke office building in the high rent area of West Los Angeles. Whilst outside the building simply displayed their logo, inside it was as if a kindergarten interior designer had been at work: the reception walls had been modelled to resemble enormous LEGO bricks, there was a huge Etch-a-Sketch in the meeting room and board-game carpets had been installed all over for the employees to play Twister, Scrabble and the pre-school game of Candyland on the floors. Even to many employees this seemed like the final sign of hubris.

At the beginning of November Toby declared to an unconvinced press, 'As we enter our peak season in 2000, I believe eToys.com has never looked better, has never been so well organized, and has never offered consumers a better overall experience than it does today.' As one analyst put it, 'eToys is going to have to climb Mount Everest to survive.'

At the same moment the share price dipped below $3, which was the trigger for the toxic convertibles to turn into shares. Until that point there had been 121 million shares of common stock, of which only about 50 million were tradable given a variety of restrictions. By the beginning of December, however, another 35 million shares had been issued, for an average of about $2 a share, so diluting the value of the existing shares. The market was being swamped with a commodity that no one wanted and the share price was being driven down in what Wall Street called a 'death spiral'.

On 8 December, *The Wall Street Journal* published an extraordinary interview with Toby. It was as if he stood on the bridge of an enormous tanker heading for the rocks and behaving as if he was unaware of his fate, for he was still talking about eToys' 'path to profitability'. Only when asked about any regrets did he admit that, 'We probably could have spent a bit less if the climate were more sane.' But Toby remained convinced that really it was others rather than himself that were to blame: 'When the speculative frenzy was out there, there was way too much capital from the venture community funding too many ideas, and too many management teams. That makes it harder for the good ideas and companies to do their jobs.' eToys, he felt, did not deserve to be 'abandoned right before the finish line, it's frustrating.'

The final part of the interview was pure Toby, still the model of an honourable captain who had taken so many risks that he was going to maintain a stiff upper lip right to the bitter end. Asked about his '5 Rules for Weathering the Dot-Com Storm' he remembered the hit book and film about a captain and his boat that had gone down in the biggest recent Atlantic storm. His parting advice was, 'Picture yourself as George Clooney in "The Perfect Storm". No matter how big the waves get, hold on to the wheel and keep your eyes on the horizon. Also, hope for a better ending than the movie.'

Just one week later, after the stock markets closed on Friday 15 December, eToys was forced to release a terrible and unexpected statement: sales had only been $125 million, half of the quarterly sales which Toby had predicted. They were obliged to tell their investors immediately as eToys' money was going to run out in March 2001. For most people, the analysts, the employees and even some of their own management, the announcement that the dream was over came as a shock.

eToys employees received a memo from their Chief Executive. Toby told them, 'I could not be more proud of what we have achieved since eToys was created just a few short years ago. We have built well-known and highly-admired consumer brands, and we have served millions and millions of customers in the US and internationally well and with pride. We should all stand tall.'

The press jumped all over them and called it 'a full-fledged disaster', or 'a fitting tribute for hubris'. For *The Washington Post* eToys' fall was proof of 'the brutalities' of e-commerce: 'Barely two years ago, the lean and smart Internet-born retailers were supposed to eat their slower and stupider off-line competition for lunch. Now they've turned out to be the feast themselves.' After the weekend the analysts downgraded the eToys stock and Lauren Cooks Levitan, of Robertson Stephens, suspended her ratings and estimates. 'They were swinging through the rafters the way they financed it,' she told *The Wall Street Journal*. 'They built a palace and ended up with a barbecue.'

eToys' shares nose-dived to just 28 cents.

On 4 January 2001, eToys announced the closing down of both their smaller warehouses and the UK branch. Seven hundred of a thousand-strong American workforce was laid off and eToys also announced that they were not going to answer the phone to creditors. Goldman Sachs was appointed to explore options to sell the business, but being saddled with at least $150 million in debt, it was difficult to find a buyer.

Still hoping to participate in the dot-com goldrush, etoy took eToys' demise badly and pushed for a final showdown. As a result, etoy's lawyer Chris Truax filed two complaints in a Californian court against eToys, one of which applied for the cancellation of the eToys trademark and the other for the transfer to etoy of the eToys.com domain. In addition etoy demanded the transfer of etoy.net, having discovered that the toy company had registered several domain names which were close to etoy.com some months before. Mirroring the previous court case's central assertion but with a switching of role from defender to plaintiff, Truax wrote that eToys' use of their trademark was 'likely to cause consumer confusion, mistake or deception and infringes on etoy Corporation's rights'. Zai, Kubli and Gramazio chose the day of eToys' disastrous earnings announcement, on 25 January, to release details of the new case to the media.

eToys responded to the court by saying that etoy had 'a vendetta' against them because of the injunction in 1999. They explained that etoy's action was 'carefully timed' to disrupt the selling of assets or the company as a whole as the lawsuit would have to be declared to potential purchasers. Bemoaning that this was 'casting a cloud' over their trademark rights and the easy transfer of the domain, eToys complained that this would all be detrimental to their business.

Few media outlets bothered to report the new lawsuit, nor did the Internet community and the cultural press greet the news with much enthusiasm. Many felt that the artists were running out of ideas, others that they more and more resembled an aggressive corporation and that they risked losing their artistic credibility. In a press release Zai, on behalf of etoy, countered that they only wanted 'to sort out some heavy problems with the old dogs in the market before we all move a step further.' Truax called the filing of the legal suit a 'defensive move' to stake out the etoy territory and told the press, 'It is not a question of revenge. It is a question of closure.'

On 7 March, eToys formally filed for Chapter 11 bankruptcy, which meant that they would keep operating under the administration of the court in order to maximise the value of their remaining assets for their investors and creditors. In a statement they said that they would close their Web site the same day. Most of the remaining 300 staff were let go. With debts of more than $400 million and assets of only $285 million eToys announced that their shares were likely to become 'worthless' and they ceased to be traded on NASDAQ. Chris Truax did not miss this opportunity to dance on the grave. As he jokily told a reporter, 'I guess you could say with the demise of eToys it's the end of an error.' The orderly winding up of the business and the demise of a thousand people's livelihoods was just another excuse to stick the boot in. He added, 'I've never seen such a long and drawn-out sort of final agony. It's been a very painful process for everyone to watch. Get it over with!'

The desultory end of the Web site came in eToys' Network Operations Centre, in a scene which bares a striking resemblance to the moment eighteen months before when Zai, Gramazio and Kubli had been forced by the Californian court to shut down their server. Some of the remaining staff had gathered for the funeral along with Shay and Rob Johnson. The engineering team had prepared a last application: on screen a picture of a child on tiptoes turning off a bedroom light underneath which was a switch simply marked 'Off'. Toby clicked the button. It was emotional and sad, particularly as so much effort had gone into building their state-of-the-art systems. Shay remembers Toby's last words being 'this sucks'.

Ridicule and contempt spilled onto many Internet message boards. 'Another DOTCOM thats DOTGONE!! Fuck what a bunch of losers!!' ranted one anonymous correspondent. Many posters remembered the Toywar, and vented their anger in vivid messages such as 'etoys is toast but etoy is still standing. now the scumbags at etoys really have gotten their comeuppance. toby you really were a little shit for what you did.' It was, as another message board poster wrote, 'What goes around comes around. It warms my heart.'

What had been the most valuable toy shop in history, whose name half of the American population could remember unaided, stopped trading forever that day in March 2001. After spending $600 million they had served 3.4 million customers. Left vacant were millions of square feet of real estate on two continents. Left over in the warehouses were piles of Barbie Fashion Avenue Party: Gold Dress with Fur, Crayon Candles and thousands of packets of AA batteries. Also up for sale was a collection of hundreds of domain names, trademarks and the transcendent brand, 'eToys, Where Great Ideas Come To You'. Toby left the company at the beginning of April, leaving other managers to deal with the final winding up and the bankruptcy.

The news of eToys' failure focused attention again onto idealab!. In the previous year Bill Gross had squandered the better part of a billion dollars buying parts of companies that he had once owned. He had bought them at the top of the market, thinking their values would continue to rise. In the week of the stock market crash itself he had filed the initial prospectus, the S-1, to take his company, valued at that time about $8 billion, public. The filing had also included the surprise addition of Jack Welch, the Chief Executive of the world's largest company, General Electric, and the pre-eminent American businessman of his generation – who had been persuaded by Bill Gross to join the board of idealab!. Six months later, however, Gross announced that the flotation was cancelled.

The Internet economy's former poster boy now found himself the object of ridicule. Whilst *Fortune* labelled him 'a tragic figure of the Internet bust' the shares of his publicly traded fledglings were on average down by more than eighty per cent from the price they had initially been sold for. Once so great a star, he was now rated 'a loser' because, as *Business Week* scornfully explained, 'his incubator has hatched nothing but rotten eggs'.

Even the business model of the 'incubator' that had once been praised as fundamentally changing business life was now pilloried.

In an ironic twist Bill Gross was now spending much of his time trying to make money out of domain names. Not only had Network Solutions proved that the registration of domains was a profitable business but they had been sold for $21 billion to the Internet security company, Verisign, just before the crash. And so Bill Gross created a number of domain companies of his own. One was called 'Dot TV', which bought the rights to register the top level domain .tv from the Pacific Island Tuvalu for four million dollars a year. Shay and Rob Johnson, who previously built eToys' Web site, were now its Chief Technical Officers.

As ever Gross himself remained optimistic and refused to be beaten. 'We have really, really great companies coming out,' he told a reporter. 'Very, very bold, world-changing.'

eToys dragged its feet whilst winding down. At the end of April 2001, they applied to the court for further permission to retain eighty employees. 'Even in bankruptcy, some dot-coms can't avoid excess', the *Dow Jones newswire* ranted. 'Are the 80 people needed to make sure a war doesn't break out between the Pokémon action figures and the Backstreet Boys dolls?' eToys also sold Babycentre to Johnson and Johnson for $10 million, a fraction of the $190 million purchase price paid just two years earlier. A firm called KB Toys bought the remaining inventory at a huge discount. After several other potentially interested parties had walked away, KB Toys also picked up a package including the eToys trademark, logos, the domain name and some software for a payment of $3.35 million – a small sum to pay for a brand which had had $100 million lavished upon it. Analysts were shocked at the rock bottom price. One cooed, 'That's a great deal. My goodness.'

According to etoy, the trademark dispute caused KB Toys some difficulty as of the $3.35 million they had to pay to eToys, half a million was put into an escrow account just in case. eToys creditors could only get hold of it after the dispute was settled, and any costs would be met from this money. At the time of writing, with eToys' declining brand-value, it seems unlikely that etoy will get their hands on much of it.

The liquidation caused some bitterness. Toby had been given a $500,000 bonus to ensure he stayed around until April. Aside from his salary, that was about all he ever made for the shares that he owned, once worth $600 million, were now worthless. In a complicated financial deal, he had even bought eToys shares as the price was collapsing using his existing shares as collateral. In the end he had to sell these and more, in order to repay the loan. Toby, who had always protested that he was creating the company for more transcendent and sublime reasons than money, did not walk away a rich man.

Most of those who remained until the end were prevented either by regulations or by Toby's power of persuasion from selling their shares. In a peculiar twist of fate those that had fallen out or found they were no longer needed by the zealous founders of the company were those that made the most money. Bill Gross and idealab! pocketed more than $200 million. eToys' first Chief Technology Officer, Rob Ferber, and their first marketing Vice President, Phil Polishook, both made between five and ten million dollars whilst their top-notch successors only pocketed their salaries. Greg McLemore and Eva Woodsmall, the founders of the first toy shop on the Internet, toys.com, were winners too, reaping something like $25 million between them from the shares they had been given as part of the buy-out. Frank Han – the co-founder with Toby – took home about a million dollars, but complained to the *Industry Standard* that he had incurred unpayable tax liabilities which neutered this windfall.

The demise of eToys together with their cohort of once valuable consumer retail 'plays' – like the pet food supplier pets.com, the grocer webvan.com and the online pharmacist planetrx.com – brought the whole value of online shopping into question. In the end, for all its technological decoration and its ability to search and find products, the Internet turned out to be little more than a glorified catalogue-retailer. It was perhaps proleptic that the grandfather of catalogue-retail, Sears Roebuck, closed its catalogue business in 1993 just as the Internet boom was beginning, having decided that it just couldn't make a decent profit despite a turnover of more than three billion dollars. It was a lesson which the Internet retailers had failed to take account of, faced as they were with the same high costs of home delivery, the aggressive pricing of the discount malls and the growing realisation that consumers actually liked the experience of going shopping. For all the excitement not enough consumers were ready to shift to use a new and unfamiliar technology to replace their familiar habits.

The truth was that it didn't matter how many millions entrepreneurs spent on growing their Internet companies because the customer base just wasn't as big or as fast to arrive as everyone had imagined. No one could force a consumer to log on, let alone buy. Whilst the millions spent on television advertising made Internet brands, like eToys, household names, in many of the homes where the name tripped off tongues there was no Internet access. Also, to the surprise of those early theorists, the winners seemed likely to be the 'incumbents' – the old order of media, manufacturing and retailing companies – which managed to re-order themselves to profit from the Web without losing their original identities. Amongst the carnage amazon.com, Toby's original model, and eBay looked set to survive.

As the bubble burst so the wider Internet euphoria faded. Ten years earlier, before anyone ever imagined that it might be sensible to sell dog food on the Net, the early ideologues and Internet evangelists had envisioned a global village, a connected world which would fertilise democracy and liberty. Challenged by the worldwide online community even businessmen would become more moral and cool. What became clear was that there was to be no wholesale redistribution of power. The Internet's journey from a free academic network to a global and commercial territory created a cyberspace which, unsurprisingly, mirrors the 'real' world. The technology proved itself to be a value-free utility on which users tended to impose their own values. The online world is now mostly dominated by businesses of all kinds. As Frank

Guerrero of ®™ark says, 'It was good to win the battle of the Toywar but it felt like we had lost the wider war.'

That said individuals and individualism do flourish around the edges: particular communities like the consumers of furry pornography or obsessive genealogists created new services for themselves; a generation of anti-capitalist activists learned to take advantage of the connected technology; and artists of all kinds found niche audiences without having to play the entertainment industry's game. One thing is certain: the mutual and equal technology of the Internet designed by Jon Postel and his colleagues all those years ago did not allow only the powerful to have a voice. So the battles continue to flare up. Whilst much of the territory has been already aggressively fought over, and fences that already existed in the real world have been erected across the digital wilderness, the fights continue about the ownership of music, the freedom of expression or the powerful new force of the free software movement. It is the technology itself that holds the seeds for most of the battles – whatever they may be.

By the summer of 2001 Zai's obsession with the business aspects of etoy was a source of increasing provocation to the members he'd fallen out with previously. Since leaving the etoy mothership each of them had found satisfaction in pursuing careers. Esposto founded micromusic.net, under the tag-line 'low tech music, for high tech people', an online community of digital music artists which received an Honorary Mention at Ars Electronica. Goldstein and Udatny had their own international Web site design consultancy, rosa, which they managed with some others. Goldstein acted as the Chief Executive while Udatny was the Chief Technology Director. Brainhard ran his own 'shock marketing' company, ubermorgen, and has collaborated with ®™ark to create and promote voteauction.com, a Web site which supposedly auctioned votes in the 2000 US election.

In the end they all grew tired of Zai's self-righteousness, and came to feel that he owed them something as he had exploited etoy's tank, brand and corporate identity which they had jointly worked so hard to create. As Zai's determined opposition to Brainhard brought them closer, they decided to create a new company, the etoy GmbH, based in Germany. Even Udatny, so reluctant to play a part ever since the others had kicked him out years before, joined the group when they apologised to him. Brainhard promised to transfer the European trademark of etoy to the new company. As Esposto put it, 'It's about justice. It is a statement to those who use the name etoy now.' Their hope was that the new company would 'secure our rights in our artistic work,' according to their Chief Executive designate, Goldstein. 'We are not out for revenge,' said Brainhard. 'We just want to be able to use the etoy brand too. From now on we will define our reality ourselves.'

Kubli is now a trainee clerk in a Zürich court and occasionally works for etoy. Gramazio remains the President of the etoy. CORPORATION as well as running his architecture practice. Zai is still the Chief Executive and lecturing at art schools. As well as defending their brand against their former friends, they have built up a new crew and secured invitations to create new projects in Tokyo and Turin.

Toby meanwhile saw literary agents in a bid to secure a book deal for his version of the eToys story. One can only imagine that the book is about a captain on a ship that is sinking in the perfect financial storm. He also joined Highland Capital Partners as an Entrepreneur in Residence.

For a long time Zai kept a message posted on the etoy.com Web site to his former adversary. 'Mr. Lenk,' it read. 'Let's try and bury the hatchet. Now that you've lost your "s", why not come and play with us? As CEO of etoy, I personally invite you to join our board. Together we are an unrivalled team. Imagine! We could really rock the party.'

The trouble was that at the Internet ball the music had stopped and there was no more dancing.

Appendix: Share Holdings

eToys' Initial Public Offering happened on 20 May 1999, almost two years after the company was founded. The IPO was the moment when all dreams and faith in the company were turned into real returns. Never before in the history of toys had such a colossal amount of money been created in such a short space of time.

As a public company, the point of eToys was to create wealth for its shareholders, whilst providing a service for its customers. And the greatest sign of achievement of that is the company's overall worth. The list of investors below, on the first day of trading, almost tells the whole story of the business itself: from a tiny family-and-friends outfit to becoming the darlings of Wall Street, its major investors the stars of the capital markets. It was difficult to say, on that day, which was more important: the credentials of those who invested or the amount of money they handed over to be part of the eToys dream.

Typically etoy has their own satiric take on this essential part of corporate engineering. As they state in their business plan, 'the only goal of the etoy.CORPORATION is to increase the etoy.SHARE-VALUE through revolutionary incubations in the field of action entertainment design, special effects, coding, music production, cultural logistics, social engineering/interaction, and art.'

For them their list of share ownership is one of their most essential elements in what they consider to be their art. It contains the names of some of the stars of their field of digital art, as well as tracing their own corporate history.

etoy.SHARES 29 April 2000

Name	Total shares	Value ($)	Percentage equity stake	Date of acquisition
Founding members				
etoy ZAI	84,800	327,328.00	13.250	January 1998
etoy GRAMAZIO	56,160	216,777.60	8.775	January 1998
etoy BRAINHARD	41,760	161,193.60	6.525	January 1998
etoy GOLDSTEIN	31,685	122,304.10	4.950	January 1998
etoy KUBLI	28,800	111,168.00	4.500	January 1998
etoy ESPOSTO	23,755	91,694.30	3.711	January 1998
etoy UDATNY	8,640	33,350.40	1.350	January 1998
Major shareholders				
Joichi Ito, Venture capitalist, Japan	17,500	67,550.00	2.734	
Suzy Meszoly, Curator, USA	8,321	32,119.06	1.300	June 1999
MIGROS, Cult. Dept., Switzerland	8,000	30,880.00	1.250	October 1998
Viktor Klima, former Chancellor of Austria	6,000	23,160.00	0.937	January 1998
Walter Rüegg, Advertising Manager, Switzerland	6,000	23,160.00	0.937	
®™ark	5,150	19,879.00	0.804	
Ruedi Zai, Architect, Switzerland	4,200	16,212.00	0.656	March 2000
UCSD-CRCA/Research Center, USA	4,200	16,212.00	0.656	June 1998
Nico Wieland, Coder, Switzerland	4,200	16,212.00	0.656	
Gottlieb Duttweiler Institut, Switzerland	4,000	15,440.00	0.625	
Rennie Pritikin, Curator Yerba Buena, USA	3,800	14,668.00	0.593	June 1999
Reinhold Grether, PhD, Germany	3,345	12,911.70	0.522	April 2000
William Linn, Curator USA	2,400	9,264.00	0.375	June 1999
Alexander Fischl, Graphic Designer, Austria	2,091	8,071.26	0.326	January 2000
Gabriela Von Wyl, Switzerland, aka Ms Monorom	2,090	8,067.40	0.326	October 1999
Other shareholders				
Peter Wild, Lawyer, Switzerland	1,200	4,632.00	0.178	February 2000
Douglas Rushkoff, Writer, USA	1,200	4,632.00	0.178	February 2000
John Perry Barlow, USA	1,200	4,632.00	0.178	February 2000
Wolfgang Staehle, The Thing USA	1,100	4,246.00	0.171	January 2000
Peter Conheim, Negativland, USA	952	3,674.72	0.148	January 2000
Richard Zach, Austria, USA	1,823	7,071.52	0.286	December 1999
Paul Miller SPOOKY, DJ, USA	1,200	4,632.00	0.178	April 2000
Lev Manovich, Professor, USA	1,200	4,632.00	0.178	June 1998

Shareholding for eToys on 20 May 1999

Names	Number of shares	Percentage	Value ($)	Purchase value ($)	Purchase date
Idealab!	18,000,000	18.00	1.4b	97,000	Jun. 1997
Highland Capital	12,411,183	12.20	950m	{ 10m	Mar. 1999
				8m	Jun. 1998
Sequoia Capital	8,131,989	7.99	622m	{ 10m	Mar. 1999
				5m	Jun. 1998
DynaFund	7,691,505	7.56	588m	1m	Dec. 1997
Intel Corporation	7,691,502	7.56	588m	1m	Dec. 1997
Idealab! Capital Partners	6,978,303	6.86	534m		Jun. 1997
Toby Lenk	7,491,000	7.36	573m	37,500	Jun. 1997
Frank Han, co-founder	2,488,752	2.45	190m		
Lou Zambello, SVP Ops	825,000	0.81	63m		Vesting
Steven Schoch, CFO	750,000	0.73	57m		Vesting
John Hnanicek, CIO	600,000	0.59	45m		Vesting
Janine Bousquette, SVP Marketing	480,000	0.47	36m		Vesting
New shareholders	8,320,000	8.17	636m	166m	
Some early shareholders	4,404,054	4.33	337m	910,171.16	Aug. 1997
Ken Deemer (angel)	247,044	0.24	18.9m	51,055	Aug. 1997
Marc D. Kozin (Toby's former boss)	98,817	0.10	7.6m	20,422	Aug. 1997
Edward Lenk (Toby's father)	98,817	0.10	7.6m	20,422	Aug. 1997
Tom Staggs, CFO Disney Corp.	248,377	0.24	19m	30,633	Aug. 1997
Arnold Whitman (Toby's brother-in-law)	123,522	0.12	9.5m	25,527	Aug. 1997
Burton and Sandra Polishook, (parents of 1st VP Mktg)	49,062	0.05	3.8m	10,139	Aug. 1997
Norman Tsang (friend of Frank Han)	49,062	0.05	3.8m	10,139	Aug. 1997
Marcee Kleinman (Bill Gross' sister)	171,720	0.17	13m	35,488	Aug. 1997
Shares distributed to management and investors of eToys.com	2,340,000	2.30	79m		

Bibliography

Much of this book is based on more than a hundred interviews on three continents with many of the central players of the story or those that witnessed events.

Whilst many of the key people in the story were co-operative there are some voices that are notably absent. Most of the senior management of eToys were unwilling to talk to us, although we are grateful to Lou Zambello, Senior Vice President Operations 1999–2000, and Phil Polishook, Vice President Marketing 1997–1999, as well as about twenty early employees. Likewise, whilst Bill Gross at idealab! insisted that he was keen to be interviewed but never found the time or the inclination to tell his story, various people with whom he had worked were prepared to be interviewed.

The existing members of etoy (Zai, Gramazio and Kubli) agreed to participate and the other founding members were happy to give up their time. In the wider stories of the Web many people gave generously of their time. Players in the capital markets, the participants in the domain wars, creators of search engines and anti-corporate hacktivists spoke to us.

Quotations in the text are taken either from our interviews or from the following printed sources.

Chapter One

Main Articles

CERN: 'History and growth', 3 December 1977

Berners-Lee, Tim: 'The Founder's Message', *Forbes ASAP*, 1 December 1997

Books

Berners-Lee, Tim: *Weaving the Web: The Past, Present and Future of the World Wide Web by its Inventor* (Orion Business, London, 1999)

Clark, Jim, with Owen Edwards: *Netscape Time: The Making of the Billion-Dollar Start-Up that Took on Microsoft* (St Martin's Press, New York, 1999)

Chilvers, Ian: *Oxford Dictionary of 20th-Century Art* (Oxford University Press, Oxford, 1999)

Ferguson, Charles H.: *High St@kes, No Prisoners. A Winner's Tale of Greed and Glory in the Internet Wars* (Three Rivers Press, New York, 1999)

Gillies, James & Robert Cailliau: *How the Web was Born: The Story of the World Wide Web* (Oxford University Press, Oxford, 2000)

Hafner, Katie and Matthew Lyon: *Where Wizards Stay Up Late: The Origins of the Internet* (Touchstone Books, New York, 1998)

Kelly, Kevin: *Out of Control* (Fourth Estate, London, 1994)

Negroponte, Nicholas: *Being Digital* (Knopf, New York, 1995)

Quittner, Joshua and Michelle Slatalla: *Speeding the Net: The Inside Story of Netscape and how it Challenged Microsoft* (Atlantic Monthly Press, New York, 1998)

Segaller, Stephen: *Nerds 2.0.1: A Brief History of the Internet* (TV Books, New York, 1998)

Chapter Two

Main Articles

Barlow, John Perry: *Declaration of the Independence of Cyberspace, 1996* (http://www.eff.org/Publications/John Perry Barlow/ barlow 0296.declaration)

Barlow, John Perry: 'Is There a There in Cyberspace', in: *Mythos Information. Welcome to the Wired World*, @rs electronica 95 (Springer-Verlag, Vienna/New York 1995)

Boulware, Jack: 'Mondo', *San Francisco Weekly*, 11 October 1995

The Economist: 'The Internet. Postel disputes', 8 February 1997

Elmer-Dewitt, Philip: 'In the Fifties it was the beatniks, staging a coffeehouse rebellion', *Time*, 1 March 1993

Froomkin, Michael: 'Wrong Turn in Cyberspace', *Duke Law Journal* [Vol. 50:17, 2000]

Gilmore, Mikal: 'Timothy Leary 1920–1996', *Rolling Stone*, 11 July 1996

Jordan, Gregory: 'Radical Nerds: The '60s Had Free Love; The '90s Have Free Information', *The New York Times*, 31 August 1996

Mansnerus, Laura: 'Timothy Leary Takes Final Trip: "Turn-On, Tune-In, Drop-Out" Guru Dies at 75', *The New York Times*, 1 June 1996

Peters, Tom: 'A Brand Called You', *Fast Company*, August 1997

Quittner, Joshua: 'The Merry Pranksters Go to Washington', *WIRED*, 1 June 1994

Sobchack, Vivian: 'New Age Mutant Ninja Hackers, Reading Mondo 2000', in: Mark Dery (ed.): *Flame Wars: The Discourse of Cyberculture*, Durham 1995, pp. 11–28.

Books

Auletta, Ken: *World War 3.0: Microsoft and Its Enemies* (Random House, New York, 2001)

Gibson, William: *Neuromancer* (Ace Books, New York, 1994)

Klein, Naomi: *No Logo* (HarperCollins, London, 2000)

Leary, Timothy: *Chaos & Cyberculture* (Ronin Publishing, Berkeley, 1994)

Leary, Timothy, with R. U. Sirius: *Design for Dying* (HarperCollins, San Francisco, 1997)

Lunenfeld, Peter: *Snap to Grid* (MIT Press, Boston, 2000)

Orwell, George: *1984* (Penguin, London, 1949)

Rheingold, Howard: *The Virtual Community* (MIT Press, Boston, 1993)

Chapter Three

Main Articles

Armstrong, Larry: 'Bill Gross, Online Idea Factory', *Business Week*, 18 June 1998

Baker, Molly and Joan E. Rigdon: 'Netscape's IPO Gets an Explosive Welcome', *The Wall Street Journal*, 9 August 1995

Baker, Molly: 'Little Stock Called Netscape Is Lofted to the Heavens In a Frenzy of Trading', *The Wall Street Journal*, 10 August 1995

Beatty, Jack: 'A Capital Life', *The New York Times*, 17 May 1998

Carbonara, Peter and Maggie Overfelt: 'The Dot-com factories', *Fortune*, September 2000

Economist: 'Business schools teach you to build one company that focuses on a few good ideas. Bill Gross never went to business school', 3 August 1997

Elmer-Dewitt, Philip: 'The Battle for the Soul of the Internet', *Time*, 25 July 1994

FitzSimon, Jane: 'Loosening Up Lotus', *Boston Globe*, 18 April 1989

Forbes: 'Promiscuous breeding', 7 April 1997

Fortune: '25 cool companies', 22 September 1993

Gilmor, Dan: 'To be an Online Company, first throw out old

rules', *St Louis Post Dispatch*, 24 February 1997 (syndicated from the *San Jose Mercury*)

Gilpin, Kenneth and Eric Schmitt: 'Plain-English Software a Project for 2 Brothers', *The New York Times*, 19 December 1985

Green, Noah: 'Weaning the Net: the feds hand cyberspace to the private sector', *The Village Voice*, 11 July 1995

Gross, Bill: 'The New Math of Ownership', *Harvard Business Review*, 11 January 1998

Hardy, Quentin: 'Netscape Plans Initial Public Offer', *The Wall Street Journal Europe*, 26 June 1995

Harmon, Amy: 'A Little Knowledge, Young Firm Aims to Make Learning a Multimedia Adventure', *Los Angeles Times*, 13 June 1994

Harmon, Amy: 'Spielberg Close to Deal', *Los Angeles Times*, 7 June 1994

Harmon, Amy: 'Agency Acts to Privatise the Internet', *Houston Chronicle*, 6 September 1994

Johnson, Johna Till: 'The Internet Opens Up to Commercial Use', *Data Communications*, 1 March 1993

Kaplan, Karen: 'Beleaguered idealab Needs to Hatch a Plan for its Survival', *Los Angeles Times*, 8 March 2001

Krantz, Michael: 'Billion Dollar Brain', *Time*, 23 September 1996

Lewis, Geoff: 'Teaching Lotus 1-2-3 to Understand English', *Business Week*, 28 October 1995

Magid, Lawrence: 'Giving Advice for a Price', *Los Angeles Times*, 1997

Martin, Michael: 'Cool Companies, Online Sale of Intellectual Property', *Fortune*, 22 September 1993

Matson, Eric: 'He Turns Ideas into Companies – at Net Speed', *Fast Company*, December 1996

McChesney, John: 'Hot Seat, Net Nursery', *Hotwired*, December 1997

McChesney, John: 'Internet Startups', National Public Radio, 7 January 1997

Nocera, Joseph: 'Why is Bill Gross Still Smiling?', *Fortune*, 5 March 2001

Platt, Charles: 'What's the Big Idea?', *WIRED*, September 1999

Rafter, Michelle: 'Internet Incubator Has Been Slow to Hatch Start-ups', *Los Angeles Times*, 21 July 1997

Silberman, Steve: 'If It's Bits It's Ideamarket's "Meat"', *WIRED News*, 11 December 1996

Steinert-Threlkeld, Tom: 'Can You Work on Netscape Time?', *Fast Company*, November 1995

Useem, Jerry: 'The Start-up Factory', *Inc.*, February 1997

Useem, Jerry: 'Entrepreneur of the Century', *Inc.*, 18 May 1999

Weber, Jonathon: 'idealab! Puts Net Concepts to Work', *Los Angeles Times*, 9 December 1996

Wrubel, Robert: 'Advantage Nerds', *Financial World Partners*, 21 January 1992

Wolff, Michael: 'Electronic Kool-aid Acid Test', *Forbes*, 2 April 2001

Books

Cringely, Robert X.: *Accidental Empires* (Addison Wesley, New York, 1992)

Himanen, Pekka: *The Hacker Ethic and the Spirit of the Information Age* (Secker and Warburg, London, 2001)

Levy, Steven: *Hackers: Heroes of the Computer Revolutions* (Penguin, London, 1984)

Malkiel, Burton G.: *A Random Walk Down Wall Street* (W. W. Norton, New York, 1999)

Packer, Randall and Ken Jordan: *Multimedia: from Wagner to Virtual Reality* (W. W. Norton, New York, 2001)

Peters, Tom: *The Tom Peters Seminar* (Vintage, New York, 1994)

Chapter Four

Main Articles

Ito, Joichi: 'Joi's point of view: Artists with "terrorist" tinge hijack users', *The Daily Yomiuri* (no date available)

Kirkpatrick, David: 'Riding The Real Trends In Technology Now That The Internet's Changed Everything', *Fortune*, 19 February 1996

Leonard, Andrew: 'Search Me', *Hotwired*, 5 August 1996

Lohse, Deborah: 'Yahoo!: Hype Builds for Wall Street Event', *The Wall Street Journal*, 19 March 1996

Marchard, Oliver: 'etoy – oder Schwachsinn hat einen Namen', *kunstradio.de*, 16 September 1996

Pinkerton, Brian: 'Finding What People Want: Experiences with the WebCrawler', paper for the Second WWW Conference in Chicago, 17 October 1994

Poulsen, Kevin: 'Hacker Mitnick released Friday', zdnet.com, 20 January 2000

Rankin, Bob: 'Interview With Brian Pinkerton, Developer Of WebCrawler', internet.com, August 1995

Rigdon, Joan: 'Yahoo! Stock Soars in Its First Day, But History Says the Issue May Tumble', *The Wall Street Journal*, 15 April 1996

Verity, John: 'What Hath Yahoo Wrought?', *Business Week*, 2 December 1996

Books

Pinkerton, Brian: 'Webcrawler, Finding What People Want', dissertation submitted for Doctor of Philosophy, University of Washington, 2000

Chapter Five

Main Articles

Andrews, Whit: 'Warehouses Emerge as Key Assets for Many Online Stores', *Internetworld*, 11 May 1998

Booth, Jason: 'Financiers Hit Jackpot With eToys', *Los Angeles Business Journal*, 19 April 1999

business2.com: 'Santa's New Helpers', 1 December 1998

Cavuto, Neil: 'eToys – CEO – Interview', *The Cavuto Business Report* (Fox News Network), 15 June 1999

Ch'ien, Evelyn: 'The aDigital Architect Profile: eToys' Frank Han', *aDigital*, 19 June 2000

Crystler, Julie: 'The Domain Game', *The Village Voice*, 14 January 1997

Doward, Jamie: 'A Gift-horse in the Mouse', *Guardian*, 24 October 1999

Fast Company: 'The Trouble with Toys', December 1998

Festa, Paul: 'Toy Seller Takes to the Web', news.com, 1 October 1997

Fry, Jason: 'etoys Story', *The Wall Street Journal*, 12 July 1999

Helft, Miguel: 'Uncle of the Board', *The Industry Standard*, 17 December 1999

Jackson, Tim: 'Shopping for Toys can be Fun', *Financial Times*, 5 October 1997

Kanter, Larry: 'Web Smurfing', *Los Angeles Business Journal*, 27 September 1997

Kanter, Larry: 'Online Toy Seller Gets Capital Infusion, Enjoys Strong Sales', *Los Angeles Business Journal*, 12 January 1998

Kaplan, Karen: 'By Other Name, Would EToys Sell the Same?', *Los Angeles Times*, 20 September 1999

Kingson Bloom, Jennifer: 'Banker Runs Off to Play On-Line with New Toy-Marketing Venture', *American Banker*, 24 April 1997

Knight, Rebecca: 'People in Focus: Toby Lenk', ft.com, 4 May 2000

Krantz, Michael: 'Billion Dollar Brain', *Time*, 23 September 1996

Macht, Joshua D.: 'Upstarts: New-Biz Watch', *Inc.*, 1 October 1998

Martin, Michael: 'The Next Big Thing', *Fortune*, 9 December 1996

Miller, Leslie: 'eToys Tops Among Virtual Toy Stores', *USA Today*, 24 December 1997

Newsweek: 'Cyberscope', 20 October 1997

Quick, Rebecca: 'Internet Addresses Spark Storm in Cyberspace', *The Wall Street Journal*, 29 April 1997

Schenker, Jennifer L.: 'A Plan To Change the Name Game Prompts High Drama on the Internet', *The Wall Street Journal*, 19 September 1997

Stoughton, Stephanie: 'A Virtual Toy Story', *Boston Globe*, 26 November 2000

Stutz, Michael: 'InterNIC Who?', *WIRED*, 16 July 1997

Useem, Jerry: 'Internet Defense Strategy: Cannibalize Yourself', *Fortune*, 6 September 1999

Weintraub, Arlene: 'He's Not Playing', *Business Week*, 24 July 2000

Winters, Rebecca: 'EToys CEO', *Time*, 30 November 1998

Books

Adams, Scott: *The Dilbert Principle* (Harper Business, New York, 1996)

Christensen, Clayton: *The Innovator's Dilemma: When New Technologies Cause Great Firms to Fail* (Harvard Business School Press, Cambridge MA, 1997)

Coupland, Douglas: *Microserfs* (Flamingo, London, 1996)

Eisner, Michael, with Tony Schwartz: *Work In Progress* (Penguin Books, London, 1999)

Frank, Thomas: *One Market Under God* (Doubleday, New York, 2001)

Gilder, George: *The Spirit of Enterprise* (Simon and Schuster, New York, 1984)

Kaplan, Jerry: *Startup: A Silicon Valley Adventure* (Houghton Mifflin Company, New York, 1995)

Micklethwait, John and Adrian Wooldridge: *The Witch Doctors* (Heinemann, London, 1996)

Peters, Tom: *The Tom Peters Seminar, Crazy Times Call for Crazy Organisations* (Vintage, New York, 1994)

Other Sources

eToys press releases

Chapter Six

Main Articles

Aitch, Ian: 'The Cussing Computer', *Independent*, 16 November 1998

AP Press: 'David Bowie Bonds with Wall Street', 14 February 1997

Arquilla, John and David Ronfeldt: 'Cyberwar is Coming!', *Comparative Strategy*, Vol. 12, No. 2, 1993, pp. 141–165

Carvell, Tim: 'Ziggy Gold Dust Good Buy Or Just A Wall Street Novelty Act?', *Entertainment Weekly*, 4 April 1997

Critical Art Ensemble: 'Electronic Civil Disobedience', 1996

Dominguez, Ricardo: 'Digital Zapatismo', thing.net

Dworkin, Andy: '"Mutual fund" Skewers Big Business', *Dallas Morning News*, 30 May 1999

Frauenfelder, Mark: 'Secret Prankster Fund Goes Public', *WIRED*, March 1997

Harmon, Amy: '"Hacktivists" of All Persuasions Take Their Struggle to the Web', *The New York Times*, 31 October 1998

McKay, Niall: 'Pentagon Deflects Web Assault', *WIRED*, September 1998

Simon, Julian: 'The Greatest Five Years for Humanity', *WIRED*, June 1998

WIRED, several authors: 'Corporate Rebels, Eight Who Made A Difference By Challenging Conventional Wisdom', May 1997

Leaving Reality Behind

WIRED: Wired 25, November 1998

Wray, Stefan: 'Electronic Disturbance Theatre News', email distributed by EDTN, 9 September 1998

Books

Eggers, Dave: *A Heartbreaking Work of Staggering Genius* (Simon and Schuster, New York, 2000)

Frank, Thomas: *One Market Under God* (Doubleday, New York, 2001)

Klein, Naomi: *No Logo* (HarperCollins, London, 2000)

Peters, Tom: *The Tom Peters Seminar: Crazy Times Call for Crazy Organisations* (Vintage, New York, 1994)

Other Sources

etoy press releases

Chapter Seven

Main Articles

Anders, George and Lisa Bannon: 'EToys to Join Web-Retailer Parade With IPO', *The Wall Street Journal*, 6 April 1999

Beckett, Paul: 'Visa Launches New Ad Campaign Touting Ease of Internet Shopping', *The Wall Street Journal*, 30 October 1998

Bicknell, Craig: 'Ebay Opens IPO Floodgates', *WIRED news*, 25 September 1998

Butcher, Andrew: 'Game On for US Virtual Toy Seller', *The Times*, 7 April 1999

Clark, Tim: 'BabyCenter Acquisition Delays eToys IPO', news. com, 20 April 1999

Davidson, Paul: 'Net Retailer eToys Faces Big Risks as its Star Rises', *USA Today*, 8 April 1999

Dugan, Ianthe Jeanne and Aaron Lucchetti: 'After Becoming Stars of the Dot-Com Boom Founders Find Fame Fleeting', TheGlobe.com, 2 May 2001

Feldman, Amy: 'Renewing Pressure on Wall Street', *The New York Daily News*, 11 January 1999

Fineberg, Seth A.: 'eToys Takes On Toy Giants', *Venture Capital Journal*, 8 January 1998

Forbes ASAP, different authors: 'Futureshop', 6 April 1998

Fry, Jason: 'eToys Story', *The Wall Street Journal*, 12 July 1999

Gillmore, Dan: Dan Gillmore Column, *San Jose Mercury News*, 14 February 1999

Glasner, Joanna: 'EToys' IPO Rocket Ride', *WIRED news*, 20 May 1999

Glassman, James and Kevin Hassett: 'Stock Prices are Still Far Too Low', *The Wall Street Journal*, 17 March 1999

Guglielmo, Connie: 'Henry Blodget', *Inter@ctive Week*, 14 August 2000

Kalin, Sari: 'Whoever Sells The Most Toys Wins', *CIO Web Business Magazine*, 1 December 1998

Kawamoto, Dawn: 'TheGlobe.com's IPO one for the Record Books', cnet.com, 13 November 1998

Krantz, Matt: 'Stocking A Giant Toy Box', *USA Today*, 24 November 1999

Krantz, Michael: 'Click Till You Drop', *Time*, 20 July 1998

Kurtz, Howard: 'Who Blew the Dot-Com Bubble?', *Washington Post*, 11 February 2001

Labate, John: 'Online Toy Retailer eToys Hopes To Raise $115 Million In Initial Public Offering', *Financial Times*, 18 February 1999

The Los Angeles Times: 'NASDAQ slide tops 10%, making it a "correction"', 26 May 1999

Mannes, George: 'Wit Capital Grabs Merril's Cohen amid Talk of IPO', TheStreet.com, 2 April 1999

Miller, Samantha and Karen Brailsford: 'In The Money: Toy Wonder Net Mogul Toby Lenk's Biz is Kid's Stuff', *People*, 11 January 1999

O'Malley, Chris: 'Jungle Fever On the Web', *Time*, 7 December 1998

Pacelle, Mitchell: 'Take Internet, Add Timing, Hit Paydirt', *The Wall Street Journal*, 19 April 1999

Pulliam, Susan and Terzah Ewing: 'Internet Stocks Drop to Bear-Market Territory', *The Wall Street Journal*, 25 May 1999

Schwartz, Peter and Peter Leyden: 'The Long Boom: A History of the Future, 1980–2020', *WIRED*, July 1997

Sellers, Patricia: 'Inside the First E-Christmas', *Fortune*, 1 February 1999

Serwer, Andrew: 'Nothing but Net', *The Wall Street Journal*, 11 October 1999

Sullivan, Jennifer: 'TheGlobe.com's Galactic IPO', *WIRED news*, 13 November 1998

Sullivan, Jennifer: 'Investor Frenzy over eBay IPO', *WIRED news*, 24 September 1998

Surowiecki, James: 'Cocktail Hour', Slate.com, 20 May 1999

Tully, Shawn: 'How to Make $400,000,000 In Just One Minute', *Fortune*, 27 May 1996

Weber, Steven: 'The End of the Business Cycle', *Foreign Affairs*, Summer 1997

Books

Brooks, David: *Bobos in Paradise: The New Upper Class and How they Got There* (Touchstone Books, New York, 2001)

Galbraith, J. K.: *The Great Crash 1929* (Penguin, London, 1954 – republished 1990)

Kindleberger, Charles P.: *Manias, Panics and Crashes, A History of Financial Crises* (Macmillan, London, 1978)

Lewis, Michael: *The Future Just Happened* (Hodder and Stoughton, London, 2001)

Nocera, Joseph: *A Piece of the Action: How the Middle Class Joined the Money Class* (Simon & Schuster, New York, 1995)

Shiller, Robert J.: *Irrational Exuberance* (Princeton University Press, New Jersey, 1999)

Chapter Eight

Main Articles

Anders, George: 'Ante Up!', *The Wall Street Journal*, 2 November 1999

AP online: 'Disney Buys Into Online Toy Retailer', 25 August 1999

Armstrong, Larry: 'The War Against eToys Is No Game', *Business Week*, 9 August 1999

Bannon, Lisa: 'eToys, Readings $20 Million Blitz To Hit Homes For The Holidays', *The Wall Street Journal*, 27 September 1999

Borden, Mark and Suzanne Koudsi: 'America's Forty Richest Under Forty', *Fortune*, 27 September 1999

Business Week: 'A New Game Plan For Toysrus.com', 30 August 1999

Cavuto, Neil: 'The Cavuto Business Report', Fox News Network, 15 June 1999

Cramer, James: 'A Different Kind of Toy Story', TheStreet.com, 23 November 1999

Doward, Jamie: 'A Gift-horse in the Mouse', *Guardian*, 24 October 1999

Fisher, Eric: 'Cyber-retail Battles Against Red Ink, *The Washington Times*, 17 August 1999

Lowell, John: 'Top Online Retailer of Children's Products eToys Announced', internetnews.com, 31 August 1999

Lucas, Sloane: 'Play Time', *Brandweek*, 9 November 1999

Ranninger, Rebecca: 'Lawyers Sue on Behalf of No One In Order To Line Their Own Pockets', *Silicon Valley/San Jose Business Journal*, 12 September 1997

Rolling Stone: 'The Pepsi Challenge', 16 October 1997

Sinclair, Tom: 'Soda Pop', *Entertainment Weekly*, 26 September 1997

Books

Heistand, Fred J. and Carol Livingston: *California's 'Unfair Competition Act' – A New Lesson in Unfairness* (Association for California Tort Reform (ACTR), Sacramento, 1997)
Locke, Christopher, Rick Levine et al.: *The Cluetrain Manifesto: The End of Business As Usual* (Perseus Press, New York, 2000)

Other Sources

eToys versus etoy: court papers filed in the Superior Court of the State of California for the County of Los Angeles
eToys versus etoy: court papers filed in the United States District Court, Central District of California
eToys press releases
etoy press releases

Chapter Nine

Main Articles

Froomkin, Michael: 'Wrong Turn in Cyberspace', *Duke Law Journal*, Vol. 50:17, 2000
Mueller, Milton: 'Rough Justice: An Analysis of ICANN's Uniform Dispute Resolution Policy', *The Information Society Journal*, forthcoming
Pearlman, Laura: 'Truth, Justice and the Dot-Com Wars', *The American Lawyer*, 31 March 2000
Stalder, Felix: 'Fences in Cyberspace', heise.de, 17 November 1999

Other Sources

eToys versus etoy: court papers filed in the Superior Court of the State of California for the County of Los Angeles

eToys versus etoy: court papers filed in the United States District Court, Central District of California

eToys press releases

etoy press releases

Chapter Ten

Main Articles

AP Press: 'Online Toy Store Under Attack', 15 December 1999

Barliant, Claire: 'E-Toy Story', *The Village Voice*, 1 December 1999

Bicknell, Craig: 'EToys Relents, Won't Press Suit', *WIRED news*, 29 December 1999

Cramer, James: 'Of eToys and Dot-Coms', TheStreet.com, 22 December 1999

Elliott, Michael: 'The New Radicals', *Newsweek*, 3 December 1999

Financial Times: 'Hackers Try to Disrupt Internet Toys Company', 18 December 1999

Financial Times: Lex Column, 'US Internet Retailers', 31 January 2000

Fry, Jason: 'Another David Fells a Goliath; Will E-Lummoxes Ever Learn?', *The Wall Street Journal*, 28 January 2000

Grimmett, John and Joe Shea: 'Clashing Domain Names Underlie Unusual Court Case', *The American Reporter*, 28 December 1999

Guglielmo, Connie: 'Protest Group Out to "Destroy" eToys', *inter@ctive Week*, 13 December 1999

Helft, Miguel: 'EToys Backs Down From Bully Stance', *Yahoo! news*, 29 December 1999

Kettman, Steve: 'Toying with Domain Names', *WIRED news*, 11 December 1999

Kettman, Steven: 'E-Riots Threaten EToys.com', *WIRED news*, 15 December 1999

Kettman, Steve: 'Be Grateful for Etoy', *WIRED news*, 17 December 1999

Kettman, Steve: 'Etoy: "The Fight Isn't Over"', *WIRED news*, 30 December 1999

Kettman, Steve: 'Etoy Balks at Olive Branch', *WIRED news*, 30 December 1999

Kettman, Steve: 'Etoy: Don't Forgive, Don't Forget', *WIRED news*, 15 January 2000

Kettman, Steve: 'Victory for Etoy Is at Hand', *WIRED news*, 26 January 2000

Leiby, Richard: 'EToys vs. Etoy: A Clash of Commerce and Art', *The Washington Post*, 10 December 1999

Leiby, Richard: 'The Fine Art of Compromise; EToys Seeks Peace in Trademark Battle With Artists' Web Site', *The Washington Post*, 31 December 1999

Messmer, Ellen: 'eToys Attacks Show Need For Strong Web Defenses', *Network World*, 20 December 1999

Miller, Greg: 'Internet Fuelled Global Interest in Disruptions', *The Los Angeles Times*, 1 December 1999

Mirapaul, Matthew: 'EToys Lawsuit Is No Fun for Artist Group', *The New York Times*, 9 December 1999

Mirapaul, Matthew: 'ISP Blocked After eToys Protest', *The New York Times*, 18 December 1999

Rötzer, Florian: 'eToys.com zieht die Klage gegen Etoy.com zurück', heise.de, 26 January 2000

Shabelman, David: 'Nothing but Net', TheStreet.com, 17 December 1999

Smith, Rebecca: 'EToys Lured Holiday-Season Shoppers But Concern About Service Hurts Stock', *The Wall Street Journal*, 18 December 1999

Sullivan, Bob: 'WTO Protest Spills Onto The Web', MSNBC, 1 December 1999

Sydney Morning Herald: 'EToys Wins Court Freeze on Etoy Site', 12 December 1999

The Wall Street Journal: 'Some Web Customers Cry: "All I Want for Christmas Is My Order!"', 13 December 1999

Young, Steve: *Moneyline News Hour*, 17 December 1999 – aired 6.30 p.m. EST

Other Sources

eToys versus etoy: court papers filed in the Superior Court of the State of California for the County of Los Angeles

eToys versus etoy: court papers filed in the United States District Court, Central District of California

eToys press releases

etoy press releases

Network Solutions Inc., Network Solutions' Domain Name Dispute Policy, Revision 03, 25 February 1998

Chapter Eleven

Main Articles

Arango, Tim: 'eToys, Offering $1 Million Bonus to Execs, Mulls Severance Cuts', TheStreet.com, 2 March 2001

Ard, Scott and Rachel Konrad: 'Net Incubator Idealab! puts IPO plans on Ice', 19 October 2000

Bannon, Lisa: 'Boss Talk: EToys CEO Toby Lenk Affirms Faith in Eventual Profitability', *The Wall Street Journal*, 8 December 2000

Bannon, Lisa: 'EToys' Disappointing Forecast', *The Wall Street Journal*, 18 December 2000

Bartlet, Bruce: 'Consider The Cause . . . Skip The Panic', *The Washington Times*, 21 March 2001

Bicknell, Craig: 'Goldman Loses Midas Touch', *WIRED news*, 10 May 2000

Braine, Bob: 'Etoys Still Plays With Creditors' Money', *Dow Jones newswire*, 2 May 2001

Buffett, Warren: 'The Oracle Was Aesop', *Berkshire Hathaway Annual Report 2000*, March 2001

Business Week: 'The Losers: Bill Gross', 8 January 2001

Business Week: 'How Some Venture Capitalists Performed', 16 April 2001

CBS Evening News with Dan Rather, 14 April 2000

Chemow, Ron: 'A Market in Need of a Broker', *The New York Times*, 16 March 2000

cnet.com: 'Milberg Weiss Announces Class Action Suit Against Three Investment Banks', 4 July 2001

cnet.com: 'Cauley Geller Bowman & Coates, LLP Announces Class Action Lawsuit', 4 January 2001

Cope, Nigel: 'More grief in dot.com land as EToys pulls plug on', *Independent*, 4 January 2001

Cope, Nigel: 'Idealab! Wields The Axe But Some Festive Season Cheer', *Independent*, 15 January 2001

Dow Jones newswires: 'Johnson & Johnson Buys BabyCenter From eToys', 2 March 2001

Economist: 'Money to Burn', 27 May 2000

Elstrom, Peter: 'The Great Internet Money Game', *Business Week*, 16 March 2001

Gentile, Gary: 'EToys Files for Bankruptcy', *AP*, 7 March 2001

Glasner, Joanna: 'eToys Epitaph: "End of an Error"', *WIRED news*, 8 March 2001

Glasner, Joanna: 'Incubating More Internet Money', *WIRED news*, 28 April 2000

Hillebrand, Mary: 'VeriSign To Acquire Network Solutions for $21B', *E-Commerce Times*, 7 March 2000

internetstocks.com: 'Etoys: A Good Play', 4 February 2000

Kaplan, Karen: 'Beleaguered idealab! Needs to Hatch a Plan for its Survival', *The Los Angeles Times*, 8 March 2001

Keller, Michele: 'No Frivolous Question: Is eToys Played?', *The Industry Standard*, 14 September 2000

Kelly, Erin: 'The Last e-Store on the Block', *Fortune*, 18 September 2000

Luening, Erich: 'eToys Unveils a Pair of Online Stores', cnet.com, 3 November 2000

Medosch, Armin: 'Toywar II', ctmagazin.com, 31 January 2001

Miles, Stephanie: 'EToys' Engineering Chief Built Grand Site, Then Helped Shut It', *The Wall Street Journal*, 16 March 2001

Miles, Stephanie: 'eToys Warns of Weak Revenue', *The Wall Street Journal*, 15 December 2000

Morgenson, Gretchen: 'Analysts Misjudge The Market', *The New York Times*, 31 December 2000

Nocera, Joseph and Ellen Florian: 'Why Is He Still Smiling?', *Fortune*, 5 March 2001

Patrizio, Andy: 'New.net Defies Domain System', *WIRED*, 5 March 2001

Rabinovitz, Jonathan: 'The End of the Beginning', *The Industry Standard*, 17 April 2000

Ratcliffe, Alice: 'European Art Group Files Suit in U.S. Against eToys', Reuters, 25 January 2001

Sandoval, Greg: 'eToys Anticipates Shutting Down in April', zdii.com, 25 February 2001

Santoli, Michael: 'The Whole Truth', *The Wall Street Journal*, 28 May 2001

Sloan, Allan: 'The $2.1 Trillion Market Tumble', *Newsweek*, 24 April 2000

Smith, Roberta: 'etoy.com', *The New York Times*, 5 May 2000

Streitfeld, David: 'EToys, Having a Disastrous Holiday Season, Puts Itself Up for Sale', *The Washington Post*, 18 December 2000

Tomkins, Richard: 'Re-inventing The Dinosaur', *Financial Times*, 8 June 1999

WIRED news: 'KB Toys Gets eToys Web Site', 17 May 2001

Books

Shiller, Robert J.: *Irrational Exuberance* (Princeton University Press, New Jersey, 2000)

Other Sources

etoy vs eToys: court papers filed in the United States District Court, Southern District of California

Web Sources

A series of links related to this book can be found at:
http://www.leavingrealitybehind.com/notes

Acknowledgements

We would especially like to thank all the people who indulged us with their time, especially Brainhard, Esposto, Udatny and Goldstein and those wry souls who lived through etoy and had a funny take and a genuine understanding of the experience. As well we would like to thank Joichi Ito for making time in his busy life for us, Douglas Rushkoff for trying to help out, and Ray and Frank from ®™ark for their time and interest.

This book would never have come about without the wonderful Patrick Walsh, and his unbounded enthusiasm, desperate encouragement and a determined eye for getting it right. We are also grateful to Emma Parry, our New York agent, for skilfully navigating the book across the ocean.

From the very start, Leo Hollis at Fourth Estate remarkably understood the idea, ceaselessly added more to it and helped guide it toward completion. Dan Halpern, at Ecco Press in New York, also helped us along. Thanks to Kate Balmforth and Monica O'Connell for disciplining the authors on their style, though the faults are our own, and to our lawyers Isabelle Vogt (Luks und Vogt) and David Daley and Simon Dowson Collins (Harper-Collins).

Also we'd like to thank various of our friends who so diligently read the whole and parts of the manuscript: Philipp Sarasin, Tim Tzouliadis, Eva Wishart, Andrea Wulf, Gillian duCharme, Steve Bowbrick, David Wishart, Paul Murphy, Andrew Hall, Stefan Turnbull, Charlotte Desai, Isabel Allen, Phillippa Bradshaw, Amy

Leaving Reality Behind

Goodyear and Steve, who thought there was a book in it in the first place. And for technical advice and support: Stuart Tiley, Robin Kearney, and Chrigel Vaterlaus.

Around the world we were grateful for the accommodation and support from the following people: Mia Sorgi, Denise Portmans, Andrew and Sarah Hall, Alex and Jean Gansa, Rachel Namsted and Robert Stanley, Andrew Newman, Mira and Reuben Gelly, Denise Langenegger, Jod and Richard Lurie, Hannes Doblhofer, and Fernandez Villa.

Photo Credits and ©: page 21, A *Los Angeles Times* Photograph by Anacleto Rapping; page 45, Roger Schneider; page 81, A *Los Angeles Times* Photograph by Iris Schneider; page 101 etoy. CORPORATION/jodi.org (ASCII art); page 134, Steve La Badessa; pages 157, 158, 288, 302, etoy.CORPORATION.

Index

All Fourth Estate books are available from
your local bookshop.

For a monthly update on Fourth Estate's
latest releases, with interviews, extracts,
competitions and special offers visit
www.4thestate.com

Or visit
www.4thestate.com/readingroom
for the very latest reading guides on our
bestselling authors, including Michael Chabon,
Annie Proulx, Lorna Sage, Carol Shields.

London and *New York*